The Evolving American Presidency

Series Editors
Michael A. Genovese
Loyola Marymount University
Los Angeles, CA, USA

Todd Belt
Department of Political Science
University of Hawaii at Hilo
Hilo, HI, USA

This series is stimulated by the clash between the presidency as invented and the presidency as it has developed. Over time, the presidency has evolved and grown in power, expectations, responsibilities, and authority. Adding to the power of the presidency have been wars, crises, depressions, industrialization. The importance and power of the modern presidency makes understanding it so vital. How presidents resolve challenges and paradoxes of high expectations with limited constitutional resources is the central issue in modern governance and the central theme of this book series.

More information about this series at
http://www.palgrave.com/gp/series/14437

Mara Oliva · Mark Shanahan
Editors

The Trump Presidency

From Campaign Trail to World Stage

palgrave
macmillan

Editors
Mara Oliva
Department of History
University of Reading
Reading, Berkshire, UK

Mark Shanahan
Department of Politics and
  International Relations
University of Reading
Reading, Berkshire, UK

The Evolving American Presidency
ISBN 978-3-319-96324-2   ISBN 978-3-319-96325-9   (eBook)
https://doi.org/10.1007/978-3-319-96325-9

Library of Congress Control Number: 2018949041

Cover credit: Paul Hennessy/Alamy Stock Photo
Cover design by Akihiro Nakayama

This Palgrave Macmillan imprint is published by the registered company Springer Nature
Switzerland AG
The registered company address is: Gewerbestrasse 11, 6330 Cham, Switzerland

ACKNOWLEDGEMENTS

This book is a collection of essays presented at the Monroe Group Inaugural Conference held at the University of Reading in May 2017. The editors wish to thank all contributors for their research, thoughtful insights and stimulating discussions. The event would have not been possible without the financial support of the British Association of American Studies (BAAS), the Vice-Chancellor's Endowment Fund, The School of Humanities, SPEIR, and the Departments of History and Politics & IR at the University of Reading.

CONTENTS

Contributors

Clodagh Harrington De Montfort University, Leicester, UK

Richard Johnson Lancaster University, Lancaster, UK

Lee Marsden University of East Anglia, Norwich, UK

Iwan Morgan Institute of the Americas, University College London, London, UK

Mara Oliva Department of History, University of Reading, Reading, Berkshire, UK

Maria Ryan University of Nottingham, Nottingham, UK

Mark Shanahan Department of Politics and International Relations, University of Reading, Reading, Berkshire, UK

Kevern Verney Edge Hill University, Ormskirk, UK

Alex Waddan University of Leicester, Leicester, UK

Mark White Queen Mary University of London, London, UK

ABBREVIATIONS

ACA   Affordable Care Act
AFDC   Aid to Families with Dependent Children
AHCA   American Health Care Act
BCRA   Better Care Reconciliation Act
BLM   Black Lives Matter
CBO   Congressional Budget Office
CIA   Central Intelligence Agency
CoS   Chief of Staff
CRD   Department of Justice's Civil Rights Division
DoJ   Department of Justice
EPA   Environmental Protection Agency
GATT   General Agreement on Tariffs and Trade
ICBM   Intern Continental Ballistic Missile
MFN   Most Favoured Nation
NAFTA   North American Free Trade Agreement
NATO   North Atlantic Treaty Organisation
NSC   National Security Council
OASDI   Old Age Social Security and Disability Insurance
OMB   Director of the Office of Management and Budget
PRC   People's Republic of China
PRWORA   Personal Responsibility and Work Reconciliation Act
RFRA   Religious Freedom Restoration Act
SNAP   Supplemental Nutrition Assistance Program
TCJA   Tax Cut and Jobs Act
TPP   Trans-Pacific Partnership

TTIP   Transatlantic Trade and Investment Partnership
VRA   Voting Right Act
WTO   World Trade Organisation

LIST OF FIGURES

CHAPTER 1

Introduction

Mara Oliva and Mark Shanahan

In May 2017, the University of Reading launched a new interdisciplinary research centre for the study of the American presidency, the Monroe Group. Co-directed by Dr Mara Oliva (Department of History) and Dr Mark Shanahan (Department of Politics and IR), its aim is to encourage dialogue between scholars in the arts, humanities, social sciences and sciences working on all aspects of the office of the US presidency. As part of its creation, the centre hosted a one-day conference on "Trump's first 100 days." Historians and political scientists from all over the UK gathered to assess the impact of a presidency like no other. The breath and the quality of the contributions prompted the organisers to put together an edited collection of the essays presented. Charting his first year from both historical and contemporary political standpoints, this book delves into key aspects of the Trump campaign promises around immigration, trade and social and

M. Oliva (✉)
Department of History, University of Reading,
Reading, Berkshire, UK
e-mail: m.oliva@reading.ac.uk

M. Shanahan
Department of Politics and International Relations,
University of Reading, Reading, Berkshire, UK
e-mail: m.j.shanahan@reading.ac.uk

© The Author(s) 2019
M. Oliva and M. Shanahan (eds.), *The Trump Presidency*,
The Evolving American Presidency,
https://doi.org/10.1007/978-3-319-96325-9_1

foreign policy and unpicks how the first year of the presidency has played out in delivering them.

The election of billionaire real estate entrepreneur and TV personality, Donald J. Trump, as 45th president of the USA in November 2016 came as a shock, to say the least, to the international community, the vast majority of the American people (he lost the popular vote by almost 3 million votes) and some would argue to him too. Back in June 2015, his announcement that he would seek the Republican nomination for the presidency was greeted with amusement by many media outlets. It was expected "the Donald" would provide some "entertainment" during the primaries but he would then quickly turn into a funny anecdote of US electoral history. Instead, Trump quickly gained popularity, not only among Republican voters, but especially among angry working-class and blue-collar white voters in battleground states, such as Florida, North Carolina and New Hampshire, and once reliably Democratic states in the Rust Belt area, such as Wisconsin and Michigan.

His aggressive campaign and skilful use of social media divided the country. Despite criticism over his authoritarian leadership style and concerns over his mental health, his promise to "Make America Great Again" by "draining the swamp," "building a wall" on the border with Mexico to control illegal immigration and renegotiating international trade deals to put "America first" appealed to that group of the American electorate that felt that the political elite had forgotten them. Presenting himself as the "I alone can fix this" candidate, he eventually overcame all odds and on election night secured the 270 electoral votes necessary to win the White House. He also produced one of the major upsets in modern political history, as the Republican Party gained control of Congress, both chambers of 32 legislatures and 33 governorships.

While aspects of the 2016 presidential race and reasons behind Trump's victory are discussed in some of the essays in this edited collection, the main aim of the book is look at how the candidate transitioned into office and how successfully, or not, his promises and plans have been implemented. In his victory speech, president-elect Trump promised unity, "I pledge to every citizen of our land, that I will be a president for all Americans." He added: "It is time for us to come together as one united people." Fifteen months into office, the country is still as divided as in 2016.

To be fair, he has been able to keep and deliver on some of the campaign promises. Congress has passed several laws that specifically aimed at rolling back some of the Obama administration's regulations. Trump had assured his voters that he would appoint a conservative to the

Supreme Court to replace the late Antonin Scalia. And he did appoint respected conservative Justice Neil Gorsuch. Since then, his team has been busy filling more than a hundred vacancies in lower federal courts. The president's response to Hurricane Harvey and Hurricane Irma in the summer of 2017 has been generally praised.

But the first year in office has mainly been a reality check for this administration and has highlighted how little prepared the president and his team were when they stepped in the White House. Domestically, he has historically low approval ratings. In April 2018, the *Washington Post* reported that just 1 out of 10 adults approves of the Trump's presidency but does not have a favourable view of him personally. According to Gallup polls, approval for the USA in the world has also fallen to a historic low with the country on a par with China.[1]

Even though supported by a Republican Congress, the president has been very slow in implementing his promised legislation. Indeed, the administration did not make significant progress until September 2017, when a possible shutdown of the federal government suddenly became a reality. Staff issues have plagued the administration from day one. Michael Flynn, who was the president's national security adviser, resigned his post over alleged contacts with the Russian ambassador to the USA before Trump even took office. This led quickly to an ongoing investigation on Trump campaign's alleged collusion with Moscow to boost his 2016 presidential chances. Appointments to important executive positions were filled very slowly impairing the administration's efforts to govern effectively and efficiently. Many positions were filled by family members, most notably, the president's daughter, Ivanka Trump and her husband, Jared Kushner. Their business background has raised questions over their competence and possible conflicts of interest.

In foreign policy, the administration is still yet to formulate a coherent strategy. During the campaign, Trump had promised he would put America first, but many of the decisions taken so far have actually damaged US economy and prestige abroad. Within days of taking office, the president sparked global outrage by signing an executive order halting all refugee admissions and temporarily banning people from Muslim-majority Iraq, Syria, Iran, Sudan, Libya, Somalia and Yemen.

[1] 'Trump's Approval Rating Is Back Near First 100 Days Levels,' *Washington Post*, 15 April 2018, https://www.washingtonpost.com/news/the-fix/wp/2018/04/15/trumps-approval-rating-is-back-near-first-100-day-levels/?utm_term=.bb5430b2dead.

Several state and local governments openly defied the order. He withdrew from the Transpacific Partnership (TPP), but he offered no replacement for the loss of trade links. Citing concerns over its impact on the US economy, in June 2017, he announced that the USA will also withdraw from the Paris Climate Accord, but again he offered no alternative plan. More recently, his twitter spat with North Korean leader Kim Jong-un and his decision to accept his invitation without consulting with any advisers, and the announcement that the USA will withdraw from the Iran deal, have left American international credibility completely shuttered.

Lack of preparation, failure in building a team to govern efficiently, reliance on family members and erratic behaviour are the themes that bind together the ten essays of this edited collection. The first part: "A Historical Perspective" compares Trump's performance against Gold-standard presidents. In the first chapter, Mark Shanahan contrasts two "Outsider" Presidents: Donald Trump, who used his rejection of DC-insiderism to win the White House, and Dwight Eisenhower, who, equally, had never held political office before his candidacy, but whose innate insiderism, gained through a career circling Washington, enabled a far easier transition to power. In Chapter 2, Mark White places the early presidency of Donald Trump in historical context by comparing his time in the White House to that of John F. Kennedy. Although Trump's confrontational style makes him appear unique among US presidents, a close comparison of Trump and JFK reveals similarities as well as differences. In Chapter 3, Iwan Morgan shows how Ronald Reagan's prior experience in government and cogent ideological convictions enabled him to make more rapid progress in his first year than the inexperienced and un-ideological Trump in setting the core agenda of his administration, appointing key personnel to deliver his vision and winning the big political battles over his taxation and spending programmes.

The second part, "Winning at Home," looks at domestic issues. In Chapter 4, Lee Marsden looks at the alt-right, conservative evangelicals and Catholics' support for Trump in the hope of pushing back against Obama reforms on LGBT, same-sex marriage, health care, reproductive rights, education and foreign policy. In Chapter 5, Richard Johnson takes stock of the Trump administration's approach to racial policy compared to that of the Obama administration. The racial symbolism of Donald Trump's election as president stood in sharp contrast to Barack Obama's election and re-election victories. In Chapter 6, Kevern Verney assesses the practical and political problems involved in the construction of a "great, great, wall" along the 1900-mile US border with Mexico during the first year of the Trump administration, together with its likely financial and environmental costs, and consideration of how, and in what ways, president Trump can deliver on his campaign promise to "make Mexico pay for that wall." In Chapter 7, Clodagh Harrington considers what the Trump presidency means for women, in terms of style and substance. Some consideration is given to Trump's tone and rhetoric both on the campaign trail and as president, along with his stated policy priorities. In Chapter 8, Alex Waddan investigates how consistently and successfully Trump's candidacy transferred into his presidency in the area of social policy. First, he establishes if Trump delivered on his promise of a "terrific" health care replacement for the Affordable Care Act and persuaded Speaker Ryan to keep his hands off Social Security and Medicare. Second, he analyses if the president's actions amount to an identifiable Trumpism in social policy. And, finally, he determines to what extent Trump's social policy diverges from, or converges with, the party of Reagan.

The final part, "Winning Away," focuses on foreign policy. In Chapter 9, Maria Ryan argues that although Trump's rhetoric of US foreign policy has remained staunchly nationalist in tone, his first months in office saw him revert to something much closer to the recent historical norm: the pursuit of American global primacy within the context of an economic and political order that is conducive to the interests of the West. In Chapter 10, Mara Oliva looks at Sino-American relations with a particular focus on trade, security, environment and human rights issues. The essay argues that despite much hype to the contrary, President Trump's foreign policy towards China is conforming to pattern, constrained by domestic and international factors.

The volume makes no effort to present anything remotely resembling the last word on the topic. It is rather a first step towards a much needed conversation on the evolution of the American presidency in the twenty-first century and its consequences.

PART I

A Historical Perspective

CHAPTER 2

Outsider Presidents: Comparing Trump and Eisenhower

Mark Shanahan

This chapter will consider the campaigns and first years in office of two contrasting characters. On the one hand is an irascible figure who deliberated for years over whether to race for the presidency; who arrived in the White House believing that he—and only he—could deliver on America's needs; and who surrounded himself in office with generals and millionaire businessmen. On the other hand, there is Donald J. Trump.

Dwight D. Eisenhower, the USA's 34th President, and Donald Trump, its 45th, would appear to have little in common. "Ike" as Eisenhower was universally known, came from hard-working mid-Western fundamental Christian stock. His mother, a River Brethren Mennonite, kept a simple home with the Bible at the centre of family life. His father managed the accounts in a local dairy in Abilene, Kansas. Ike's route out was a scholarship to West Point, built more on a prowess for football than on early academic achievement, and a career in the Army.

M. Shanahan (✉)
Department of Politics and International Relations,
University of Reading, Reading, Berkshire, UK
e-mail: m.j.shanahan@reading.ac.uk

© The Author(s) 2019
M. Oliva and M. Shanahan (eds.), *The Trump Presidency*,
The Evolving American Presidency,
https://doi.org/10.1007/978-3-319-96325-9_2

An effective staff officer between the wars, he rose to prominence only when he came under the wing of General George C. Marshall running his planning office in Washington, DC in the run-up to World War Two. Having risen painfully slowly through the ranks of the officer corps over the previous two decades, Eisenhower was propelled into the front lines of military command, first leading the USA's Operation Torch invasion of North Africa before subsequently leading the Allied Invasions of Sicily and the Italian mainland and then, in perhaps his finest hour, masterminding the Normandy Landings on D-Day, and the allied drive across France and the Low Countries into Germany to help bring an end to the War in Europe.

Trump, of an age to fight in Vietnam, didn't go to war. Despite schooling at the New York Military Academy, he preferred to collect rents for his housing developer father Fred Trump than be drafted for service overseas. He registered for the Draft in 1964, but his decision to take an undergraduate degree at Fordham University ensured he deferred.[1] He passed an Army physical in 1968, after transferring to an undergraduate business degree course at the Wharton School within the University of Pennsylvania, but was reclassified as 1Y, and thus unfit for active service, shortly afterwards citing bone spurs on each heel.[2] Perhaps those foot anomalies account for his having to hold UK Prime Minister Theresa May's hand as he walked down the shallow slope along the White House Colonnade on May's visit on 27 January 2016?[3]

Trump grew up in considerable wealth in the less than fashionable New York borough of Queens. Even in his Penn days, he had his sights set on making his fortune in property development, taking on the reins of the family business from his father. This he duly did, and the rise and fall of his financial fortunes alongside the growing marketability of the Trump brand has been the subject of immense scrutiny elsewhere. For this study, suffice to say it put him in a position where a run for the presidency was much more than a pipe dream.

---

[1] M. Kranish and M. Fisher, *Trump Revealed* (New York: Simon & Schuster, 2016), p. 44.

[2] Ibid., p. 48.

[3] R. Mendick and P. Dominiczak, *Daily Telegraph*, 28 January 2016, http://www.telegraph.co.uk/news/2017/01/28/revealed-real-reason-donald-trump-theresa-may-held-hands-not/ [last accessed 2 January 2018].

That pipe dream was built on a character sold to the US public. It has been a long time since Trump's development business morphed into a licensing operation garnering its income from putting the Trump name in big bold letters on everything from Chinese-made ties to a golf club in Dubai. The awareness of brand-Trump was built in the consciousness of the American public less through his property deals than through his near-ubiquity on US TV screens, first as the playboy-about-town on the chat show circuit and then for over 15 years as host of *The Apprentice* and *Celebrity Apprentice*.[4] Meanwhile, by the time Eisenhower was acclaimed as Republican nominee in 1952, without any kind of pre-Convention personal campaign, he was a hero in the eyes of voters all across America. Despite a bruising Convention when he battled the conservative forces coalesced around Senator Robert Taft, as soon as his name was on the ticket, he was a shoe-in for victory—despite the image sold to the public being a little different from the reality of the man.

EISENHOWER'S RUN FOR OFFICE: STARTING AT THE GUILDHALL

By 1945, Eisenhower had spent his whole career in the Army. With a stint in Washington, DC, working for the Secretary of the Army in the 1930s, and executive officer experience supporting US Army luminaries such as John J. Pershing, Fox Conner, Douglas F. MacArthur and Marshall, he was well-set for a post-forces career in a senior role in government administration. But the period from 1942 to 1945 caused him to set his sights higher as he worked first-hand with President Franklin D. Roosevelt, Soviet Premier Joseph V. Stalin, British Prime Minister Winston Churchill and French President Charles De Gaulle. While understanding he needed more rounded experience beyond the Army to establish his credibility as a candidate, Ike was convinced that his intellect, outlook and character would enable him to lead the USA through the post-war years. What he also had on his side was a complete mastery of the logistics of war. Ike was no battlefield general but was astute in collecting the forces and materiel necessary to prosecute war effectively. If he could apply that "master logistician" aptitude in peace, he would offer the country a level of management experience unmatched by any other emerging candidate.

---

[4] *NBC* Television, 15 series aired from 2004 to 2017 with Donald Trump hosting the first 14.

But Eisenhower was not a Beltway politician and needed to test the water to gauge the likelihood that the public perception of him squared with his own view of his skill set. That opportunity occurred in the summer of 1945 following the cessation of hostilities in Europe. In one week, he made two speeches that captured media, political and popular attention across both the UK and USA. On June 12, he addressed the UK's political, civic and business leaders on being made a Freeman of the City of London. Six days later, he addressed the US Congress.

In London, Eisenhower set out the basis for the foreign policy he pursued during his presidency—waging peace. And he did so in a way that elevated the UK–US "Special Relationship" to an apogee at odds with the still-endemic US mood of isolationism. On 18 June, in Washington, DC, the hero Eisenhower, son of the heartland, was accorded the kind of tumultuous reception that presidents can only dream of. His report on the successful completion of his mission in Europe sounded less like a soldier's summary than a message to America from a leader in waiting.

The 1945 speeches were a great opportunity for Eisenhower to test his credibility as a future candidate. He had worked with the free world's political leaders since 1942 and could certainly hold his own with them. Now, he could gauge the reaction of domestic politicians and the public to his presence, thinking and mode of public address. The reaction was laudatory, and Eisenhower filed it away as part of a plan for his future.

MOTIVATION, OPPORTUNITY AND APPEAL

What does it take to become a president? I would suggest motivation, opportunity and appeal. So where did Eisenhower stand on those counts in June 1945? Far from the reluctant candidate driven only by the duty James David Barber described in his model of presidential characteristics, Eisenhower was a man on a mission.[5] He firmly believed he had the knowledge and personality to be president. What he needed was leadership experience in peacetime, and opportunity delivered through the continued goodwill of the American people. His speeches in the heady days of June 1945 went a very long way to establish that goodwill.

---

[5] J. D. Barber, *Presidential Character* (Englewood Cliffs: Prentice-Hall, 1972), pp. 6–9.

Eisenhower had a good war. In 1939, when Britain entered the war, he was a Lieutenant Colonel, a rank he had held since 1936. Back then, he was personal assistant to General Douglas MacArthur preparing the Filipino Army for independence. In 1941, after two Chief of Staff positions, he was promoted to Brigadier General and went to work for General Marshall in the War Department in Washington, DC. Within six months, he'd jumped two ranks and become Commander of European Operations based in London. On 8 November, Eisenhower commanded the Allied Invasion of North Africa.

By February, he had been promoted to the temporary rank of full General. Next up, he commanded the invasion of North Africa in May and directed the invasion of Sicily in July and August. On 30 August 1943, he received a permanent promotion to Brigadier General and immediately to Major General—not a bad day's work. The following month, he commanded the invasion of Italy and two months later attended the Cairo and Tehran Conferences with FDR. In December, FDR appointed Eisenhower as Supreme Commander of Allied Expeditionary Forces to command Operation Overlord, the invasion of Europe. Ike arrived in London in January 1944 to set up Supreme Headquarters. He directed the invasion of Normandy on 6 June, D-Day, and on 20 December, was promoted to General of the Army and received his fifth star. By VE Day, he was acclaimed throughout the Western world as a hero—the man who'd won the war in Europe.

His was a precipitous rise. As Jean Edward Smith pointed out in *Eisenhower in War and Peace*, Eisenhower had been promoted over the heads of more than 200 officers who outranked him in 1940. He had little field experience and was seen by such figures as Field Marshall Bernard L. Montgomery and General Omar N. Bradley as a poor battlefield general. But that was not Ike's role. He was a political general, a man with an innate sense of how to manage difficult—and often competing—egos among both the military and political commands. He had become an essential right hand to Roosevelt from the Cairo Conference onwards. He had the strength of character to win Churchill's admiration—and he could manage the notoriously difficult De Gaulle. Somehow, he even managed to keep Montgomery and General George S. Patton from ripping out each other's throats as the Allied invasion broke out of Normandy and headed for the German frontier in late 1944.

Eisenhower had then emerged as an individual thinker through his decisions to liberate Paris (thus getting De Gaulle's support) and advance on a broad front, rather than Monty and Patton's competing desires for narrow front attacks. He had reacted, just about in time, to marshal his troops effectively to counter the German surge in the Ardennes and had made the decision to hand the attack on Berlin to the Soviets. In all these cases, he was politicking on two fronts: first with his military commanders and second with the Allies' political leaders. He could hold his own with both.

After VE Day, while commanding the US occupation zone in Germany, Eisenhower commenced a valedictory tour of European capitals, before a short, triumphant visit home to the USA. The highpoint of his European tour was his Guildhall speech in London, while his address to the joint chambers of Congress was unprecedented.

THE PREPARATION

There was little spontaneous about either the London or Washington events, or the speeches that Eisenhower delivered. He worked very hard on both starting first with a response to an invitation from Churchill. On 19 May, Eisenhower wrote:

> I have just been thinking over the proposal you suddenly presented to me just before I left your delightful luncheon table the other day, to the effect that I should participate in a formal celebration in London. As I told you then, I think that some simple ceremony along this line might have a pleasing effect at home, but I sincerely hope that the arrangements would be such as to avoid over-glorification of my own part in the victories of this allied force. For three years I have earnestly attempted to stress the value of team play and I have religiously kept from the public eye those affairs and decisions which necessarily had finally to be the responsibility of one man, myself.[6]

Ike then continued by setting out the arrangements *he* would like for the event: bringing a "small but representative section of my Staff....symbolical of the British-American team....roughly half and half from British and Americans, including ground, air and naval personnel."[7]

---

[6]DDE to Winston Churchill, 19 May 1945, Box 22, Pre-Presidential Papers 1916–1952, Dwight D. Eisenhower Presidential Library, Abilene, KS, USA.

[7]Ibid.

This was Ike responding to Churchill's invitation—but Eisenhower was the one setting the tone and style of the event. But what is interesting is how the event benefitted both big beasts. This was appreciation by association—the kind of relationship that served Eisenhower well throughout his military career and had delivered an equal result for Churchill through his wartime premiership. Unlike the unplanned, spontaneous celebration of VE Day, the Guildhall event was planned to the nth degree. Eisenhower was to be awarded the Freedom of the City of London. He was to be driven through the streets with all the pomp and circumstance Churchill could summon up at three weeks' notice, in a city still pockmarked with the effects of six years of war.

Harry Butcher, Eisenhower's naval aide noted in his diary that Eisenhower would make the principal speech to "every high ranking military and civil official in the United Kingdom."[8] Butcher also noted that Eisenhower crafted the speech over a three-week period and rehearsed it with him over and over again until he had it off pat. On the day, Ike delivered his address without notes. But rather than being spontaneous, it was carefully constructed and memorised in full. The speech was brief—less than two and a half pages. In terms of textual analysis, Caudle Travers, writing in 2010 concluded: "Although Eisenhower's overt purpose...was to accept recognition for his war efforts....his speech transcended the immediate situation and audience by depicting his vision for both future British–American relations and (American) international diplomacy initiatives writ large."[9]

This was Eisenhower who was criticised throughout his presidency for his jumbled speech: for not being well read and for being a poor communicator. But what he delivered was clarity: language with more than a hint of classical, even biblical, allusion and an evocative use of the present and the past to conjure a vision for the future. What strikes the reader most is that this is a political speech: the humility in ascribing his success to the joint labours of the overall allied forces; the praise

---

[8] H. C. Butcher, Diary Entry, 2 June 1945, Box 6, Harry C. Butcher Papers, 1910–1959, DDE Library.

[9] C. Caudle Travers, 'Cementing Alliances in Epideictic Oration: Eisenhower's Guildhall Address of 1945,' *Paper Presented at the Annual Meeting of the NCA 96th Annual Convention*, Hilton San Francisco, San Francisco, 13 November 2010, supplied to M. Shanahan by the author, 11 June 2015.

both for Londoners and for British forces and the wider population; the introduction of the First and Second Amendment rights—that one for the American ear—and the vision for the future of a joint enterprise that will beat swords into ploughshares. This was not the speech of a military man, but the careful construction of a statesman in waiting.

THE IMPACT

The day after the Guildhall Address, *The Times* called Ike's words "a masterpiece of oratory" and likened them to the Gettysburg Address.[10] That was, frankly, more than a little over the top. On 13 June, the proto-statesman departed London with the beginnings of a foreign policy on record; with the successful shoring-up of the UK–US "Special Alliance"; and with every high-ranking military and civil official in Britain firmly on his side. Was this necessary for a General? Not really. For a future, if undeclared, politician? Absolutely.

After a goodwill tour around the capitals of Europe, Eisenhower headed back to the USA for a series of speeches before he addressed a joint session of Congress. Ike's greeting in Washington was rapturous, and he delivered some very safe platitudes to the Congress. The War was still on, with the focus turned to Japan. Eisenhower could celebrate the triumph in Europe, but had to be acutely aware of the continuing threat to American lives in the Pacific.

However, the acclaim he enjoyed from the massed ranks of politicians as well as the nation's outpouring of gratitude in every city he visited was evidence to be stored up that he had the appeal to be a successful presidential candidate if he still had the motivation when the opportunity occurred. That opportunity could have presented itself in 1948. But Eisenhower never committed to a battle, he wasn't sure he could win. In 1948, while President Harry S. Truman declared he would stand aside if Eisenhower headed the Democratic ticket, the likes of Tom Dewey and Robert Taft were at the height of their powers, and Eisenhower (who would never have run as a Democrat) had no guarantee he would win the Republican candidacy. In 1948 too, he still had no experience beyond the Army. He would soon gain that as an academic administrator, as President of Columbia University. Nor did he have

---

[10]Editorial, unattributed (though probably E. H. Carr), *The Times*, London, 13 June 1945, p. 4.

sufficient international standing outside a wartime environment. That was to follow when, ironically, he accepted Truman's order to return to the Army as the first Supreme Commander of the North Atlantic Treaty Organisation (NATO) based in Paris.

The year 1952 brought him opportunity. First, Truman was no longer in the race—a combination of the 22nd Amendment and a poor performance in the New Hampshire primary persuading him not to run for a third term. Second, America was at war in Korea, and the belief was that the only man who could end it was Eisenhower. With an impending presidential election looming, experience, appeal and opportunity aligned. The road to the White House, which started at the Guildhall, was now a highway to victory. Eisenhower was a formidable character. He was more complicated, more irascible and much more calculating figure than many who write about him perceive. Most of all, he was a strategist. He knew his classics and he knew his bible. He could quote Clausewitz and Sun Tzu. He used them all—more so in London than Washington, DC—as part of his long plan; his political strategy to become president—and on his terms.

In war, Eisenhower never committed to a battle unless he knew that the winning odds were stacked in his favour. His presidential race trod the same path. His "campaign" was largely won before he entered it. Despite numerous entreaties from Tom Dewey and others throughout 1951, he did not formally commit to the Republican cause until he was convinced there was a groundswell of support in his favour. There was more than an echo of this with Trump in 2015, although few within the GOP were looking for him to lead them from the electoral wilderness. Even in 1952, however, the GOP were not unanimous in their acclaim for a liberal outsider. M. Stephen Weatherford has noted: "They (The Republican Party) already had a strong standard bearer in Robert Taft.....an experienced legislator with broad appeal in a diverse state would appeal to an electorate tired of the ethical shortfalls of Truman and the Democrats."[11] Eisenhower would defeat Taft on the first ballot at the Republican Convention, but it took a personal appeal from the

---

[11] M. Stephen Weatherford, 'The Eisenhower Transition,' in *The Eisenhower Presidency: Lessons for the 21st Century*, ed. A. J. Polsky (Lanham, MD: Lexington Books, 2015), p. 65.

aviator Jackie Cochran who flew to Paris where Ike was the first Supreme Commander of NATO with a film of a midnight rally which attracted 30,000 people to New York's Madison Square Gardens to persuade the General to run.[12]

CPAC-MAN

So where and when did Donald Trump's campaign start? Not in June 2015, when he glided down into the Trump Tower Lower Lobby to be acclaimed by a crowd claimed to have been rented for the occasion.[13] Nor, though his strategy has subsequently been underpinned by a desire to rollback every policy President Barack H. Obama put in place, was the catalyst for the campaign the Washington Correspondents' Dinner of 2011 when Trump was famously roasted by both Obama and comedian Seth Myers. However, another 2011 event is crucial in siting Trump's belief that a run for the presidency was more than a hook to glean TV time on the chat show couches of America.

That event occurred on 10 February 2011, when Trump addressed conservative activists at the Conservative Political Action Conference in Washington, DC. That day, taking aim at China, Opec and Obama; claiming to be pro-life, pro-gun and anti-Obamacare, Trump found his base. His 13-minute speech, part-scripted and part-ad-libbed offered the same substance-free swipes his 2016 campaign became famed for but showed how his mix of braggadocio and populist rhetoric, heavy on the pathos and light on the logos, had the power to connect with an audience already at odds with Washington insiderism. A comparison of that speech with its 2016 successors shows a startling similarity and evidences one factor that swung Trump the 2016 race. He has an exceptional ability with a TV-sized sound bite. The genesis of "MAGA" is in that speech when he closed by saying: "Our country will be great again."[14]

---

[12] News announcement regarding the New York campaign rally, February 12, 1952, Jacqueline Cochran Papers, Eisenhower Campaign Series, Box 1, Eisenhower-General File 1952, DDE Library.

[13] P. Bump, *Washington Post*, 20 January 2017, https://www.washingtonpost.com/news/the-fix/wp/2017/01/20/even-the-firm-that-hired-actors-to-cheer-trumps-campaign-launch-had-to-wait-to-be-paid/?utm_term=.c66744d0bc65 [last accessed 17 February 2018].

[14] Transcript sourced from E. Appleman, Democracy in Action, http://www.p2012.org/photos11/cpac11/trump021011spt.html [last accessed 17 February 2018].

While Trump sensed the appeal of his message in 2011, the opportunity was not clear-cut. The Republican shift to the right was still a work in progress, and Obama remained a likely winner whoever the GOP set to run against him. Trump's appeal–motivation–opportunity triangle would not coalesce until Obama was off the scene and any Trump run would be most likely against Hillary Clinton, the most prepared but least admired candidate the Democrats could field.

Eisenhower and Trump shared one attribute in their race for the White House: their ability to use the media to get one over on their opponent. For Ike, it was his use of TV advertising—a first for a presidential campaign. For Trump, social media, and in particular his use of Twitter, enabled him to set the media agenda on a daily basis.

Eisenhower used a series of stilted TV messages responding to voter questions as the mainstay of his early ads. But his breakthrough came with a one-minute cartoon slot: his "I like Ike" advertisement. The cartoon was created by Walt Disney Studios, while the "I like Ike" song was a progression of an earlier song written by Irving Berlin called "They like Ike."[15] Irritatingly catchy, the tune, paired with a cartoon GOP elephant marching past a succession of downbeat Democrats, including Dean G. Acheson, Truman and the candidate Adlai S. Stevenson, became a living room hit with the new generation of American TV owners and established "I like Ike" as the slogan of the campaign.[16] It would be usurped to an extent only late in 1952 when Ike announced "I shall go to Korea"—the campaign message that connected so strongly with voters to ensure a landslide when America went to the polls.

Truman had unwisely used an October speech to call Eisenhower out on what he would do to unblock the stasis of the war in Korea where forces on both sides were bogged down in a conflict more reminiscent of World War One than any more modern conflict. Eisenhower, having ensured his speech a week later on 24 October 1952 in a Masonic Temple in Detroit, would have national live TV coverage responded that ending

---

[15] I. Berlin, music and lyrics, from *Call Me Madam*, which premiered on Bradway in 1950.

[16] By 1952, more than 15 million US households had TVs, with over 6 million more added to the total in 1953 alone. By 1961 when Eisenhower left office, the number of US households owning a TV had passed 45 million. RETMA TV Handbooks Volumes 18 and 27, published 1954 and 1962, respectively.

the war: "requires a personal trip to Korea. I shall make that trip. Only in that way could I learn how best to serve the American people in the cause of peace. I shall go to Korea."[17] The response from voters was such that Stevenson might as well have given up campaigning that day. When voters went to the polls, they elected Ike by a 55–45% majority. Eisenhower won 39 of the 48 States taking 442 Electoral College votes to his opponent's 89. The level of landslide that Trump could only dream of.

But that Trump won at all is arguably a far greater feat. Eisenhower, who really campaigned only from 1 September 1952 to the October Korea pronouncement, travelled the country more on a pre-victory parade than a campaign. While liberal politicians criticised him for selling out to the right wing of the GOP, in the eyes of Americans, he was already a hero set to take his rightful place at the country's helm.[18] Trump, by contrast, reinvented himself, inserting his bullish anger into a stale debate, blindsiding his political opponents by changing the campaign paradigm. Content to trade policy for insult, debate for personal attack and rationality for emotion, he tapped into a well of anger at the system and gave those more attracted to reality television than executive policy a totem. The un-politician became an unlikely rallying point for the disaffected and those bypassed by Obama's global view. While Trump was nothing like his core voter, he was more like them than Hillary, the politics wonk. By using Twitter to set the news agenda each day, he quite simply relegated the norms of a political campaign to the status of also-ran.

Outsiders but Not Outliers

Both Eisenhower and Trump can be described as outsider presidents. Eisenhower, the soldier, had held no political office before running for president, but he was hardly an outlier, having served the previous administrations of Herbert C. Hoover, Roosevelt and Truman and worked in DC for significant periods in his career. Trump, having no experience in civic engagement, arrived in the White House seemingly as the great outlier. However, is that truly the case?

---

[17] Sourced online from DDE Library, https://www.eisenhower.archives.gov/education/bsa/citizenship_merit_badge/speeches_national_historical_importance/i_shall_go_to_korea.pdf [last accessed 18 February 2018].

[18] P. McKeever, *Adlai Stevenson, His Life and Legacy* (New York, 1989), p. 242.

Trump has been characterised as the first celebrity president. To take that at face value certainly discounts Ronald Reagan. Much has been made of The Donald's philandering, yet he may have found it hard to keep up with John F. Kennedy. And what about his strategy of surrounding himself in his first year with billionaires and generals? The parallel here is with Eisenhower himself, whose first Cabinet has been summed up as "eight millionaires and a plumber."[19]

At a very surface level too, they have significant parallels in the White House. Neither can be regarded as religious. Both enjoyed their leisure time in the first year in office, and both demonstrated a passion for golf. Yet in what they planned and delivered in their first year, they differed greatly. Most pointedly, Eisenhower stopped a war. At the head of a turbulent Executive, Trump's tin-eared rhetoric could quite easily have started one. In each instance, Korea was the focus of presidential attention.

The massive difference in tone and intent was set with each president's Inaugural Address. Eisenhower, who had his personal faith but was not a church member until becoming president, struck a biblical tone in his address. After an opening prayer, he addressed citizens, noting: "We sense with all our faculties that forces of good and evil are massed and armed and opposed as rarely before in history...Seeking to secure peace in the world, we have had to fight through the forests of the Argonne to the shores of Iwo Jima and to the cold mountains of Korea."[20] Continuing, he "beseeched God's guidance" to take on "the responsibility of the free world's leadership."[21] Eisenhower offered an eight-point "rules of conduct" plan built upon an overarching aim to "deter the forces of aggression and promote the conditions of peace."[22] And within this, he set out to strive to make the UN an "effective force."[23]

---

[19] Associated Press, syndicated 19 January, 1953. When Charles E. Wilson was sworn in as Defense Secretary, the Cabinet became Nine Millionaires, while the Plumber, Martin Durkin, remained.

[20] DDE Inaugural Address, 20 January 1953, The American Presidency Project, www.presidencyucsb.edu/ws/index.php?pid=9600 [last accessed 4 April 2018].

[21] Ibid.

[22] Ibid.

[23] Ibid.

The USA has always required an existential threat—and at the start of 1953, that was still Stalin's Soviet Union: the focal point of the communist threat. Eisenhower was committed to countering this threat, but through hope, and belief that "an earth of peace may become not a vision, but a fact."[24] Newspapers recall that as Eisenhower spoke, the clouds parted and the sun came out.[25] His words of hope for peace drew almost universal praise with the Eisenhower Presidential Library boxing 2015 pages of letters in response to the Address; 2000 were positive.[26]

Contrast that to the snarling, dystopian venality of the Trump's Inaugural in January 2017. It is interesting that this was not so much in the words—at least the top and tail of the speech are the classic invocation of one nation under God—but in the way Trump delivered them. Trump provided a staunchly populist address stating he was "transferring power from Washington, DC, and giving it back to you, the people."[27] Yet after this nod to his MAGA campaign promise, he lurched into 17 minutes of Alt-Right rhetoric devoid of hope and filled with blame and bile against the political classes. Trump, in a weak echo of Reagan, attacked the "Establishment" and offered up his presidency to the "forgotten men and women of this country."[28] Quite a claim to make as he simultaneously filled his White House not with Eisenhower's millionaires, but with billionaires including Betsy DeVos, Steven Mnuchin and Rex Tillerson.

Much of the core of the speech focused on Trump's America First rhetoric. Unlike Eisenhower who made a point of stressing the value of other nations and the commitment to work together for peace, Trump's global hostility was captured through sentiments such as: "We've made other countries rich while the wealth, strength, and confidence of our country has dissipated over the horizon. One by one, the factories shuttered and left our shores with not even a thought about the millions and millions of American workers that were left behind."[29] Again the populist claim that would appeal to his disaffected base, but one that is at odds

[24] Ibid.

[25] E. T. Folliard, *Washington Post*, 21 January 1953, Section A01.

[26] DDE Records as President 1953–1961, Personal Files, Boxes 584–586, Dwight D. Eisenhower Presidential Library.

[27] Trump Inaugural address, 20 January 2017 https://www.whitehouse.gov/briefings-statements/the-inaugural-address/ [last accessed 4 April 2018].

[28] Ibid.

[29] Ibid.

with a reality that saw most traditional American jobs lost to technology rather than other nations. But the phrase that resounded most from the speech came at the end of a section highlighting the crime and drug epidemics Trump saw sweeping America. Offering not the usual platitudes of hope and redemption, Trump asserted: "This American carnage stops right here and stops right now."

The reaction to the Inaugural Address is notable and the startling unsuppressed anger of the new president was captured most pithily by a predecessor, George W. Bush, who reacted: "That was some weird shit."[30] The glee with which much of the news media savoured Bush's remark reflected the increasingly attritional relationship Trump "enjoyed" with the US media throughout his first year. To a far greater degree than any president before him, he both sidestepped the media *and* set the media agenda through his use of Twitter. While it ensured his personal agenda led the news cycles, he was by no means alone in being a White House incumbent frustrated by the media's treatment of him.

Unlike Trump, Eisenhower never played the victim at the hands of the media. But editorialising frustrated him. As he saw it, he expected what he said to be reported—unfiltered. Of course, even in the 1950s, journalists did not work in that way. The White House lobby would listen to Eisenhower, distil his message and present it to readers and listeners in a manner most likely to sell more newspapers or get more people to listen to their shows. Over time, Eisenhower was able to limit the distortion he felt the media offered by inviting TV cameras into the White House and ensuring the key networks either took the feed live or replayed whole news conferences in full. However, this practice did not start until 1955. On first entering the White House, the president had the advantage of a full-time Press Secretary for the first time in presidential history. Seasoned New York newsman Jim Hagerty took on that role and, unlike Trump's equivalents, stayed with the president throughout his two terms in office. And he was more than just a press spokesman. Throughout his tenure, Hagerty was part of the Eisenhower's inner circle: part of a very small group of trusted advisers who sourced, shaped and salted Eisenhower's key messages to try to ensure they elicited the right response from the American people.

[30]Y. Ali, *New York Magazine*, 27 March 2017, http://nymag.com/daily/intelligencer/2017/03/what-george-w-bush-really-thought-of-trumps-inauguration.html [last accessed 18 February 2018].

Keeping on top of the media's critique was not always easy for Ike. He had been used to a deferential press during wartime. When meeting reporters, he told them what to write, and they wrote it. But the White House lobby was different. While still respectful, and much less adversarial than today's reporters, they were not wholly compliant and saw their role as much in holding the president to account as in amplifying his policy messages. As Paul Johnson noted, one of Eisenhower's key tools in managing this, employed both directly and through Hagerty, was to obfuscate. "He enjoyed the deliberate mangling of syntax and got a particular relish from clever imitations of his inarticulate use of English."[31] The result was that Eisenhower could be vague on key issues: a vagueness that gave him the space to make decisions and manage White House priorities without the constant line-by-line critique of journalistic influence.

By contrast, Trump appeared in his first year to be in constant battle with "MSM"—mainstream media. He moved very quickly to denounce any media mention that did not match his narrative as "fake news," and in so doing both undermined the authority of the fourth estate in holding him to account, but also shifted the paradigm of an honest White House into one where exaggerations, volte-faces and downright lies became so common that they normalised a dishonest presidency to the point that objective truths became ever more scarce and hardly valued. Trump's modus operandi has been to tweet early most mornings, ensuring the items he wanted to prioritise became the lead stories on the morning TV shows and got massive direct contact with Americans—and notably his base of conservative supporters—through retweeting and endless comments. On average, Trump tweets around five times a day, and in his first 12 months in the White House, his favourite topics were "fake news" (his ongoing battle with a less-than-supportive media), the Clinton family (much of 2017 was spent re-fighting the presidential campaign) and Russia (a complicated relationship, but most tweets focused on refuting any links between the Trump campaign and President of Russia Vladimir V. Putin's forces during the election campaign).[32] The campaign slogans resurfaced on a regular basis with "MAGA,"

[31] P. Johnson, *Eisenhower: A Life* (New York: Penguin Books, 2014), p. 96.

[32] B. McNamara, *1 Year of Trump's Tweets Analyzed*, *Teen Vogue*, 22 January 2018, https://www.teenvogue.com/story/trump-tweet-analysis [last accessed 24 January 2018].

"Build the Wall" and "Drain the Swamp," given regular airings, while Trump also used the 140-character (latterly 280) format to attack opponents and demean his perceived enemies. His second most popular tweet stated: "Why would Kim Jong-un insult me by calling me "old," when I would NEVER call him "short and fat?" Oh well, I try so hard to be his friend - and maybe someday that will happen!"[33]

I would argue that the approaches taken by Eisenhower and Trump to dealing with the media in their first year in office reflected their wider management style. In my book *Eisenhower at the Dawn of the Space Age*, I present a picture of the Eisenhower White House as one where the president was in executive charge, setting policy direction and making the key policy decisions, but where the day-to-day operational business was conducted by "helping hands," these being "subtly different like-minded advisers from beyond partisan political elites run almost on military lines."[34] Ike's speechwriter Stephen Hess noted that the Eisenhower's White House consisted of "just fifty-six posts with just eighty-eight staff filling these roles across the eight year of Eisenhower's presidency."[35] It would appear that Trump has had almost that many press spokespeople alone in his short duration to date. Whereas Eisenhower operated along military lines, Trump brought the practices of a mid-sized family builder to the Oval. For decades, he has operated through a system of personal favour where loyalty was bought, and where family outweighed expertise. The essential Trump set-up was for him to work on the fun stuff that interested him and to be surrounded by payrolled-sycophants and family loyalists who managed the business in return for salaries and benefits that may well have overvalued their talents.

Such an approach does not work where many of the inherited staff are career civil servants, and where the presidential appointees were working in effect not for Trump, but for the country. As a consequence, what we witnessed in Trump's first year in office was a chaotic White House with little leadership and consequent battles for the president's ear. In *Fire and Fury*, observer Michael Wolff captured the chaotic structure stating: "There was no real up and down structure, but merely a figure at the top and then everyone scrambling for his attention. It wasn't

---

[33] http://www.trumptwitterarchive.com/ [last accessed 24 January 2018].

[34] M. Shanahan, *Eisenhower at the Dawn of the Space Age* (Lanham, MD: Lexington Books, 2017), p. 8.

[35] Ibid.

task-based so much as response-oriented—whatever captured the boss's attention focused everybody's attention."[36] In sum, it was the antithesis of the Eisenhower operation. As a result, West Wingers and Executive Officers left in droves, with the highly oiled revolving door on 1600 Pennsylvania Avenue spinning breezily behind no fewer than 22 key figures in the administration by the end of March 2018, including Michael Flynn, Steve Bannon, Reince Priebus, Gary Cohn, Rex Tillerson and HR McMaster—as well as the potential obstacles to the Trump powertrain, James Comey and Andrew McCabe.

A Year of Contrasts

Domestically, Eisenhower enjoyed a quiet first year. While the Taft-led wing of the GOP pushed for tax cuts and a rollback on both Truman's Fair Deal policies and the longer-established New Deal policies brought in under Roosevelt, Eisenhower preferred to focus on balancing the budget and there were no significant economic moves in Year 1 of his presidency. Like Trump, he made meeting his key campaign promise the most important item on the agenda, and in Ike's case, that was bringing the Korean War to a close.

The Trump presidency, which had started with a snarl, settled into a routine of non-routine. Yet, with hindsight, it might come to be recognised as the most honest presidency of modern times. Trump had a simple two-pronged strategy—deliver on his (albeit broad-brush) campaign promises and rollback virtually anything Obama had put in place, whether for the good or to the detriment of the nation. What Trump soon found was how hard it was to deliver radical change in Washington. But it must not be said that he achieved nothing.

During a campaign stop in Dallas in September 2015, Trump declared: "Obamacare. We're going to repel it, we're going to replace it, get something great. Repeal it, replace it, get something great!"[37] As discussed elsewhere in this volume, it became the totem policy for the early months of the Trump presidency, yet it was ultimately rejected. Travel bans for

[36] M. Wolff, *Fire and fury* (New York, 2018), p. 108.

[37] D. Trump, *America a Dumping Ground for the Rest of the World*, Campaign Speech, *Dallas*, 14 September 2015, as reported by CBS News, http://dfw.cbslocal.com/2015/09/14/trump-america-a-dumping-ground-for-the-rest-of-the-world/ [last accessed 7 April 2018].

predominantly Muslim countries were proposed—and knocked back by *got through now or proposed again?* the independent judiciary. Meanwhile, funding for the Southern Border Wall proved very hard to come by despite a year of tweets and anti-Hispanic immigrant rhetoric. However, the president scored a major victory with conservatives with his nomination, and successful confirmation, of Neil Gorsuch to the Supreme Court. And while Mexico proved more than a little reluctant to corral its citizens by paying for Trump's Wall, he did ensure a significant increase in the deportation of illegal immigrants.

Domestically, Trump's biggest deliverables were in rolling-back regulation and in cutting taxes for some taxpayers. Trump's officials claimed the rollback in financial, environmental and health regulation would save $570m per year in regulatory costs.[38] While this infuriated environmentalists and consumer protection groups, it appeared to curry favour with the business community. This squared with Trump's biggest apparent domestic success, which was the Congressionally delivered tax cuts authorised through the Tax Cuts and Jobs Act, described by the president as a "big beautiful Christmas present" for Americans.[39] How big and for how many Americans remain to be seen, but the passing of the Act and subsequent paycheque bonuses for many Americans led to Trump's approval rating rising from a low of 33% at the start of December 2017 to a high of 40% at the end of the month. This had risen to 45% at the end of January, when many Americans received their first paycheques benefiting from the cuts, although the upswing in approval was short-lived as Trump's figures headed down to 39% by 26 March 2018.[40]

His global approval rating was no doubt inhibited by the final point of Eisenhower/Trump comparison in this chapter: their contrasting actions with regard to Korea. Eisenhower based his major foreign policy activity in 1953 on the fulfilment of his campaign promise to end the war in Korea. Trump, by contrast, seemed, for much of his first year,

---

[38] E. Lipton and D. 'Ivory, *Trump Says His Regulatory Rollback Already Is the 'Most Far-Reaching'* Politics,' *New York Times,* 14 December 2017, https://www.nytimes.com/2017/12/14/us/politics/trump-federal-regulations.html [last accessed 7 April 2018].

[39] D. Trump, White House Address to Media, 2 November 2017, www.reuters.com/video/2017/11/02/trump-calls-gop-tax-bill-big-beautiful-c?videoId=372891597 [last accessed 9 April 2018].

[40] D. Trump Presidential Approval Rating, Gallup, December 2017–March 2018, http://news.gallup.com/poll/203198/presidential-approval-ratings-donald-trump.aspx [last accessed 9 April 2018].

hell-bent on starting a war on that self-same peninsula. When one assesses Eisenhower's achievement in enabling the Korean Armistice by July 1953, there is no doubt that he got lucky. Key to the North Korean decision to return to the Paris peace talks was the death of Stalin in March 1953. The new Soviet leadership saw no virtue in continuing a stalemated conflict and pressured Mao and the North Korean regime to work towards a peaceful solution, thus reducing the temperature of the Cold War.[41] This undoubtedly benefited Eisenhower. Shortly after Stalin's death, Georgy Malenkov had addressed the Supreme Soviet saying: "At the present time there is no dispute or unresolved question that cannot be settled peacefully by mutual agreement of the interested countries. This applies to our relations with all states, including the United States of America."[42] Eisenhower's response was one of his greatest feats of oratory across his career—his speech on 16 April to the American Society of Newspaper Editors subsequently known as "The Chance for Peace." While the speech overall set about undermining Soviet barbarism and focused on two roads to peace—one blocked and one perilous—it made a concrete provision for working towards peace as Eisenhower told his audience:

> The first great step along this way must be the conclusion of an honorable armistice in Korea. This means the immediate cessation of hostilities and the prompt initiation of political discussions leading to the holding of free elections in a united Korea.[43]

Broadcast live on radio and television, the White House also ensured transcripts were disseminated to all major foreign governments and media outlets. This was the fulcrum of a peace offensive designed to drive the North Koreans to the peace talks table. As it happened, the North Koreans proved not to be the sticking point in delivering the Armistice, formally signed on 27 July 1953. The last hurdle was to get South Korean President Syngman Rhee to co-operate. This Eisenhower achieved quite simply by cutting off Rhee's access to fuel and ammunition for his forces.

[41] Z. Shen, *Mao, Stalin and the Korean War: Trilateral Communist Relations in the 1950s*, trans. N. Silver (London: Routledge, 2012), pp. 196–202.

[42] Quoted in Smith, *Eisenhower in War and Peace*, p. 572.

[43] 'The Chance for Peace' Address Delivered Before the American Society of Newspaper Editors, 16 April 1953, DDE Library, www.eisenhower.archives.gov/all_about_ike/speeches/chance_for_peace.pdf [last accessed 9 April 2018].

Trump did not have a useful Malenkov equivalent to assist his cause in 2017. But then, his cause—finding an existential enemy to promote as the "other" for Americans to fear and challenge—was one quite singular to Trump. Having flailed around to identify enemies among the Muslim and Hispanic communities during his election campaign, Trump used the transition, and his preferred diplomatic tool—Twitter—to define an enemy his base could buy into: a racially different foreign power with a history of antagonism to the USA and one so odd that it made a far-from-normal US President appear the rational actor. On 2 January 2017, Trump tweeted: "North Korea just stated that it is in the final stages of developing a nuclear weapon capable of reaching parts of the U.S. It won't happen!"[44] Seemingly undeterred, and perhaps goading the USA into action, the Kim regime in North Korea responded with a series of ballistic missile launches between February and April 2017. Trump's response was a show of strength punctuated by dropping a massive non-nuclear device on Afghanistan and ordering a strike group of ships to the Sea of Japan (although it actually did not arrive there for almost three weeks). But being Trump, the goading seemed to have an opposite effect, and after meetings with the Prime Minister of Japan, Shinzo Abe, and China's Xi Jinping, his tone towards North Korean Kim Jong-un was suddenly one of describing him as a "smart cookie."[45]

Trump's tone changed again beyond mid-year as Kim launched two very provocative ICBMs that appeared to prove the capability of North Korea to reach US soil with nuclear weapons if they could marry a warhead to the rocket—a feat the Pyongyang regime trumpeted on 8 August. This, of course, prompted the now notorious Trump response that he would unleash "fire and fury" if North Korea continued to threaten the USA. It is notable that this became the title for Michael Wolff's fly-on-the-wall expose of Trump's early months in office. Notable not least in that the book gives only a brief couple of mentions to North Korea, using "fire and fury" as a set-up for a description of Trump's weak and watery response to the white supremacist show of strength at Charlottesville.[46]

---

[44] D. Trump Tweet, 2 January 2017.

[45] D. Trump, *Face the Nation, CBS* Television, 1 May 2017.

[46] Wolff, *Fire and Fury*, pp. 291–93.

But what really emerged later in 2017 and into 2018 was Trump's motivation for facing off against Kim. Since the first moves towards a campaign, Trump has been most motivated not by policy success, but by ratings—the amount of exposure he gets on TV; the number of column inches set against his opponents; and the favourability of his base towards him. Attacking Kim gave him good numbers. We have already seen that it provoked his second most popular tweet response, and indeed, it also generated his third most popular response when he wrote: "North Korean Leader Kim Jong-un just stated that the 'Nuclear Button is on his desk at all times.' Will someone from his depleted and food starved regime please inform him that I too have a Nuclear Button, but it is a much bigger & more powerful one than his, and my Button works!"[47] It was a crude and undiplomatic, but a typically boastful way for Trump to start the New Year. While it may have amused those in the Heartland who he seemingly cannot offend, it drew scorn from Pyongyang. The North Korean response was: "This is the spasm of a lunatic."[48] Pithy, but it did call into question who was the grown up in the Trump/Kim relationship.

CONCLUSION

The spat with North Korea may have been all about ratings for Donald Trump who, seemingly, had next to no understanding of Kim's policy intent and even less on the destabilising effect of his own sabre rattling. As such, it presents a microcosm of the Trump strategy—weaving coverage from chaos by jumping from policy to outrage to phony wars to sackings all to be the number one news item of the day. This strategy is Trump's one means of making America interested…without asking too many deep questions about the lack of policy success or the creeping flames of the Mueller inquiry. It is reflective of the position Trump was in entering the White House in comparison with Eisenhower. Dwight D. Eisenhower was elected as a hero. The man who defeated Hitler was regarded as the firm hand on the tiller who could keep Communism at bay and ensure the continuance of the American Dream. Of course, that was a massive over-simplification, but one that enabled him to trounce Stevenson in the general election. His first year in office was not without controversy,

---

[47] D. Trump Tweet, 3 January 2018.

[48] From *Rodong Sinmun* (DPK Official News), reported in *South China Morning Post*, 16 January 2018, p. 1.

particularly as he stood outside the fray as Senator Joseph McCarthy (R-WI) flared in the TV lights before finally fizzling in the Army Hearings of 1954. But what Eisenhower had promised to do in his campaign, he did: he ended the war in Korea and brought the troops home.

Trump entered not as a hero but as a change maker determined to Make America Great Again. His brash narcissism has ensured his White House grates on many and a year in, the focus is definitely on soap opera rather than the Citadel on the Hill. But the sense by the end of the year was that the Mueller investigation aside, Trump was actually beginning to enjoy the presidency more. Rather than dealing with a small, tight staff picked by others, as per Eisenhower, he was finally surrounding himself with a team of acolytes far more likely to say "yes" to him than to schedule (Priebus), harangue (Bannon) or lecture (McMaster) a president with a notoriously short attention span. With the Tax and Spending legislation on the books, he finally had a significant policy success. And having been flattered in Paris, across Asia and at Davos, he was more comfortable dealing with foreign Heads of State, with a strong belief that he was still the world's foremost dealmaker. That final point brings him closer to Eisenhower, a character less brash and more emotionally intelligent, but still steadfastly convinced he was the one person who could solve America's problems in the 1950s.

Eisenhower's greatest success at the height of the Cold War was waging peace—keeping America out of war and himself in office across two terms. Trump has far to go if he is to match either achievement. Whereas domestically, Eisenhower's greatest challenge was Joe McCarthy, the demagogue in the Senate, Trump's likely downfall will be his own demagoguery. James David Barber highlighted Ike's prime virtue as his sense of duty to the nation.[49] Trump, by contrast, operates by a pervasive sense of a duty only to himself and his own brand. He has normalised lies and insults as within the presidential paradigm. Clinging to the coat-tails of power, Congressional Republicans have supported the president so far. One suspects though that the foundations of Trump's House of Cards are weak. A poor performance in the November 2018 midterms for the GOP could weaken it to the point of collapse—if Special Counsel Mueller or even "Little Rocket Man" hasn't got there first.[50]

---

[49] J. D. Barber, *The Presidential Character* (Englewood Cliffs: Prentice-Hall, 1972), p. 160.

[50] D. Trump, Presidential Rally, Huntsville, Alabama, 22 September 2017.

REFERENCES

Barber, J. D. *Presidential Character*. Englewood Cliffs: Prentice-Hall, 1972.

Johnson, P. *Eisenhower: A Life*. New York: Penguin Books, 2014.

Kranish, M., and Fisher, M. *Trump Revealed*. New York: Simon & Schuster, 2016.

McKeever, P. *Adlai Stevenson, His Life and Legacy*. New York: William Morrow and co, 1989.

Shanahan, M. *Eisenhower at the Dawn of the Space Age*. Lanham, MD: Lexington Books, 2017.

Shen, Z. *Mao, Stalin and the Korean War: Trilateral Communist Relations in the 1950s*, trans. N. Silver. London: Routledge, 2012.

Stephen Weatherford, M. *The Eisenhower Transition, in the Eisenhower Presidency: Lessons for the 21st Century*, ed. A. J. Polsky. Lanham, MD: Lexington Books, 2015.

Wolff, M. *Fire and Fury*. New York: Little, Brown, 2018.

CHAPTER 3

Style and Substance:
Trump in the Context of Camelot

Mark White

Comparison is a valuable analytical tool for any historian as it develops an important relative perspective. To compare the start of John F. Kennedy's presidency to that of Donald J. Trump, however, would seem to be of questionable value, for Trump appears to be a president *sui generis*. His abrasive style, hostile rhetoric and constant attacks on the press and judiciary are unique in the history of the American presidency. So how can Kennedy be juxtaposed with Trump when the brash New Yorker leads in a manner so different to that of his presidential predecessors?[1]

It would be easy to believe, therefore, that any similarities between Kennedy and Trump would be few and far between. That assumption, however, is not necessarily sound. In Alan Bennett's 2004 play *The History Boys*, the teacher Irwin encourages his students always to

---

[1] For the analytical value of presidential comparison, see Mark J. White, ed., *Kennedy: The New Frontier Revisited* (New York: New York University Press, 1998), pp. 10–12.

M. White (✉)
Queen Mary University of London, London, UK
e-mail: m.j.white@qmul.ac.uk

© The Author(s) 2019
M. Oliva and M. Shanahan (eds.), *The Trump Presidency*,
The Evolving American Presidency,
https://doi.org/10.1007/978-3-319-96325-9_3

consider the possible validity of the opposite to that which they assume to be the case. That counter-intuitive approach, he suggests, can yield unsuspected truths. Indeed, a careful comparison of JFK and Trump in the first year of their presidencies reveals a number of commonalities as well as differences. This chapter, then, will compare the early presidency of Trump to that of Kennedy, utilising a wide range of sources, including the *Public Papers of the Presidents*, newspapers, archival materials, White House press releases, and that veritable treasure trove for historians, the Trump Twitter Archive. The aim is to help shape the initial phase of the Trump historiography by identifying some key issues that historians will need to address.[2]

The differences between Kennedy and Trump were no more apparent than in their Inaugural Addresses. Inaugural speeches are important because they enable a leader, with the whole nation, indeed entire world, looking on, to give rhetorical definition to their presidency at its outset. In signposting his priorities in a speech written by his influential adviser Steve Bannon, Trump emphasised his determination to reduce America's international commitments in order to focus on the nation's domestic needs. 'From this day forward,' he said, 'a new vision will govern our land. From this moment on, it's going to be America First.' That declaration chimed with the sentiments he had expressed on the campaign trail about withdrawing from free-trade agreements, compelling other North Atlantic Treaty Organisation (NATO) countries to contribute more so as to reduce America's financial commitment to the Western alliance, building a great wall on America's Southern border to stem the flow of illegal immigration from Mexico, and avoiding the sorts of wars that had characterised recent US foreign policy. It was a vision of America redolent of the 1930s when isolationist sentiment was to the fore, and his use of the phrase 'America First' came directly from the lexicon of that decade.[3]

[2] Alan Bennett, *The History Boys* (London: Faber and Faber, 2004), p. 35.

[3] Michael Wolff, *Fire and Fury: Inside the Trump White House* (London: Little, Brown, 2018), p. 44; Donald J. Trump, inaugural address, 20 January 2017, https://www.whitehouse.gov/briefings-statements/the-inaugural-address/ [accessed on 23 January 2018]; Joshua Green, *Devil's Bargain: Steve Bannon, Donald Trump, and the Storming of the Presidency* (London: Scribe, 2017), pp. 190–91. For an example of his rhetoric in the 2016 campaign, see transcript, Trump's speech at the Republican National Convention, 21 July 2016, https://www.politico.com/story/2016/07/full-transcripts-donald-trump-nomination-acceptance-speech-at-rnc-225974 [accessed on 23 January 2018].

Kennedy, by contrast, used his Inaugural Address to present an *internationalist* vision for America. Foreign policy was the salient theme of his speech, and he stressed his resolve to uphold America's overseas obligations and meet the challenges posed by its adversaries. 'Let every nation know, whether it wishes us well or ill, that we shall pay any price, bear any burden, endure any hardship, support…any friend, oppose any foe to assure the survival and the success of liberty.' 'Let us never negotiate out of fear,' he added. 'But let us never fear to negotiate,' indicating that his foreign policy would be a melange of diplomacy and more forceful tactics. Hence, Kennedy made clear that his determination to lead the 'free world' was absolute. Allies were reassured; adversaries duly warned.[4]

The initial approach of Trump and of Kennedy to foreign policy, as expressed in their Inaugural Addresses, was as compatible as oil and water. But one of the striking features of Trump's first hundred days was the rapidity with which he abandoned his professed isolationism. It is one thing to anticipate a presidential term, as candidates do during a campaign, quite another to *experience* it in the White House when circumstances and events can prompt a change in perspective. This is precisely what would happen to Kennedy as his a thousand days or so in the White House unfolded. In the case of Trump, he soon indicated his strong support for NATO in meetings with British Prime Minister Theresa May and NATO chief Jens Stoltenberg, albeit with a reaffirmation of his desire to get allies to contribute more to the defence of the West. 'In the coming months and years,' he promised at his press conference with Stoltenberg, 'I'll work closely with all of our NATO allies to enhance this partnership.' Expressing outrage at Syrian President Bashar al-Assad's use of chemical weapons, he authorised a retaliatory strike against the airfield from which this attack had been launched. He also ordered the use of the most powerful weapon deployed since the atomic bombs were dropped on Japan in 1945 against an extensive underground ISIS base in Afghanistan. Subsequently, he moved to thwart the nuclear ambitions of North Korea. His foreign-policy team, comprising generals and businessmen who were all internationalists apart from National Security Advisor Michael Flynn (soon replaced by another

[4]John F. Kennedy, inaugural address, 20 January 1961, *Public Papers of the Presidents, The American Presidency Project* (this and all other documents from the *Public Papers of the Presidents* were accessed via www.presidency.ucsb.edu/ws/ between August 2017 and February 2018).

internationalist H. R. McMaster), clearly influenced Trump's approach to these issues. In effect, Trump has at times played America's usual, post-1945 role as global superpower and leader of the Western world. This could not have been anticipated on the basis of what he had said about foreign policy in 2016.[5]

At other times, however, Trump has followed the 'America First' path that he mapped out during his campaign. Convinced that free-trade agreements hurt the American worker, he announced only a few days into his presidency the withdrawal of US participation from the Trans-Pacific Partnership (TPP), which consisted of eleven Pacific Rim nations that controlled 13.5% of the world economy. He announced US withdrawal from the landmark 2015 Paris climate change agreement, which had been signed by almost 200 countries. Amongst other things, he believed it restricted the development of clean coal in America. He also imposed substantial tariffs on the import of washing machines and solar panels, again to protect American industry—a decision criticised by the two countries whose trade with the USA would suffer most, China and South Korea. So Trump's foreign policy has comprised both internationalist and 'America First' elements, yet the internationalist dimension has been more pronounced than anticipated.[6]

---

[5] May press conference with Trump, 27 January 2017, https://www.gov.uk/government/speeches/pm-press-conference-with-us-president-donald-trump-27-january-2017 [accessed on 23 January 2018]; Jim Garamone, 'Trump, Stoltenberg Discuss NATO Issues in Advance of May Summit,' 13 April 2017, U.S. Department of Defense, https://www.defense.gov/News/Article/Article/1150674/trump-stoltenberg-discuss-nato-issues-in-advance-of-may-summit/ [accessed on 23 January 2018]; Joint Press Conference of President Trump and NATO Secretary General Stoltenberg, 12 April 2017, White House, Briefings & Statements (this and other such White House releases were accessed via https://www.whitehouse.gov/briefings-statements between October 2017 and February 2018); statement by President Trump on Syria, 6 April 2017, U.S. Embassy & Consulates in the U.K., https://u.k.usembassy.gov/statement-president-trump-syria/ [accessed on 23 January 2018]; Helene Cooper and Mujib Mashal, 'U.S. Drops "Mother of All Bombs" on ISIS Caves in Afghanistan,' *New York Times*, 13 April 2017 (this and all other *New York Times* articles were accessed via www.nytimes.com between March 2017 and February 2018); Michael Nelson, *Trump's First Year* (Charlottesville and London: University of Virginia Press, 2018), p. 116.

[6] David Smith, 'Trump Withdraws from Trans-Pacific Partnership Amid Flurry of Orders,' *Guardian*, 23 January 2017, accessed via www.theguardian.com on 26 February 2018; Statement by President Trump on the Paris Climate Accord, 1 June 2017, White House, Briefings & Statements; Tracy Lee, 'China, South Korea Protest Trump's Steep Tariffs on Washing Machine, Solar Panel Imports,' *Newsweek*, 25 January 2018, www.newsweek.com/trade-us-china-trum-south-korea-790770 [accessed on 26 February 2018].

Kennedy's foreign policy was more uniformly internationalist. The roots of that approach went back to the late 1930s when he reflected on the issue of appeasement for his undergraduate thesis at Harvard. It was published in the summer of 1940 as his first book, *Why England Slept*. Rejecting his father Joseph P. Kennedy's isolationist views, he argued that Neville Chamberlain's ill-conceived appeasement of Hitler showed that democracies such as the USA needed to be tough, and in particular militarily prepared, in dealing with totalitarian foes. This would remain the cornerstone of his foreign-policy ideology for the rest of his life, and after World War II, he would reiterate these arguments in a Cold War context, substituting the Soviet Union for Nazi Germany.[7]

A notable overlap between the early foreign policy of Kennedy and of Trump was the focus on combatting communist adversaries. Elected in 1960, when meeting the communist challenge was the major international issue for America, Kennedy thought a good deal about how to handle his Russian counterpart, Nikita S. Khrushchev. How should he respond to Khrushchev's troubling 6 January 1961 speech in which he declared his support for wars of national liberation? On the other hand, how should he react to Khrushchev's private overtures indicating that he wanted more cordial relations with Washington? Kennedy also considered the idea of convening an early summit meeting with Khrushchev. He did indeed meet with the Soviet premier in Vienna in June 1961 and was compelled to deal that summer with a major crisis over Berlin as Khrushchev demanded that the USA leave the German city by the end of the year.[8]

In his first hundred days, however, the key Cold War issue facing Kennedy was the perceived threat from Fidel Castro's Cuba. During the 1960 presidential campaign, Kennedy had showed his generally hardline views on foreign policy, indicated he was not another 'soft' liberal like Adlai E. Stevenson, and sought to suggest he would wage the Cold War more robustly than his Republican opponent Richard M. Nixon by

---

[7]John F. Kennedy, *Why England Slept*, 2nd ed. (New York: W. Funk, 1961); U.S. Department of State, *Foreign Relations of the United States, 1940* (Washington, DC: U.S. Government Printing Office, 1958), pp. 35, 37.

[8]Khrushchev speech, 6 January 1961, osaarchivum.org/files/holdings/300/8/3/text/58-4-307.shtml [accessed on 23 January 2018]; Stevenson to Kennedy, 22 November 1960, in Walter Johnson, ed., *The Papers of Adlai E. Stevenson* (Boston: Little, Brown, 1977), pp. VII, 585.

accusing the Eisenhower-Nixon administration of 'losing' Cuba to the communists in 1959, and pledging bold action to overthrow Castro. Briefed on intelligence issues as a matter of traditional courtesy by CIA Director Allen W. Dulles during the campaign, Kennedy learnt—before his election victory—about the CIA's plan to use Cuban exiles in an invasion of Cuba, what would later become the Bay of Pigs operation. Given his campaign promise to oust Castro, it was convenient for JFK that there was already a plan designed to achieve that objective.[9]

At the start of his presidency, the major foreign-policy decision Kennedy needed to make was whether to authorise the implementation of this plan. He had great faith in the ability of the boys from Langley to get things done. His fascination with the world of espionage was revealed, trivially, by his penchant for the James Bond novels of Ian Fleming, whom Kennedy met in 1960 and whose advice on handling Castro he solicited; he knew that the CIA had succeeded in 1953–1954 in overthrowing governments in Iran and Guatemala. He was concerned that Castro would encourage left-wing revolutions throughout Latin America, if allowed to stay in power. He was almost certainly aware of the CIA plots to assassinate Castro. At least one such plot was scheduled around the time of the Bay of Pigs. Kennedy may well have believed that Castro would be killed, political instability in Cuba would ensue, and in that context, this invasion by a small brigade of anti-Castro Cuban exiles could be successful. For all these reasons, therefore, JFK authorised an invasion at the Bay of Pigs. It turned out to be an ignominious failure, as Castro's forces soon routed the exile army.[10]

After this defeat, Kennedy had to decide whether to live with Castro or continue to work for his overthrow. He plumped for the latter approach, deciding at a 5 May National Security Council (NSC) meeting to do all he could to oust the Cuban leader with the exception of the direct use of US force—though even that was to be kept as a policy option. This general desire to undermine the Castro government

[9] Mark J. White, *The Cuban Missile Crisis* (Basingstoke and London: Macmillan, 1996), pp. 8–13; Allen W. Dulles to Eisenhower, 3 August 1960, box 88, and Dulles memorandum for the record, 21 September 1960, box 89—both in Papers of Allen W. Dulles, Seely Mudd Library, Princeton University, Princeton, New Jersey.

[10] Seymour Hersh, *The Dark Side of Camelot* (London: HarperCollins, 1998), pp. 173–74; Michael R. Beschloss, *The Crisis Years: Kennedy and Khrushchev, 1960–63* (New York: Edward Burlingame, 1991), pp. 137–39.

was given precise definition in November 1961 when Kennedy launched Operation Mongoose, a well-resourced, top-secret CIA programme to destabilise the Cuban government, spark an anti-Castro uprising and then dispatch American forces to the Caribbean island in support of that insurgency in order to ensure Castro's removal from power.[11]

Confronting a communist regime was, then, the major international issue facing Kennedy at the start of his presidency. Even though he was less concerned with the ideological issues involved in a contest between communism and democratic capitalism, this was also the case with Trump as Communist North Korea's programme to develop nuclear weapons greatly troubled him. In dealing with a North Korean state that is a relic of the Cold War, led by an erratic dictator with clear ambitions to become a nuclear power, Trump decided that it was in the security interests of the USA to confront Pyongyang. Accordingly, he announced that the days of America's 'strategic patience' with North Korea were over. Military collaboration between the USA and South Korea was furthered. Trump himself negotiated with Chinese Premier Xi Jinping at his own tackier version of Camp David, Mar-a-Lago, in an attempt to persuade Beijing to pressure Pyongyang to abandon its nuclear programme. He also revealed that all options, including the use of force, were being considered.[12]

On 21 June 2017, Trump announced the continuation of the state of national emergency originally declared by the USA against North Korea in 2008. That same month, he conducted negotiations with South Korean President Moon Jae-in on how to deal with the North. He carried out a broader diplomatic effort, with various Asian governments and at the United Nations, to enlarge sanctions against North Korea. Then, in November, he officially declared that North Korea was a state sponsor of terrorism, to be added to an infamous list that included Iran, Syria

---

[11] National Security Action Memorandum No. 2422, 'U.S. Policy Toward Cuba,' 5 May 1961, National Security Files, box 313, John F. Kennedy Library, Boston, MA; Memorandum From President Kennedy, 30 November 1961, in *Foreign Relations of the United States, 1961–1963*, vol. X, http://history.state.gov/historicaldocuments/frus1961-63v10/d275 [accessed on 26 January 2018].

[12] Trump tweets, 11 April, 30 June 2017, Trump Twitter Archive (this and all other Trump Twitter Archive materials were accessed via www.trumptwitterarchive.com between January and February 2018).

and Sudan. North Korea responded by launching an intercontinental ballistic missile further than with any of their previous missile tests.[13]

Much was written in the media about the incendiary nature of Trump's policies towards North Korea. To be sure, his rhetoric was brash, belligerent and at times juvenile. He threatened to unleash 'fire and the fury' against North Korea. He mocked Kim Jong-un as a 'short and fat' 'Rocket Man.' On 22 September, he tweeted that the North Korean leader was 'obviously a madman who doesn't mind starving or killing his people.' At the start of the New Year, he tweeted that his 'Nuclear Button' was 'much bigger & more powerful' than Kim's. However, Trump neither invented nor exaggerated a threat from Pyongyang that was grave. So regular had been North Korea's nuclear testing that the UN Security Council had felt compelled to impose nine rounds of sanctions since 2006. In August and September 2017 alone, the North had, provocatively, fired two missiles over Japan. In fact, the threat posed by North Korea in 2017 was greater than that represented by the Castro government in 1961 for it was not until the autumn of 1962 that JFK had to deal with the prospect of a nuclearised Cuba.[14]

Trump's general approach, moreover, largely mirrored Kennedy's. He applied a policy of 'maximum pressure' against Pyongyang that included strict economic sanctions. He did not launch a direct attack on the North but kept that as a policy option, informing GOP Senator Lindsey Graham that he would rather start a war with North Korea than permit it to become a nuclear power. On 11 August, he tweeted: 'Military solutions are now fully in place, locked and loaded, should North Korea act

---

[13] Donald J. Trump, 'Notice—Continuation of the National Emergency with Respect to North Korea,' 21 June 2017, *Public Papers of the Presidents*; Trump, 'Remarks During an Expanded Bilateral Meeting with President Moon Jae-in of South Korea,' 30 June 2017, *Public Papers of the Presidents*; Nicholas Kristof, 'Slouching Toward War with North Korea,' *New York Times*, 4 November 2017; Michael D. Shear and David E. Sanger, 'Trump Returns North Korea to List of State Sponsors of Terrorism,' *New York Times*, 20 November 2017; Mark Landler, Choe Sang-Hun, and Helene Cooper, 'North Korea Fires a Ballistic Missile, in a Further Challenge to Trump,' *New York Times*, 28 November 2017.

[14] Wolff, *Fire and Fury*, p. 292; Trump tweets, 17 and 22 September, 11 November 2017, Trump Twitter Archive; Peter Baker and Michael Tackett, 'Trump Says His "Nuclear Button" Is "Much Bigger" Than North Korea's,' *New York Times*, 2 January 2018; Landler, Sang-Hun, and Cooper, 'North Korea Fires a Ballistic Missile.'

unwisely.' The *New York Times* reported on 4 November that those military contingency plans included US air strikes on the North.[15]

Kennedy had adopted the same approach. 'Maximum pressure' in the case of his Cuban policies included the Bay of Pigs invasion, Operation Mongoose, ejecting Cuba from the Organization of American States, and—like Trump with North Korea—sanctions (a strict economic embargo was imposed in February 1962) and the development of contingency plans for an attack on the rogue state. In addition, the CIA devised and tried to implement various assassination plots against Castro, almost certainly with JFK's approval. In summary, Trump's outlandish rhetorical flourishes should not mask the surprising overlap between the way he met the major communist challenge of the first year of his presidency and how Kennedy handled his. Both implemented hardline policies, utilised sanctions, authorised the development of military contingency plans, and retained the option of a direct attack on their adversary.[16]

Beyond North Korea, a key foreign-policy issue for Trump was America's relationship with Russia and, more specifically, his personal relationship with President Vladimir Putin. His love affair with the Russian leader went back to 2013 when he speculated via his Twitter account whether Putin would become his best friend during the upcoming Miss Universe Pageant in Moscow. During the 2016 campaign, he spoke openly of his admiration for Putin, even arguing that he was a better leader than Obama. Speculation as to the reasons for his stated admiration for Putin included his penchant for authoritarian strongmen, business dealings with Russia, and even that Moscow had incriminating information about Trump and was blackmailing him. A week into his presidency, Trump received a congratulatory call from Putin, and a White House press release described that conversation as 'a significant start to improving the relationship between the United States and Russia that is in need of repair.' A week later, Trump spoke to Bill O'Reilly of *Fox News* of his respect for the Russian leader. These warm sentiments created the prospect of a US-Russian rapprochement during the Trump years, but this became politically problematic for the new president as evidence mounted of Russian interference in the 2016 campaign to

---

[15] Kristof, 'Slouching Toward War with North Korea'; Trump tweet, 11 August 2017, Trump Twitter Archive.

[16] White, *Cuban Missile Crisis*, pp. 22–59.

assist Trump and of possible collusion between Moscow and the Trump team, including his own family. An investigation of the matter proceeded under the leadership of Special Counsel Robert Mueller and in Congress. Trump sought to counter this claim by asserting that it was 'fake news.' In addition, the press began to talk in terms of a new Cold War, fuelled by Russian aggression, manifest in Moscow's cyber meddling in other countries.[17]

Despite the pressure on Trump to distance himself from Putin, he did not do so. In July, he repeated as trustworthy Putin's insistence to him that Moscow had not interfered in the 2016 election. At the Asia-Pacific Economic Cooperation summit in Vietnam in November, he held informal talks with his Russian counterpart. That same month, it became clear that Trump had essentially ceded post-war planning for Syria to Putin who met in Sochi with officials from Iran and Turkey, but not the USA, to discuss the issue. On 14 December, Trump thanked Putin in a phone conversation for the praise he had lavished on his economic policies at his annual news conference in Moscow. Putin also revealed that the two men were on first-name terms.[18]

A perhaps charitable summary of Trump's Russian policy is that, conceptually, it has been a fusion of the approach of Franklin Roosevelt, in terms of its emphasis on conciliation with Moscow, and Richard Nixon,

---

[17] Brian Klaas, *The Despot's Apprentice: Donald Trump's Attack on Democracy* (London: Hurst & Co., 2017), p. 211; Andrew Kaczynski, Chris Massie, and Nathan McDermott, '80 Times Trump Talked About Putin,' *CNN Politics*, March 2017, edition.cnn.com/interactive/2017/03/politics/trump-putin-russia-timeline/ [accessed on 28 February 2018]; Wolff, *Fire and Fury*, pp. 99–102; Readout of the President's Call with Russian President Vladimir Putin, 28 January 2017, White House, Briefings & Statements; Trump, 'Interview with Bill O'Reilly of Fox News,' 3 February 2017, *Public Papers of the Presidents*; Trump, 'President's News Conference,' 16 February 2017, *Public Papers of the Presidents*; Trump tweet, 16 February 2017, Trump Twitter Archive; Evan Osnos, David Remnick, and Joshua Yaffa, 'Trump, Putin, and the New Cold War,' *New Yorker*, 6 March 2017, www.newyorker.com/magazine/2017/03/06/trump-putin-and-the-new-cold-war [accessed on 10 December 2017].

[18] Trump tweet, 9 July 2017, Trump Twitter Archive; Andrew Restuccia and Nancy Cook, 'Trump Careens Off Script on Russia After Putin Meeting,' *Politico*, 11 November 2017 (this and all other *Politico* articles were accessed via www.politico.com between March 2017 and February 2018); Michael Crowley, 'Trump Cedes Syrian Postwar Planning to Putin,' *Politico*, 21 November 2017; Henry C. Jackson, 'In a Phone Call, Trump Thanks Putin for Praise, Looks for Help on North Korea,' *Politico*, 14 December 2017.

in terms of the underlying Realpolitik conviction that, whatever the ethical shortcomings of the Russian state, Moscow could help in handling various international problems in a manner congenial with American interests. In a Twitter message sent after his Vietnam talks with Putin, he explained, 'I want to solve North Korea, Syria, Ukraine, terrorism, and Russia can greatly help!'[19]

In comparison with Kennedy, Trump's approach to Russia was less robust. Kennedy emphasised the gravity of the threat posed by Communism in general and Russia in particular. Trump could have done the same given Russian policy in the Ukraine and the credible evidence of Moscow's interference in elections in the USA in 2016 and elsewhere. He refused, however, to countenance the possibility of Russian assistance in his own election. Even if Moscow did possess compromising information on him (and hence, his pro-Putin stance was tactical), Trump's Russian policy has been more naïve than Kennedy's. JFK confronted the reality of the Russian challenge but exhibited sufficient tactical flexibility to move after the Cuban missile crisis towards a more accommodating approach that included the 1963 Test Ban Treaty. The oddest example of Trump's naivety came on 9 July 2017 when he tweeted that he and Putin had discussed 'forming an impenetrable Cyber Security unit so that election hacking…will be guarded,' an idea he abandoned—presumably on the advice of national security staff—before the day was out.[20]

On the domestic scene, a focus for both the Trump and Kennedy presidencies was race. With JFK, this was due not so much to the emphasis placed by him on racial matters—international affairs were always his priority—but to a Civil Rights Movement that had gathered momentum. In the years preceding his election as president, the Supreme Court outlawed segregation in public schools in the landmark Brown v. Board of Education decision. The Montgomery Bus Boycott resulted in not only the desegregation of transport in that Alabama city but brought Martin Luther King to the fore. Civil rights legislation was passed in Congress in 1957 and 1960. The proliferation of the 'sit-in' movement through the South in 1960 helped make race a major political issue by the start of the new decade in a way that it had not been say during the New Deal years.

[19] Trump tweets, 13 April, 11 November 2017, Trump Twitter Archive.
[20] Trump tweet, 9 July 2017, Trump Twitter Archive.

As president, Kennedy had to respond to the reality of an increasingly potent Civil Rights Movement.[21]

With Trump, race became a prominent issue because of his controversial handling of various race-related issues that emerged, including the decision of some black NFL players to kneel during the national anthem. But the context is important in understanding the underlying dynamics of the race issue in 2017, in terms of both the scepticism felt by many Americans about Trump's bona fides on racial matters and the resonance of his message on race to some white Americans. That scepticism was due largely to the way he had queried whether Barack Obama had been born in the USA (and so had the right even to run for president). Trump's participation in the Birther Movement seemed a deliberate attempt to delegitimise America's first African-American president. This damaged his reputation with minorities, with whom he had been popular as his TV show *The Apprentice* often portrayed ethnic contestants in a positive, upwardly mobile fashion. The appeal of Trump's stance on race was due to an important long-term trend: the increasing sense of alienation of the white working class. The impact of globalisation, the rise of economic rivals such as China, the loss of blue-collar jobs overseas and the very slow growth in wages had created a palpable anger and hopelessness. The most striking symptom of this has been the increasing mortality rate amongst middle-aged white non-Hispanics, after decades of improving lifespans. The research of Princeton economists Anne Case and Angus Deaton has shown that these 'deaths of despair' have often been from drug or alcohol abuse or suicide. Whilst economic insecurity was at the root of this despair, there has been a discernible 'white rage' at African-American progress, especially after Obama's election. Trump's campaign pledge to bring back blue-collar jobs met the economic concerns of many white working-class voters, and his indelicate use of language—describing Mexican migrants as rapists, for example—pandered to those prejudices. As journalist Michael Wolff put it, Trump (influenced by Bannon) had 'come closer than

[21] For excellent coverage of this phase of the Civil Rights Movement, see Taylor Branch, *Parting the Waters: America in the King Years, 1954–63* (New York: Simon & Schuster, 1988).

any other major national politician since the Civil Rights movement to tolerating a race-tinged political view.'[22]

Trump's handling of a series of issues in 2017 confirmed for his detractors his crass insensitivity on racial matters, and to his supporters his refreshing willingness to eschew politically correct cant. A week into his presidency, he signed an executive order on immigration and travel, banning Muslims from seven countries from entering the USA. 'This is not about religion,' he claimed, 'this is about terror and keeping our country safe.' The result, however, was outrage at home and abroad. When in August clashes erupted in Charlottesville, Virginia, between Klan and American Nazi supporters on the one hand and Black Lives Matter protestors on the other, he refused to condemn the white nationalists. Rather he chided the excesses of the overtly racist group *and* those protesting a spate of recent police shootings of black Americans. He condemned 'hatred, bigotry, and violence on *many* sides.' His tweets merely called for the 'swift restoration of law and order,' and lamented that the situation was, 'So sad!' He also attacked those NFL players who sought to draw attention to the twin issues of racism and police brutality by refusing to stand during the national anthem. 'The issue of kneeling has nothing to do with race,' Trump claimed in a 25 September tweet. 'It is about respect for our Country, Flag and National Anthem. NFL must respect this.' He even called those players 'son of a bitch,' and demanded that the NFL suspend for the remainder of the season Oakland Raiders running back Marshawn Lynch for wearing a 'Trump vs. everybody' t-shirt. Once again Trump had succeeded in appealing to his base. As one journalist put it, 'Despite efforts by NFL players to frame their protests as targeting racial issues in the U.S., Trump has successfully turned

---

[22] Green, *Devil's Bargain*, p. 39; Susan B. Glasser and Glenn Thrush, 'What's Going on with America's White People?' *Politico* (September/October, 2016); Anne Case and Angus Deaton, 'Rising Morbidity and Mortality in Midlife Among White Non-Hispanic Americans in the 21st Century,' *Proceedings of the National Academy of Sciences*, 112 (December 2015), 15078–83; Wolff, *Fire and Fury*, p. 138. For an excellent analysis of the increasing alienation of both young and old white men, see David Frum, *Trumpocracy: The Corruption of the American Republic* (New York: Harper, 2018), pp. 192–204, and for his appeal to white Americans, see T. J. Coles, *President Trump, Inc.: How Big Business and Neoliberalism Empower Populism and the Far-Right* (West Hoathly: Clairview, 2017), p. 31.

them into a front on the culture wars that played such a dramatic role in his campaign.'[23]

Controversy broke out once more following Trump's phone call to Myeshia Johnson, the widow of a black Army Sergeant La David Johnson, to convey his condolences. Trump's comments impressed neither Johnson nor family friend House Representative Frederica Wilson. They said that the president had forgotten the slain soldier's name. Trump responded by calling Wilson 'wacky' and suggesting Myeshia Johnson had lied. Trump's sensitivity to black America was again called into question when he backed for the vacant Alabama Senate seat Republican candidate Roy Moore, who had not only been accused of paedophilia but also had extolled the virtues of America at the time of slavery, arguing that families were more close-knit then and that 'our country had a direction.' All of this was of no concern to Trump. Moore sounded 'like a really great guy who ran a fantastic campaign,' he tweeted.[24]

Not surprisingly, many black Americans took umbrage at Trump's insensitivity and, especially when considering his reaction to the white nationalist rally in Charlottesville, even bigotry. And black America responded. Black Republican Sophia Nelson, who had worked for George W. Bush, wrote an article for *Politico* in which she lambasted the president for his 'disdain for black women,' describing him as 'the bully in the White House.' In the Virginia gubernatorial race in November, high levels of black political engagement were reported with African Americans determined to send a message to Trump in the wake of the Charlottesville controversy. When Trump spoke at the opening of the Mississippi Civil Rights Museum, civil rights leader and Georgia House Representative John Lewis boycotted the event, saying in a joint statement with Congressman Bennie Thompson that 'President Trump's

[23]Wolff, *Fire and Fury*, pp. 65, 292–94; President Donald J. Trump Statement Regarding Recent Executive Order Concerning Extreme Vetting, 29 January 2017, White House, Briefings & Statements; Louis Nelson, 'Trump Revives His Twitter Fights with Black Athletes,' *Politico*, 22 November 2017; Trump tweets, 12 August (2), 25 September 2017.

[24]Sophia Nelson, 'What's Trump's Problem with Black Women?' *Politico*, 26 October 2017; Nancy Cook, 'Boycotted by Black Leaders, Trump Speaks at Civil Rights Museum Opening,' *Politico*, 9 December 2017; Trump tweet, 27 September 2017, Trump Twitter Archive.

attendance and his hurtful policies are an insult to the people portrayed in this civil rights museum.'[25]

A defence of Trump's leadership on race could be constructed. Perhaps his version of his conversation with Myeshia Johnson was more accurate than hers. It could well be the case that he was genuinely offended by what he perceived as the lack of patriotism apparent in the refusal of NFL players to stand for the national anthem. But his unwillingness to draw a distinction in Charlottesville between the racism of the far right and those protesting that racism was egregious. Trump had failed to provide the appropriate moral leadership. It stood in sharp contrast to Kennedy's civil rights address on 11 June 1963, following racial disturbances in Birmingham and at the University of Alabama, in which he described racial equality as 'a moral issue' that was 'as old as the scriptures and…as clear as the American Constitution,' and introduced legislation to end segregation. In contrast, Trump had prioritised pandering to disaffected whites rather than showing support for causes such as Black Lives Matter.[26]

Although Kennedy's commitment to civil rights in 1961 was not as pronounced as it would become two years later after the Birmingham crisis, his rhetoric and approach on race differed markedly from Trump's at the start of his presidency. In 1961, the major civil rights issue that JFK had to confront was the Freedom Rides. Organised chiefly by the Congress of Racial Equality, black and white activists journeyed by bus through Alabama in May in order to challenge segregation in interstate transportation. Passengers were savagely beaten in Anniston and Birmingham. There was evidence of KKK participation. The local authorities, including Governor John Patterson and the police, did nothing to prevent these heinous acts. The statement issued by JFK on 20 May was morally neutral in urging all sides to prevent further violence. But in their actions, the president and Attorney General Robert F. Kennedy showed their increasing determination to protect the protesting passengers. They dispatched federal marshals to Alabama to do precisely that. Robert Kennedy's Justice Department exhorted the KKK,

[25] Nelson, 'What's Trump's Problem with Black Women?'; Kevin Robillard, 'Activists Eye Post-Charlottesville Surge in Black Voting in Virginia,' *Politico*, 5 November 2017; Cook, 'Boycotted by Black Leaders, Trump Speaks at Civil Rights Museum Opening.'

[26] Kennedy, 'Radio and Television Report to the American People on Civil Rights,' 11 June 1963, *Public Papers of the Presidents*.

as well as the National States Rights Party, to desist from interference. Influenced by pressure from Robert Kennedy, which must have been applied at JFK's behest, the Interstate Commerce Commission ordered an end to the practice of segregation at interstate bus terminals. At this point, the president did not propose legislation to bring fundamental change to racial relations in the South. Nevertheless, he displayed early signs of the moral authority he would bring to bear in 1963 when introducing the civil rights bill. The appointment of more blacks, notably Robert Weaver and Thurgood Marshall, to significant positions in his administration and the judiciary and the numerous lawsuits brought by the Justice Department's Civil Rights Division to ensure black voting rights were other early signs of the enlightened trajectory of the Kennedy administration's policies on race. This stands in stark contrast to an incipient Trump approach that exacerbated racial tensions in America.[27]

Beyond policy, the first year of the presidencies of Trump and JFK displayed some common features. The first was a communications strategy that shared the same basic objective. Trump continued to make full use of his Twitter account, as he did during the presidential campaign. His tweets had a clear purpose: to circumvent the traditional media by communicating directly with his supporters. As of February 2018, those followers totalled 47.9 million. That enabled him to sustain the support he received from his base. So a major advantage of Twitter is it allowed Trump to communicate a message to the American people unfiltered by a censorious television and print media that he had come to loathe. Trump's understanding of this accounts in part for the overt hostility of himself and his aides to the press, including the risible reprimand given by his pugnacious Press Secretary Sean Spicer to the journalists at a White House press conference on 21 January 2017 for underestimating the apparently limitless throngs that attended Trump's inauguration. Why be obsequious to a press whose power and influence had been eroded by the advent of Twitter?[28]

---

[27] Herbert S. Parmet, *JFK: The Presidency of John F. Kennedy* (Harmondsworth: Penguin, 1984 reprint), pp. 252–56.

[28] Sean Spicer press conference, 21 January 2017, https://edition.cnn.com/videos/politics/2017/01/21/sean-spicer-entire-defends-inauguration-crowd-size-sot.cnn [accessed on 30 December 2017]. For an example of Trump's antipathy towards the press, see Wolff, *Fire and Fury*, pp. 48–50, for an account of his angry speech before CIA officials on 21 January 2017.

Bypassing the press to communicate directly with the voters— Kennedy had the very same idea. Having dazzled in the television debates with Nixon in the 1960 campaign, JFK's Press Secretary Pierre Salinger hatched a plan to exploit Kennedy's telegenic appeal: regular live televised press conferences. Confident in his ability to avoid any embarrassing gaffes on live television, Kennedy accepted Salinger's proposal. Hence, on 25 January 1961, in the State Department auditorium, the new president held the first of what would turn out to be numerous live televised press conferences. They were very successful. Kennedy consistently impressed. His assiduous preparation enhanced the quality of his performances. He would learn reams of relevant facts, field likely questions from his aides; sometimes, Salinger would speak to the journalists beforehand, find out what issues were of concern to them, and convey this information to Kennedy so that he could anticipate the sorts of questions he would be asked. Even the visual impact of these press conferences was considered and enhanced. The back wall of the State Department auditorium was adjusted through the use of partitions, if less journalists than usual attended, so that the room always looked full. These news conferences account in part for the high approval ratings JFK enjoyed during his presidency, despite the narrowness of his electoral victory over Nixon.[29]

A major reason why Kennedy so favoured live televised news conferences was the opportunity it afforded him to communicate directly with the American people. To be sure, he needed to respond to questions from the press that were not always straightforward. But compared to a newspaper or television news report, what he was saying in a live televised press conference was less filtered by the Fourth Estate. (For that reason, some newspapers were appalled by the idea of live TV news conferences, believing it reduced their own influence.) Americans could hear his words and see how he said them as he spoke. Later in his presidency, when journalist and friend Benjamin C. Bradlee commented on how well a 17 December 1962 television interview of Kennedy had been received, JFK responded: 'Well, I always said that when we don't have to go through you bastards, we can really get our story over to the American people.' Trump would no doubt endorse that sentiment. His penchant for Twitter reflected a conviction, which he shared with Kennedy, that it

---

[29] Pierre Salinger, *With Kennedy* (Garden City, NY: Doubleday, 1966), pp. 53–54, 56, 135–41; Kennedy, news conference, 25 January 1961, *Public Papers of the Presidents*.

is in the presidential interest to communicate directly with the American people and to diminish the influence of the press.[30]

Another similarity between Kennedy and Trump is the centrality of family to the image each sought to project. For Kennedy, the cultivation of an appealing image had always been a key objective. Before reaching the White House, he had constructed a powerful, multifaceted image as man of letters, war hero, sex symbol and a symbol of the family. With a prominent family—his father was one of the richest businessmen in America, his mother was daughter of the mayor of Boston—JFK was always seen not so much as an individual politician but as the represent-ative of a dynasty. His marriage to Jacqueline Bouvier and their young children enlarged this sense of JFK as a familial symbol. The images of him in the 1950s that adorned the covers of magazines such as *Life* and *Time* were often with Jackie and their daughter Caroline. Robert Kennedy's role in running his 1960 presidential campaign forged an even greater sense of JFK as an emblem of the family.[31]

The start of his presidency bolstered Kennedy's image as a familial symbol. Robert Kennedy became attorney general, his closest adviser, and the second most powerful man in America. The inauguration was important for the way it showcased the Kennedy family as JFK was sworn in as president. Journalists were struck by just how many Kennedys were in attendance, and in their articles, they highlighted the dynastic signifi-cance of the inauguration. As one writer put it, JFK's inauguration was 'more than just a change-over of administration and a party victory; it is the proclamation of a new American dynasty – the Kennedys.' The notion that the Kennedys constituted America's royal family was thus created at the start of JFK's presidency. Jackie Kennedy would entrench that idea a week after the assassination in Dallas by invoking the legend of Camelot in the interview she granted *Life* magazine.[32]

---

[30]Benjamin C. Bradlee, *Conversations with Kennedy* (New York: Pocket, 1976), p. 123.

[31]For an overview of the construction of JFK's image, see Mark White, 'Apparent Perfection: The Image of John F. Kennedy,' *History: Journal of the Historical Association* 98 (April 2013), 226–46.

[32]Richard Reeves, *President Kennedy: Profile of Power* (London and Basingstoke: Papermac, 1994), p. 35; Victor Lasky, *J.F.K.: The Man and the Myth* (New York: Macmillan, 1963), pp. 11–12; Theodore White, typed notes of conversation with Jackie Kennedy on 29 November 1963, 19 December 1963, Papers of Theodore H. White, box 59, Kennedy Library.

Family has also been central to how the American people and the media have viewed the Trump White House. During his presidential campaign, he relied on his daughter from his first marriage, Ivanka, and his son-in-law Jared Kushner as key advisers. Despite the risk of provoking accusations of nepotism, as did JFK with his choice of Bobby as attorney general, he proceeded to appoint Ivanka Trump as a presidential assistant and Kushner as senior adviser. She attracted enormous attention from the media, became the de facto First Lady, and on 25 April 2017 attended a Berlin conference on women's issues—sharing the stage with German Chancellor Angela Merkel and IMF Managing Director Christine Lagarde. Trump used his Twitter account to sing her praises. 'I am so proud of my daughter Ivanka,' he said on 11 February. 'To be abused and treated so badly by the media, and to still hold her head so high, is truly wonderful!' And he often retweeted her tweets. His public praise for her was sincere; in private, they got along well. Behind closed doors she even disclosed her plan to use her elevated status in her father's administration to become, one day, the first woman president.[33]

Despite having no diplomatic experience, Kushner's policy remit included US relations with China, Mexico, and Canada, as well as the Israeli-Palestinian dispute. On 27 March 2017, his role in the new administration expanded even further when Trump put him in charge of the Office of American Innovation that would prune federal bureaucracy. The American people and the media, therefore, came to view the Trump White House as a family business, as they had the Kennedy presidency. So in that sense the images of Kennedy and Trump overlapped.[34]

Other similarities between Trump and JFK can be identified. In the area of defence, both announced vast military build-ups. In Kennedy's case, his commitment to bolstering America's military power derived from his examination as a Harvard student of the failure of the British appeasement of Germany. His conviction on the importance of countering totalitarian foes, be it Nazi Germany or Communist Russia, with a strong defence resulted in his consistent support for increases in US military spending during his years in Congress. As president, Kennedy called

---

[33] Simon Shuster, 'Ivanka Trump's Booing in Berlin Leaves Angela Merkel Red-Faced,' *Time*, 25 April 2017, time.com/4754369/ivanka-trump-boo-berlin-angela-merkel/ [accessed on 23 February 2018]; Trump tweet, 11 February 2017, Trump Twitter Archive; Wolff, *Fire and Fury*, pp. 69, 79.

[34] Wolff, *Fire and Fury*, pp. 180–81.

for a substantial increase in military expenditures in 1961, a determination to fortify the nation's defences that was enlarged by the superpower crisis over Berlin that summer. This defence appropriation of $46.66 billion was the largest since the Korean War.[35]

Trump's resolve to augment defence spending was no less considerable. It was part of his critique of what he perceived to be Obama's failure to maintain America's strength and greatness that his predecessor had permitted the nation's military power to atrophy. In the context of the 2007–2008 financial crash, Great Recession and huge government debt, military expenditures had been cut. Trump vowed to restore the strength of the US military. He argued that this was especially important given the North Korean threat. In December 2017, he signed a bill that vastly increased defence spending. He had called for a $668 billion budget for the military. In the end, the Republican-controlled Congress produced a bill amounting to $700 billion. A jubilant Trump signed it into law at a White House ceremony in which he explained, 'We need our military. It's got to be perfecto.' 'We're working very diligently on … building up forces,' he added. A key part of the legislation, as Trump told the press, was the bolstering of America's missile defence systems in order to 'continue our campaign to create maximum pressure on the vile dictatorship in North Korea.'[36]

In the area of economic policy, Trump championed tax cuts as a way of generating growth. In 2016, he had promised a major tax cut to help ordinary working Americans, a fiscal commitment consistent with the overall theme of his campaign of championing forgotten blue-collar and middle-class workers. Having failed in late July 2017 to secure a congressional repeal of Obamacare, which he had described as a 'nightmare,' he depended on the passage of his tax bill to be able to claim a major domestic policy achievement in the first year of his presidency. So, along with GOP leaders in Congress, he began to focus on large corporate

---

[35] Kennedy, *Why England Slept*; Kennedy, 'Radio and Television Report to the American People on the Berlin Crisis,' 25 July 1961, *Public Papers of the Presidents*; New York Times Chronology: Defense & Military, Kennedy Library, www.jfklibrary.org/Research/Research-Aids/Ready-Reference/New-York-Times-Chronology/Defense-and-Military-in-progress.aspx [accessed on 16 January 2018].

[36] Darlene Superville, 'Trump Signs $700 Billion Military Budget into Law,' *Washington Post*, 12 December 2017 (this and other *Washington Post* articles were accessed via www.washingtonpost.com between June 2017 and February 2018); Trump tweet, 28 November 2017, Trump Twitter Archive.

tax cuts as an approach that would receive widespread support from Republicans on Capitol Hill. On 27 September, Trump's White House and Republican leaders unveiled a plan called 'Unified Framework for Fixing Our Broken Tax Code,' which proposed inter alia slashing corporate tax from 35 to 20%. Nonpartisan pundits said that the plan would benefit mainly the affluent, although Trump claimed the contrary.[37]

As the final plan took shape, this trend towards prioritising corporate tax cuts over working- and middle-class tax reduction continued. A $300 'family flexibility credit' to assist the poor was cut from ten to five years in duration so that the corporate tax cut could be made permanent. In effect, $200 billion was transferred from families to corporate America. On 16 November, the House of Representatives passed the tax bill. Senate deliberations served only to enhance its regressive features. 'Pass through' tax reductions for businesses that paid tax via the individual code were incorporated: they would benefit mostly the top 1% of wage earners. In short, the tax cut for corporations was vast and permanent whilst for the poor and middle class it was mostly temporary and far smaller than promised by Trump in 2016 (8.9%, not 35% as pledged). This did not deter him from declaring on Twitter his great pride in a tax bill that he claimed would boost US business in the forthcoming year. In the context of a rapidly growing economy and booming stock market, Trump could claim a major accomplishment in domestic policy. His background as a high-profile businessman added a sense of credibility to this major economic reform.[38]

Ultimately, championing tax cuts was a common theme of the Trump and Kennedy presidencies. Encouraged by the Keynesians in his administration, such as Chairman of the Council of Economic Advisers Walter Heller, to stimulate the sluggish economy by cutting taxes, JFK was initially reluctant given the need for self-sacrifice he had emphasised in the 1960 campaign. However, he came to believe that a tax cut would ameliorate the economy. Hence, on 13 August 1962, he delivered a television address informing Americans of his intention to introduce a tax bill

---

[37] Statement by President Donald J. Trump on the Senate Supporting the Motion to Proceed on Healthcare, 25 July 2017, White House, Briefings & Statements; Damian Paletta, 'As Tax Plan Gained Steam, GOP Lost Focus on the Middle Class,' *Washington Post*, 9 December 2017.

[38] Paletta, 'As Tax Plan Gained Steam'; Trump tweets, 22 and 26 December 2017, Trump Twitter Archive.

in Congress in early 1963. By summer 1963, the Kennedy administration was backing a bill that would reduce taxes and introduce depreciation allowances and an investment tax credit. The bill did not pass in his lifetime but it did in 1964 with President Lyndon B. Johnson actively supporting it.[39]

It is striking that in the essential thrust of their fiscal policy (tax cuts) and defence policy (military build-up) the Trump and Kennedy presidencies overlapped. These similarities on policy should not be exaggerated, however. In domestic affairs, JFK unveiled a liberal agenda encompassing a housing programme, medical care for the aged and an increase in the minimum wage. For his part, Trump embarked on a range of conservative policies, including the rolling back of both Obamacare and environmental-protection policies.[40]

Despite a turbulent private life that remained hidden from the American people, JFK always comported himself in public with a dignity and grace conspicuously absent from Trump's presidency. That helps account for another notable difference between these two presidents. Despite the Bay of Pigs, Kennedy ended his first hundred days with approval ratings from the American people of 83%—the highest on record. He would go on to enjoy very high approval ratings throughout his presidency. Trump, by contrast, had exceedingly low approval ratings during his first year in office. At the start of 2018, a Gallup poll revealed that only 37% of Americans approved of his job performance, whilst 58% disapproved. That suggests a clear majority of the American people regarded Trump's early presidency as a failure.[41]

Despite his public gracefulness, Kennedy's private life was as tawdry as Trump's. Character has become an important theme in presidential

---

[39] James Hillyer, 'Promoting Keynesian Liberalism: Walter W. Heller and US Economic Policy, 1933–1987,' unpublished Ph.D. thesis (UCL, 2017), passim; Kennedy, 'Report on the National Economy,' 13 August 1962, *Public Papers of the Presidents*; Parmet, *JFK*, p. 246.

[40] Irving Bernstein, *Promises Kept: John F. Kennedy's New Frontier* (New York: Oxford University Press, 1991); Trump tweet, 14 February 2017, Trump Twitter Archive; Fact Sheet, 'President Trump: Putting Coal Country Back to Work,' 16 February 2017, White House, Briefings & Statements.

[41] Kennedy, Presidential Job Approval, *The American Presidency Project*; polling data, President Trump's Job Approval, Real Clear Politics, https://www.realclearpolitics.com/epolls/other/president_trump_job_approval-6179.html#polls [accessed on 9 February 2018].

studies. In his 1991 work on Kennedy, *A Question of Character*, historian Thomas C. Reeves argued that it should be viewed as central to an understanding of JFK's presidency. A dissolute private life, he claimed, was evidence of an ethical deficiency—a lack of understanding of the basic difference between right and wrong—that damaged his presidency, whether it was by escalating the arms race or espousing civil rights with an unimpressive timidity. The most striking feature of JFK's private life was its sexual hedonism. In 1961, he continued an affair with Californian socialite Judith Campbell, to whom Frank Sinatra had introduced him in early 1960, that was ill-judged as she became close to Chicago crime boss Sam Giancana. Hence, there was the risk of blackmail by the Mob. He also started an affair with bohemian artist Mary Meyer. They took drugs together, smoking marijuana in the White House.[42]

With Trump, the true nature of his presidential private life will most likely emerge only after he has left the White House. What is known is that prior to his presidency he was a philanderer of prodigious proportions. Along with his three marriages was his disclosure to *NBC* host Billy Bush, caught on tape and released during the 2016 campaign, that when it came to women, 'I don't even wait.... You can do anything... Grab them by the pussy': in effect, this was an admission of sexual assault. Numerous women came forward in the 2016 campaign to claim that they had been victims of a predatory Trump, allegations that were handled by his adroit lawyer Marc Kasowitz. Trump also boasted about how one of the most satisfying things in his life was bedding his friends' wives. A former British intelligence officer disclosed that, according to his Russian sources, Putin's intelligence services had compromised Trump by taping him with prostitutes at the time of the 2013 Miss Universe contest in Moscow.[43]

---

[42] Thomas C. Reeves, *A Question of Character: A Life of John F. Kennedy* (New York: Free Press, 1991), pp. 1–17, 413–21; Judith Exner, *My Story* (New York: Grove, 1977); Nina Burleigh, *A Very Private Woman: The Life and Unsolved Murder of Presidential Mistress Mary Meyer* (New York: Bantam, 1998), pp. 207–8, 211–13.

[43] Wolff, *Fire and Fury*, pp. 13, 23, 280; Green, *Devil's Bargain*, p. 220; Jon Swaine and Shaun Walker, 'Trump in Moscow: What Happened at Miss Universe in 2013,' *Guardian*, 18 September 2017, www.theguardian.com/us-news/2017/sep/18/trump-in-moscow-what-happened-at-miss-universe-in-2013 [accessed on 26 February 2018].

A key difference between Trump and JFK on this character issue of private conduct is the shifting role played by the media. Kennedy was president in an era of press deference that meant journalists neither investigated nor reported his shenanigans. Strict Catholics Florence and Leonard Kater, neighbours of Kennedy lover Pamela Turnure, collected evidence of this affair and sent it to numerous newspapers that ignored the scandal. Trump's presidency has taken place in an era in which Vietnam and Watergate had long destroyed the media deference enjoyed by Kennedy. So despite having private lives of striking similarity, personal conduct did not become a political issue for JFK but has been a major part of the press coverage of Trump as man and leader. In February 2018, for instance, his alleged affairs in 2006 with Playboy model Karen McDougal and porn star Stormy Daniels were widely reported. In this way, the Trump presidency resembles more that of Bill Clinton than of JFK. As with Kennedy scholarship, this issue of character will necessarily become a salient theme in the emerging Trump historiography.[44]

A comparison of Trump and Kennedy reveals a number of surprising similarities. Both took a hard-line with a communist adversary, North Korea in the case of the former and Cuba in the case of JFK. Despite Trump's rhetorical hyperbole, he used the same sort of tactics as Kennedy, from sanctions to military contingency planning. Both made family a key part of the image they sought to project. Both tried to bypass the media in order to communicate directly with the American people; Trump used Twitter for this, whereas Kennedy scheduled live televised press conferences. Both had private lives notable for sexual excess. Both championed tax cuts and a military build-up. To be sure, Kennedy sought liberal reform on housing, education, health care and aid to depressed areas; Trump did not. Trump's foreign policy was less wholeheartedly internationalist. But the surprising degree of imbrication between their presidencies suggests that the greatest difference between

---

[44]Seymour Hersh, *The Dark Side of Camelot* (London: HarperCollins, 1998), pp. 106–10; Ronan Farrow, 'Donald Trump, a Playboy Model, and a System for Concealing Infidelity,' *New Yorker*, 16 February 2018, https://www.newyorker.com/news/news-desk/donald-trump-a-playboy-model-and-a-system-for-concealing-infidelity-national-enquirer-karen-mcdougal [accessed on 20 February 2018]; Michael Rothfield and Joe Palazzolo, 'Trump Lawyer Arranged $130,000 Payment for Adult-Film Star's Silence,' *Wall Street Journal*, 12 January 2018, www.wsj.com/articles/trump-lawyer-arranged-130-000-payment-for-adult-film-stars-silence-1515787678 [accessed on 20 February 2018].

the two men was stylistic. Trump's boorish manner was reminiscent of Joe McCarthy—it is interesting to note that one of Trump's early mentors was ruthless McCarthy aide Roy Cohn—whilst Kennedy's grace and good manners evoked Cary Grant. Those stylistic differences should not conceal the substantive truth that in espousing tax cuts, a defence build-up and a tough foreign policy (towards North Korea), Trump's presidency is hardly unique in modern American history. Future generations of historians will need to grapple with this key issue, namely the extent to which the Trump presidency is unprecedented in US political history.[45]

REFERENCES

Bernstein, Irving. *Promises Kept: John F. Kennedy's New Frontier.* New York: Oxford University Press, 1991.

Beschloss, Michael R. *The Crisis Years: Kennedy and Khrushchev, 1960–63.* New York: Edward Burlingame, 1991.

Branch, Taylor. *Parting the Waters: America in the King Years, 1954–63.* New York: Simon & Schuster, 1988.

Burleigh, Nina. *A Very Private Woman: The Life and Unsolved Murder of Presidential Mistress Mary Meyer.* New York: Bantam, 1998.

Coles, T. J. *President Trump, Inc.: How Big Business and Neoliberalism Empower Populism and the Far-Right.* West Hoathly: Clairview, 2017.

Frum, David. *Trumpocracy: The Corruption of the American Republic.* New York: Harper, 2018.

Green, Joshua. *Devil's Bargain: Steve Bannon, Donald Trump, and the Storming of the Presidency.* London: Scribe, 2017.

Hersh, Seymour. *The Dark Side of Camelot.* London: HarperCollins, 1998.

Klaas, Brian. *The Despot's Apprentice: Donald Trump's Attack on Democracy.* London: Hurst & Co., 2017.

Kranish, Michael, and Marc Fisher. *Trump Revealed.* London: *Washington Post*, 2017.

Lasky, Victor. *J.F.K.: The Man and the Myth.* New York: Macmillan, 1963.

Nelson, Michael. *Trump's First Year.* Charlottesville and London: University of Virginia Press, 2018.

Parmet, Herbert S. *JFK: The Presidency of John F. Kennedy.* Harmondsworth: Penguin, 1984 reprint.

---

[45]For Roy Cohn's relationship with Trump since the 1970s, see Michael Kranish and Marc Fisher, *Trump Revealed* (London: *Washington Post*, 2017), pp. 60–69.

Reeves, Richard. *President Kennedy: A Profile of Power*. London and Basingstoke: Papermac, 1994.

Reeves, Thomas C. *A Question of Character: A Life of John F. Kennedy*. New York: Free Press, 1991.

White, Mark J. *The Cuban Missile Crisis*. Basingstoke and London: Macmillan, 1996.

White, Mark J., ed. *Kennedy: The New Frontier Revisited*. New York: New York University Press, 1998.

Wolff, Michael. *Fire and Fury: Inside the Trump White House*. London: Little, Brown, 2018.

CHAPTER 4

Make America Great Again: Ronald Reagan and Donald Trump

Iwan Morgan

Donald J. Trump supposedly authored the "Make America Great Again" slogan that defined his 2016 presidential campaign the day after Republican standard-bearer Mitt Romney lost to incumbent Barack Obama in the 2012 election. Seeing his way now open for a White House run four years hence, he immediately registered the catchphrase for his own exclusive use with the US Patent and Trademark Office. In fact, Ronald Reagan had used a very similar slogan, "Let's Make America Great Again," in his presidential campaign of 1980. Whether this resonated in Trump's subconscious can never be known—he claimed to have no recollection of it and asserted bragging rights with the comment that Reagan "didn't trademark it."[1] Despite their similar slogans, there were

---

[1] Karen Tumulty, 'How Donald Trump Came up with "Make America Great Again,"' *Washington Post*, 18 January 2017, https://www.washingtonpost.com/politics/how-donald-trump-came-up-with-make-america-great-again/2017/01/17/fb6acf5e-dbf7-11e6-ad42-f3375f271c9c_story.html?postshare=831484737469175&utm_term=.317b73a9d4f4.

I. Morgan (✉)
Institute of the Americas, University College London, London, UK
e-mail: i.morgan@ucl.ac.uk

© The Author(s) 2019
M. Oliva and M. Shanahan (eds.), *The Trump Presidency*,
The Evolving American Presidency,
https://doi.org/10.1007/978-3-319-96325-9_4

major differences between how Reagan and Trump operated in their first year as president, but also some important similarities. This chapter compares the two through exploration of: what they meant by making America great again; their administration-building; their White House organization; their leadership styles; and how far they advanced their make-America-great-again agendas.

Making America Great Again

Ronald Reagan used "Let's Make America Great Again" to link his public philosophy with his promise to renew America's prosperity and power after the setbacks of the 1970s. The onset of stagflation (simultaneous stagnation and inflation) in mid-decade had defied solution by Keynesian fiscal measures, the orthodox governmental response to economic problems since World War II. The situation had reached crisis point in 1980 when inflation was running at 12.5%, a recession had pushed unemployment to 7%, and the prime borrowing rate hit 20%. These were the worst economic indicators in any election since Democrat Franklin D. Roosevelt inflicted landslide defeat on President Herbert Hoover in 1932. Portraying President Jimmy Carter as the agent of outdated liberal doctrines that had led America into economic decline, Reagan promised to renew prosperity through initiatives that embodied the new doctrine of supply-side economics. He identified tax cuts, deregulation and federal spending retrenchment as necessary incentives for business, investors and workers to expand the economy's productive potential free from the dead hand of government.[2]

Meanwhile, America appeared to be losing the Cold War. After Vietnam was finally lost to communism in 1975, the Soviet Union and its clients made sweeping gains elsewhere in Southeast Asia and parts of Africa during Gerald Ford's presidency. Worse followed on Jimmy Carter's watch as Moscow expanded its influence in Central America, the Horn of Africa and—most damagingly—Southwest Asia through the December 1979 invasion of Afghanistan. By 1980, a senior CIA official noted, "[T]he sense that the Soviet Union and its surrogates were on the march around the world was palpable in Washington and elsewhere."[3] Holding Carter's pursuit of détente with Russia responsible for this state of affairs, a critique that ignored this strategy's Republican origins under Richard Nixon, Reagan promised to mobilize America's vastly superior military and economic resources to turn Cold War retreat into advance. An arms race, he told one journalist, is "the last thing [the Soviets] want from us because they are running as fast as they can and we haven't started running." Equally important, seeing the Cold War as a global struggle between freedom and tyranny, he looked to restore America's moral resolve to resist the expansion of its communist adversary anywhere in the world.[4]

More than any modern president, political scientist Hugh Heclo observed, Reagan brought to office a clear-cut public philosophy that defined the way he saw issues and the policies he adopted to address them.[5] In focusing on a tight-knit agenda of restoring the free market and resisting communism, Reagan's make-America-great-again vision embodied the conservative philosophy that he had developed in the 1950s and first brought before a national audience in his "Time for Choosing" television address on behalf of Barry Goldwater's presidential candidacy in 1964. He had further showcased his ideological convictions in the 1970s through regular radio spots, public speaking and campaign speeches that established him as the nation's foremost conservative. He possessed a blueprint for his economic agenda as president—in August 1979, aide Martin Anderson had drawn up a summary of his boss's ideas for restoring prosperity under the title "Policy Memorandum No. 1." Possessing equally well-developed foreign policy ideas, Reagan envisaged a "peace through strength" strategy of building up US power in order to negotiate with the Soviets from a position of military superiority. Once its threat to the free world was turned back, Reagan expected communism to collapse of its own contradictions because the human desire for freedom could

[3] Robert Gates, *From the Shadows: The Ultimate Insider's Story of Five Presidents and How They Won the Cold War* (New York: Touchstone, 1996), p. 194.

[4] Elizabeth Drew, '1980: Reagan,' *The New Yorker*, 24 March 1980, https://www.newyorker.com/magazine/1980/03/24/1980-reagan; Iwan Morgan, *Reagan: American Icon* (London: Tauris, 2016), pp. 127–30.

[5] Hugh Heclo 'Ronald Reagan and the American Public Philosophy,' in W. Elliot Brownlee and Hugh Davis Graham, eds., *The Reagan Presidency: Pragmatic Conservatism and Its Legacy* (Lawrence: University Press of Kansas, 2003), pp. 17–39.

never be stifled. "The West," he avowed early in his presidency, "won't contain communism, it will transcend communism … It will dismiss it as some bizarre chapter in human history whose last pages are even now being written." [6]

There was nothing to suggest that the pre-presidential Donald Trump had an ideological core within his political self. What he developed instead was a bite-sized and intuitively emotive message that showed marketing genius in targeting disaffected blue-collar Democrats in key states but was free of philosophy. Some of Trump's advisers—notably Steve Bannon, who served briefly as his White House chief strategist—could envisage how "Make America Great Again" might be parlayed into advocacy of conservative nationalism. [7] Whether Trump himself had any conception of using what was essentially a marketing brand in this way is doubtful. Unwilling to share it with conservative ideologues, he got his lawyers to fire off copyright warnings when Republican presidential nomination rivals Senator Ted Cruz of Texas and Governor Scott Walker of Wisconsin began using it. Days before being inaugurated his efforts to define the slogan in policy terms in a *Washington Post* interview exposed his lack of a public philosophy: "It actually inspired me because to me, it meant jobs. It meant industry, and meant military strength. It meant taking care of our veterans. It meant so much." His inaugural address was heavy on visceral populism in holding the Washington establishment to blame for the loss of American jobs abroad but light on everything else. His "America first" promise that henceforth "[e]very decision on trade, on taxes, on immigration, on foreign affairs, will be made to benefit American workers and American families" hardly embodied a substantive governing vision. [8]

In marked contrast to Reagan, therefore, Trump lacked a strong public philosophy that could infuse his presidential agenda with coherence, cogency and consistency from its outset. He also lacked a real economic or international crisis to lend impetus to his policymaking. Barack Obama's legacy was a steadily expanding economy that had recorded six

[6] Martin Anderson, *Revolution* (San Diego: Harcourt Brace Jovanovich, 1988), pp. 111–21; Ronald Reagan, 'Address at Commencement Exercises at the University of Notre Dame,' 17 May 1981, Online by Gerhard Peters and John T. Woolley, *The American Presidency Project* [Henceforth *APP*], http://www.presidency.ucsb.edu/ws/?pid=43825.

[7] 'America First and Last,' *The Economist*, 4 February 2017, pp. 17–18.

[8] Tumulty, 'Trump'; Donald J. Trump, 'Inaugural Address,' *APP*, 20 January 2017, http://www.presidency.ucsb.edu/ws/?pid=120000.

years of solid job growth and an international situation in which America did not face an existential threat. The America of 2017 was therefore in a very different situation to the America of 1981.

ADMINISTRATION-BUILDING

Every new president faces the challenge of building an administration through appointment of personnel with the ability and dedication to convert his ideals into policy. Though not without flaws, Reagan's operation ranks as the most efficient of recent times, while Trump's stands out as the most chaotic.

In the summer of 1980, veteran Reagan aide Edwin Meese commissioned top headhunter Pendleton James to organize a pre-election personnel operation that matched CVs to government posts. Once Reagan had won, suggested nominations for Cabinet department and agency heads and the 550 or so sub-Cabinet political appointments were screened by a group of long-standing Reagan associates, who ranked loyalty to conservative ideals equal in importance to ability in their review. The nominees then received final vetting from the troika of top presidential aides, Chief of Staff [CoS] James Baker, presidential counsellor Ed Meese and Deputy CoS Michael Deaver, each of whom had been appointed before any other post was decided. Reagan only involved himself in the selection of those heading departments and agencies vital to his core agenda (State, Defense, Central Intelligence Agency, National Security Council, Treasury and Office of Management and Budget).[9]

With some exceptions, the appointments system worked well to select competent conservatives, most of whom had either served in past Republican administrations, or had close Republican associations, or had conservative think-tank affiliations. Its most glaring failure was choosing James Watt as Interior Secretary (a third choice after two others turned down the job), a fervent advocate of unrestrained development who was utterly out of his depth in Washington. Nearly as problematical was the appointment as Environmental Protection Agency [EPA] director of free marketeer Anne Gorsuch Burford, who promptly slashed departmental personnel by nearly one-third and drastically reduced

[9] Edwin Meese, *With Reagan: The Inside Story* (Washington, DC: Regnery Press, 1993), pp. 57–59; James Pfiffner, 'The Paradox of President Reagan's Leadership,' *Presidential Studies Quarterly*, 43 (March 2013), 82–84.

anti-pollution prosecutions. Watt's alienation of his own department and the environmental lobby's allies in Congress plus his public-statement gaffes resulted in his departure in late 1983. Burford had earlier resigned because of a scandal over misuse of a superfund for toxic waste clear-up.[10]

The selection of General Alexander Haig as Secretary of State was ill-starred for different reasons. Urged by disgraced former President Richard Nixon to appoint his onetime CoS to this post—in the hope of gaining influence in administration circles—Reagan overruled his aides' preference for George Shultz, the sole instance he went against them. Haig's egotistical desire to run administration foreign policy and lord it over other national security principals rubbed everyone, including the president, up the wrong way. In mid-1982, Reagan finally accepted one of the Secretary of State's several offers of resignation at not getting his own way, commenting in his diary, "It's amazing how sound he can be on complex international matters but how utterly paranoid with regard to the people he must work with."[11] George Shultz got the job that always should have been his, but was soon at odds with Secretary of Defense Caspar Weinberger and CIA director William Casey over their unrelenting hawkishness towards the Soviet Union. It required a strong National Security Assistant [NSA] to impose order on the quarrelling principals and ensure that the president received advice untainted by bureaucratic politics. Reagan would in all be served by six NSAs, the first four of whom got drawn into supporting the hawks instead of acting as honest broker because they lacked bureaucratic experience and foreign policy expertise. Frank Carlucci (1986–1987) and Colin Powell (1987–1988) were more effective, but the president had effectively resolved the hawk-versus-dove debate by then through his arms-limitation negotiations with new Soviet leader Mikhail Gorbachev.[12]

Each of Reagan's successors, including Trump, followed his example of establishing a pre-election executive recruiting group. However, Trump is the only one to have replaced his after being elected—he thought it too closely connected to the Republican establishment that

---

[10] Patrick Allitt, *A Climate of Crisis: America in the Age of Environmentalism* (New York: Penguin, 2014), pp. 161–65.

[11] Ronald Reagan, *The Reagan Diaries* [Henceforth *RD*], ed. Douglas Brinkley (New York: HarperCollins, 2007), p. 88 (14 June 1982).

[12] Morgan, *Reagan*, pp. 154–56.

had been cool towards his presidential candidacy. A new transition team understood that loyalty to the president-elect and his anti-Washington impulses was the overriding consideration for personnel selections in domestic departments. Trump consequently ended up with an unusually high number of appointees who were hostile to the missions of the bodies they headed. These included Scott Pruitt as EPA director, someone who had frequently sued the agency when Oklahoma Attorney General, former Texas governor Rick Perry as Energy Secretary, a department whose abolition he had urged when seeking the presidency in 2012, and billionaire Republican donor Betsy DeVos as Secretary of Education despite her long-standing support for private and charter schools over public ones. These appointees were soon at odds with their own officials to the detriment of departmental efficiency and morale. Whereas Reagan's two maverick picks—Watt and Gorsuch Burford—were eventually axed, the strength in numbers of Trump's will probably save most of them from this fate, even though an ethics scandal led to Pruitt's resignation in mid 2018. Nevertheless, media reports soon told of permanent officials pursuing a coordinated resistance to slow down or obstruct changes sought by their new bosses. "People here will resist and push back against orders they find unconscionable," asserted one unnamed Justice Department official.[13]

Another highly unusual aspect of Trump's administration-building is that of the 630 top political appointments subject to presidential nomination, 140 were awaiting confirmation, and about 240 lacked even a nominee at the end of his first year. To have so many important positions with no one projected to fill them at this juncture of a presidency is unprecedented. Among the consequences, the White House Drug Control Office, meant to deal with the opioid crisis, had no director, State lacked any regional assistant secretaries, and key nuclear oversight positions were unfilled in Energy. For Trump, this was unproblematic—he reassured reporters, "I'm a businessperson. I tell my people, when you don't need to fill slots, don't fill them." Perhaps this strategy will make government more efficient but is more likely to make it dysfunctional. Moreover,

[13]Juliet Elperin, Lisa Rein, and Marc Fisher, 'Resistance from Within: Federal Workers Push Back Against Trump,' *Washington Post*, 31 January 2017, https://www.washingtonpost.com/politics/resistance-from-within-federal-workers-push-back-against-trump/2017/01/31/c65b110e-e7cb-11e6-b82f-687d6e6a3e7c_story.html?utm_term=.34c25d4eb405.

temporary replacements are only allowed a 300-day tenure by law, so many officials operating on this basis, including the acting Assistant Secretary of State for East Asian and Pacific Affairs whose regional remit includes North Korea, technically lacked legal authority to do so.[14]

Another distinctively Trumpian approach to administration-building, one generally praised not criticized, is the number of generals, active and retired, in his administration, which reflects his admiration for military leaders as patriotic warriors. Some commentators hailed the trio of General James Mattis as Secretary of Defense, General John Kelly as CoS (initially Secretary of Homeland Security) and Lieutenant-General H. R. McMaster as NSA (replacing Lieutenant-General Michael Flynn who quit within four weeks of taking office after being caught fibbing about contacts with Russian officials – but was himself replaced by John Bolton in March 2018 because Trump wanted a more hawkish adviser) as pro-alliance counterweights to Trump's nationalist aspirations. To former Obama Administration Defense Secretary Leon Panetta, they represented "the best hope we have to restrain this president and to keep him on a more traditional foreign-policy path." In his Senate confirmation hearings, Mattis insisted it was in the national interest to stay within the Iran nuclear freeze deal that Trump wanted to scrap and eventually abandoned in May 2018. He was more successful in persuading his boss not to follow Steve Bannon's advice to use the threat of American troop withdrawal from South Korea to get its government to reduce that country's trade surplus with America. Trump's national security team was therefore more united than Reagan's for his first fifteen months in office but the advent of John Bolton in place of H. R. McMaster underlined Trump's determination to forge a more assertive stance on America's national security interests. Even without this particular personnel change, the generals were unlikely to become a permanent restraint on Trump. If he issued an absolute order that they disliked, they would be honour-bound to obey their commander-in-chief.[15]

[14] 'Hundreds of Top Government Jobs Under Trump are Unfilled. So Whose Running Things?' *PBS News Hour*, 29 January 2018 [Lisa Desjardins Transcript], https://www.pbs.org/newshour/show/hundreds-of-top-government-jobs-under-trump-are-unfilled-so-whos-running-things.

[15] 'Counsel of Warriors: Donald Trump's Generals Cannot Control Him,' *The Economist*, 9 November 2017, https://www.economist.com/news/briefing/21731112-americas-president-loves-men-uniform-and-they-often-give-him-sound-advice-it-mr; Greg Jaffe and Missy Ryan, 'Trump's Favourite General: Can Mattis Check an Impulsive President and

ORGANIZING THE WHITE HOUSE

According to political scientist Fred Greenstein, a president's ability to get the best out of his staff through effective White House organization is critical to his success. As he notes, Ronald Reagan had little input into how his presidency was organized, but first-term aides created a system that played to his strengths.[16] In contrast, Trump's White House initially lacked an orderly decision-making and the man brought into resolve matters himself soon became part of the problem.

Reagan had been well-served as California governor by a power-sharing arrangement among key staff. This was successfully replicated in his first-term White House, wherein CoS James Baker and presidential counsellor Ed Meese agreed a division of labour formalized in a co-signed memorandum dated 17 November 1980. The former managed political affairs and organized the White House, while the latter oversaw policy development. A political fixer by inclination, Baker proved craftier than the devoutly conservative Meese in their occasional turf wars. Meese established five Cabinet Councils to devise policy in specific areas. The Legislative Strategy Group, Baker's fiefdom, guided proposals from those bodies into law and often made unilateral adjustments to gain congressional support—notably in cutting deals with legislators to win votes in the Democrat-controlled House of Representatives in the 1981 battle to retrench domestic spending. As such, he demonstrated better understanding that policy was as much about implementation as initiation. More media-savvy than his rival, Baker also got the press on his side through his aptitude for well-timed leaks.[17]

By and large, Reagan's initial White House organization worked well, particularly compared to the change of system and personnel implemented by new CoS Don Regan in the second term. While there were tensions among rival aides, these did not spill out into open warfare.

Still Retain His Trust,' *Washington Post*, 7 February 2018, https://www.washingtonpost.com/world/national-security/can-jim-mattis-check-an-impulsive-president-and-still-retain-his-trust/2018/02/07/289297a2-0814-11e8-8777-2a059f168dd2_story.html?utm_term=.eed66d97be5a.

[16] Fred Greenstein, *The Presidential Difference: Leadership Style from FDR to Clinton* (New York: Free Press, 2000), p. 156.

[17] James Baker, *Work Hard, Study ... and Keep Out of Politics! Adventures and Lessons from an Unexpected Life* (New York: Putnam's, 2006), pp. 122–41; David Cohen, 'From the Fabulous Baker Boys to the Master of Disaster: The White House Chief of Staff in the Reagan and G. H. W. Bush Administrations,' *Presidential Studies Quarterly*, 32 (September 2002), 463–83.

Uninterested in detail, the president let Baker and Meese manage the intricacies of policy and politics, but insisted on their fealty to his core principles. Accordingly, he would not sacrifice the third annual tranche of personal income tax cuts contained in the Economic Recovery Tax Act of 1981 to win the votes of deficit-conscious Democrats in the House of Representatives. Nor would he agree to scale back his defence expansion when its consequences for massive budget deficits became evident in the fall of 1981.[18]

Whereas Reagan's tenure as California governor ensured he understood the need for good staffing, Trump had no experience in office to guide him. Nor was his business background of much help in organizing the presidency. Having run what was effectively a family enterprise with franchised offshoots, his habitual mode of operation was personal and informal based on face-to-face interactions with subordinates and deal-making with those outside the company. Unsurprisingly, Trump sought to recreate a familiar model of doing business in the White House, but he allowed too many staffers access to him and resisted delegation of authority to CoS Reince Priebus to manage the policy process.[19] One damaging outcome of this freewheeling style was Trump's decision to meet FBI director James Comey alone in the Oval Office on 14 February 2017 to discuss the agency's investigation of his aides' possible collusion with Russia in the 2016 election campaign. With no one able to verify what they discussed, the president's later sacking of Comey inevitably looked like payback for refusing to toe the line on the Russia affair.[20]

[18] David Stockman, *The Triumph of Politics: Why the Reagan Revolution Failed* (New York: Harper & Row, 1986), pp. 269–99; Richard Darman, *Who's in Control? Polar Politics and the Sensible Center* (New York: Simon & Schuster, 1996), pp. 93–97.

[19] Fareed Zakaria, 'The Problem with Trump as CEO of America: Government Is Not a Business,' *Washington Post*, 5 May 2016, https://www.washingtonpost.com/opinions/the-problem-with-trump-as-ceo-of-america-government-is-not-a-business/2016/05/05/146cc1a0-12f5-11e6-8967-7ac733c56f12_story.html?utm_term=.bb10fffa583c; James Pfiffner, 'The Unusual Presidency of Donald Trump,' *Political Insight* (September 2017), http://journals.sagepub.com/doi/abs/10.1177/2041905817726890.

[20] Josiah Ryan, 'Why Did Trump Want to Meet Comey Alone? Senator Susan Collins Offers Theory,' *CNN Politics*, 9 June 2017, https://edition.cnn.com/2017/06/09/politics/senator-new-theory-comey-cnntv/index.html; 'Fallout over FBI Chief Comey Sacking,' *BBC News*, 12 May 2017, http://www.bbc.co.uk/news/live/world-us-canada-39866259.

In contrast to Reagan, Trump's White House organization facilitated rather than forestalled factionalism. Without a CoS empowered to run the show, competing centres of power were quick to emerge. A former congressman, Priebus himself was at the centre of one group that hoped to mould Trump into an agent for partisan Republican goals; another consisted of conservative nationalists headed by chief strategist Steve Bannon, who sought deconstruction of the administrative state and retreat from international commitments; and a third, grouped around the president's daughter and son-in-law, Ivanka Trump and Jared Kushner, was largely pragmatic in outlook.[21]

Hoping to bring much-needed order to the White House, Trump moved General John Kelly from Homeland Security to replace Priebus as CoS in late July 2017. The military man was instrumental in removing Bannon and his ally, national security aide Sebastian Gorka, from office, limiting access to the president and establishing tighter control over leaks without wholly stemming the flow. Over time, however, the CoS himself became increasingly controversial—instead of restraining Trump's often intemperate language, he appeared as insensitive as his boss in his own public statements regarding Confederate commemoration, immigration and abuse of women. His response to domestic abuse allegations against Staff Secretary Rob Porter, a White House ally who had to resign over the matter, was particularly clumsy in the light of how revelations of sexual harassment were reshaping American public life. In essence, Kelly became prone to the kind of rhetorical indiscipline and botched management he was appointed to put right. Of course, the ultimate responsibility for internal White House tumult lay with the president himself who was to say the least, a difficult, disloyal and disorganized boss [22]

---

[21] Larry Buchanan and Karen Yourish, 'The Shifting Alliances and Rival Factions Inside Trump's White House,' *New York Times*, 14 April 2017, https://www.nytimes.com/interactive/2017/04/14/us/politics/the-shifting-alliances-and-rival-factions-inside-trumps-west-wing-bannon-kushner.html.

[22] Greg Price, 'Trump Feels "Isolated" Following Chief of Staff John Kelly's White House Moves, Gorka Says,' *Newsweek*, 29 August 2017, http://www.newsweek.com/kelly-trump-isolated-gorka-white-house-656639; Stephen Collinson, 'John Kelly's Latest Blunder Is Protecting an Accused Abuser,' *CNN Politics*, 8 February 2018, http://www.newsweek.com/kelly-trump-isolated-gorka-white-house-656639; Ezra Klein, 'Why There's so Much Chaos in the Trump Administration,' *Vox*, 13 February 2018, https://www.vox.com/policy-and-politics/2018/2/13/17004108/.

LEADERSHIP STYLE

Reagan took office at a time when the presidency was considered by some pundits to be unmanageable for one man. After Vietnam and Watergate revealed the dangers of an overly powerful "imperial presidency," failure to resolve stagflation and resist Soviet expansionism suggested that an "imperilled presidency" was too weak to lead the nation. By the end of his first year, however, Reagan had re-established presidential authority. According to Richard Neustadt, dean of presidency scholars, he restored the office as "a source of programmatic and symbolic leadership, both pacesetter and tonesetter, the nation's voice both to the world and us, and—like or hate the policies—a presence most of us loved to see as Chief of State."[23] In contrast, some commentators have expressed concern that Trump will end up destroying the presidency, a far-fetched scenario but the fact that it is even being discussed is significant. According to one analyst, "We have never had a president so ill-informed about the nature of his office, so openly mendacious, so self-destructive, or so brazen in his abusive attacks on the courts, the press, Congress (including members of his own party), and even senior officials within his own administration."[24]

Reagan offers an interesting test of competing scholarly hypotheses about presidential power. Is it dependent, as Richard Neustadt argues, on the power of persuasion that reflects each president's political skill, public prestige and reputation with the Washington community? Or, as George Edwards contends, on strategic opportunity based on independent variables like electoral mandate, party control of Congress and the economic and international contexts?[25] The evidence from Reagan's first year supports the former, but later developments tend to support the latter.

---

[23] Richard Neustadt, *Presidential Power and the Modern Presidents: The Politics of Leadership from Roosevelt to Reagan* (New York: Free Press, 1990), p. 269.

[24] Jack Goldsmith, 'Will Trump Destroy the Presidency?' *The Atlantic* (October 2017), https://www.theatlantic.com/magazine/archive/2017/10/will-donald-trump-destroy-the-presidency/537921/.

[25] Neustadt, *Presidential Power*, pp. 29–90; 'Resolved: Presidential Power Is (Still) the Power to Persuade,'—Pro: Matthew Dickinson; Con—George Edwards in Richard Ellis and Michael Nelson, eds., *Debating the Presidency: Conflicting Perspectives on the American Presidency* (Washington, DC: CQ Press, 2014), pp. 117–42.

Despite losing control of the Senate in the 1980 elections, the Democrats were still the majority in the House of Representatives. Their leaders were confident of blocking a new president they considered an amiable tyro innocent in the ways of Washington from achieving his conservative agenda. "You're in the big leagues now," Speaker Tip O'Neill of Massachusetts told Reagan, but he would soon eat his words.[26] In his first six months, Reagan promoted enactment of the largest tax reduction in US history, the largest-ever cutbacks in domestic federal spending and the biggest increase in defence outlays since the Korean War. He skilfully used the presidential podium to rally public opinion behind his programme, beginning with his televised address to the nation on 5 February and followed by his first address to Congress on 18 February. Surviving an attempted assassination on 30 March helped his poll numbers no end. Though still weak from his wound, Reagan followed aides' advice to exploit popular admiration by addressing Congress again on 28 April on his economic proposals. The president was also an adept behind-the-scenes negotiator in efforts to peel conservative Southern Democratic congressmen away from O'Neill in return for being granted constituency benefits.

With Reagan building the most successful first-year legislative record of any post-1945 president, the Speaker privately admitted, "I'm getting the shit whaled out of me." The Democrats never underestimated him again. As House Majority Leader James Wright of Texas grudgingly admitted, "We haven't really laid a glove on [Reagan].... What he preaches is economic pap glossed with uplifting homilies and inspirational chatter. Yet so far the guy is making it work. Appalled by what seems to me a lack of depth, I stand in awe nevertheless of his political skill. I am not sure that I have seen its equal."[27]

However, the Democratic leadership would enjoy greater success in resisting Reagan as his first term progressed. A severe economic recession—the result of Federal Reserve monetarist strategy to choke off inflation—and escalating Cold War tensions that aroused popular concern about nuclear conflict dented presidential poll approval. Accordingly, Southern Democrats became less willing to support Reagan, while Republican failure to capture the House of

[26] Ronald Reagan, *An American Life* (New York: Simon & Schuster, 1990), p. 233.

[27] John Farrell, *Tip O'Neill and the American Century* (Boston: Little, Brown, 2001), p. 558; James Wright Diary, 29 July 1981, James Wright Papers, Texas Christian University.

Representatives in the 1982 midterms encouraged liberal Democrats to stand fast against him. After the legislative blitzkrieg of 1981, Reagan thereafter found himself engaged in trench warfare just to hold the ground gained in that *annus mirabilis*.

Trump appears the polar opposite of Reagan in the politics of persuasion. He simply does not understand that the presidency is an inherently weak institution with limited powers of command. For a supposedly skilled salesman, he has made little effort to bargain for votes in Congress, even from wavering members of his own party in the unsuccessful effort to repeal and replace Barack Obama's Affordable Care Act (ACA). His public rhetoric does not hold a candle to Reagan's. Instead of being uplifting, it is often mean-spirited, exemplified by remarks blaming both sides for the violent clashes between white supremacists and anti-racist protesters at Charlottesville, Virginia, in August 2017. Trump can also display an uncanny knack for misjudging an audience as when he gave a nakedly political address to the non-political Boy Scouts of America in July, prompting the Chief Scout to issue an apology to scouts' parents angered by the president's words.[28]

Instead of courting the media, Trump has conducted a war against critical journalists for peddling "fake news." No president has truly loved the press, of course, but none has attacked sections of it in the manner of Trump—other than the ill-fated Richard Nixon. Most presidents have at least tried to woo it to get their message over to the public. Trump, in contrast, has used tweets to circumvent what he sees as an implacably hostile liberal media. "The Fake News Media hates when I use what has turned out to be my very powerful Social Media - over 100 million people! I can go around them," he messaged on 16 June 2017. Trump's tweets certainly hearten his base, but their offensive tone is a turn-off for many other Americans.[29]

---

[28] Jonathan Bernstein, 'The 1960 Book That Explains Why Trump Is a Failure,' *Bloomberg View*, 16 August 2017, https://www.bloomberg.com/view/articles/2017-08-16/the-1960-book-that-explains-why-trump-is-a-failure.

[29] Chris Cillizza, 'The Fallacy at the Heart of the Defense of Trump's Tweeting,' *CNN Politics*, 30 June 2017, https://edition.cnn.com/2017/06/30/politics/trump-twitter-polling/index.html; Paul Farhi, 'Trump's Bizarre Communications Strategy: Constantly Upstaging His Own Agenda,' *Washington Post*, 28 July 2017, https://www.washingtonpost.com/lifestyle/style/trumps-bizarre-communications-strategy-constantly-upstaging-his-own-agenda/2017/07/27/29546ed0-72e2-11e7-8f39-eeb7d3a2d304_story.html?

Trump appeared blind to the reality that his first-year average approval rating was the lowest in polling history. Having won just 46% of the popular vote to win office, the rational response would have been to try to broaden his appeal with an eye to re-election. Instead, Trump's strategy aims only to satisfy his core supporters, who constitute a minority of voters. This largely explains why his approval rating throughout the second half of 2017 was stuck between 37 and 42%. Presidents usually have a honeymoon with public opinion in their first year, but Trump is an exception. Another habitual source of presidential popularity—a strong economy—did nothing to boost him in 2017. If he has found his natural level of poll approval, this does not augur well for the remainder of his term—or for his re-election.[30]

POLICY AGENDAS

The Initial Actions Project, a White House staff report, asserted that Ronald Reagan's best hope of effecting change lay in making a strong start to his presidency. "How we begin will significantly determine how we govern," it advised. Following this game plan, Reagan had a laser-like focus on economic renewal to the extent that foreign policy was a secondary element of his early agenda. Furthermore, he invested no political capital in advancing socio-moral issues dear to his Christian right supporters. As he commented in his memoirs, "In 1981 no problem the country faced was more serious than the economic crisis [...] because without a recovery we couldn't afford to make the country strong again."[31] Trump, by contrast, sought to advance on a broad, uncoordinated front in pursuit of the 2-page "Contract With the American Voter" issued in his very own Gettysburg address on 22 October 2016.[32]

The instrument for delivering Reagan's economic programme was the Fiscal 1982 budget plan, presented to Congress on 10 March 1981. Hitherto new presidents had broadly accepted the lame-duck budget

[30] Ariel Edwards-Levy, '5 Things the Polls Show About Trump's First Year,' *Huffington Post*, 20 January 2018, http://www.huffingtonpost.co.uk/entry/donald-trumps-first-year-polls_us_5a636231e4b0dc592a092bab.

[31] White House Staff, *Ronald Reagan's Initial Actions Project* (New York: Threshold, 2009), pp. 5–6; Reagan, *American Life*, p. 333.

[32] Deroy Murdock, 'Trump's Gettysburg Address Overflows with Conservative Ideas,' *National Review*, 26 October 2016, http://www.nationalreview.com/article/441458/donald-trumps-contract-american-voter-gettysburg-address.

plan of their predecessor because major overhaul of a budget that had taken close to a year to prepare was deemed impossible. They waited until their second year to make their own mark on fiscal policy. Thanks to the punishing schedule worked by the Office of Management and Budget under new director David Stockman, Reagan was able to submit a plan embodying his own priorities of tax reduction, domestic retrenchment and defence expansion within 50 days of taking office. The enactment by the end of July of measures embodying these priorities seemed to many pundits to constitute a "Reagan Revolution" that spelled the reversal of the New Deal tradition of activist liberal government launched in the 1930s. Reagan further cemented his transformational reputation by becoming the first president since Grover Cleveland in 1894 to break a strike. When the Professional Air Traffic Controllers Organization struck for a new contract in August in defiance of prohibitions on federal workers doing so, he ordered them back to work in two days or be fired. Half the membership stayed out in the belief Reagan was bluffing because of the danger to air safety but ended up losing their jobs and the union lost its federal certification. The president therefore won popular kudos for standing up against an inflationary settlement sought by a well-paid group of public employees and discouraging private-sector unions from following their example.[33]

While focusing on economic renewal, Reagan could not ignore the world. His wrong-headed conviction of a Soviet plot to implant Marxism in Central America meant that he allocated this region more importance than anywhere except Europe. In his view, Jimmy Carter's emphasis on human rights had weakened authoritarian regimes to the consequent benefit of pro-Soviet insurgents in Nicaragua and El Salvador. At the first meeting of his National Security Council on 6 February, Reagan avowed determination to support anti-communist regimes of any ilk: "We don't throw out of our friends because they can't pass the 'saliva test' on human rights. I want to see that stopped." An infusion of US weaponry and other aid propped up El Salvador's military dictatorship against rebel

[33] Iwan Morgan, *The Age of Deficits: Presidents and Unbalanced Budgets from Jimmy Carter to George W. Bush* (Lawrence: University Press of Kansas, 2009), pp. 83–91; Rowland Evans and Robert Novak, *The Reagan Revolution* (New York: Dutton, 1981); Joseph McCartin, *Collision Course: Ronald Reagan, the Air Traffic Controllers, and the Strike That Changed America* (New York: Oxford University Press, 2011).

fighters. On 1 December 1981, Reagan also authorized $19 million in aid to set up a Contra army to harry Nicaragua's Sandinista regime that was suspected of being a conduit for Soviet and Cuban aid reaching Salvadorean insurgents.[34] This was the first step down the slippery slope that would eventually embroil Reagan in the Iran-Contra scandal that nearly destroyed his presidency in 1986–1987.

In the Middle East, Reagan's most important early initiative was to approve the largest foreign-arms sale in American history to strengthen Saudi Arabia as a bulwark against Soviet regional advance through surrogates like Syria and safeguard it from Iranian-directed Islamic militancy. The inclusion of five Airborne Warning and Control Systems (AWACS) aircraft in the deal aroused opposition from Israel, which urged its congressional supporters to block the sale. The Democrat-led House voted to do so, but a presidential counter-lobby prevented the Senate following suit. There were economic as well as geopolitical reasons for Reagan's very active part in winning congressional support. In return for the arms, the Saudis quadrupled their oil production, so that world prices dropped from $30 a barrel in 1981 to $12 in 1985 to the benefit of Western economies but not the oil-exporting Soviet Union.[35]

Other than sanctioning an intensification of CIA covert operations, Reagan held back from openly confronting Moscow until it instigated a crackdown on the pro-democracy Solidarity movement in Poland in December 1981. In response, he authorized economic sanctions against both Poland and Russia. Reagan saw the issue as a test of America's commitment to act on behalf of freedom. "We are the leaders of the Western world," he told the National Security Council on 21 December. "We haven't been for years, several years, except in name, but we accept that role now."[36] This signalled an intensification of Soviet-US tensions that would reach dangerous levels in the so-called year of living dangerously in 1983.

[34]NSC-1: The Caribbean Basin, Poland, 6 February 1981, in *The Reagan Files: Documentary Collections: National Security Council and National Security Planning Group Meetings* (Henceforth *TRF: NSC*), ed. Jason Saltoun-Ebin, http://www.thereaganfiles. com/; *RD*, 52 (1 December 1981).

[35]Peter Schweizer, *Reagan's War: The Epic Story of His 40-Year Struggle and Final Triumph over Communism* (New York: Doubleday, 2002), pp. 239–41; Morgan, *Reagan*, p. 205.

[36]NSC-33: Poland, 21 December 1981, *TRF-NSC*.

If Trump could not match the scale of Reagan's first-year success in advancing his agenda, he did make strides in meeting campaign promises. Amateur in the White House he may have been, but he had two significant assets that helped him do so. Firstly, Obama had increasingly resorted to executive actions because it was difficult to secure his legislative priorities in the polarized political environment of his second term. Accordingly, it was easy for Trump to rescind many of his predecessor's initiatives, notably regarding immigration, abortion aid, gun control and environmental protection through issuing his own executive orders. In total, he signed 58 executive orders in his first year (a few of which fell afoul of the courts), a higher number than any president from Reagan onwards.[37] Meanwhile, government agencies all but stopped writing new rules in 2017.

Trump's other great asset was Republican control of both houses of Congress, something denied Reagan. This did not save him from failure to replace the ACA, but he ended 2017 on a high with enactment of a massive tax-reduction bill that also abolished the individual mandate at the heart of Obamacare.[38] Moreover, congressional Republicans enabled Trump to make progress on his promised creation of a conservative federal judiciary. Although Reagan had wanted to transform the bench, the conservative legal movement was in its infancy during his presidency. His first-year Supreme Court pick, Sandra Day O'Connor, honoured a campaign pledge to appoint the first woman justice, but she was pro-choice on abortion. In contrast, Trump may well add to his first-year selection of the strongly conservative Neil Gorsuch (to fill the holdover position created by Senate Republicans' refusal to hold hearings on an Obama's nominee in 2016) if ageing liberal justices Stephen Breyer and Ruth Bader Ginsburg were to retire soon. The retirement of swing justice Anthony Kennedy at the end of the 2018 Supreme Court session has at least enabled him to consolidate the conservative majority on this body. His impact on the federal lower courts, where law is now most hotly contested, will likely be greater still. The Republicans used their control of the Senate, regained in the 2014 midterms, to confirm just 22 judges in the 114th Congress of 2015–2016, the fewest since the 82nd Congress of 1951–1952, in the hope of getting a GOP president in 2017. This strategy

[37]'Executive Orders: Washington to Trump,' *APP*, http://www.presidency.ucsb.edu/data/orders.php.

[38]Jim VandeHei and Mike Allen, 'Trump Triumphant: A Consequential Lasting End to 2017,' *Axios*, 20 December 2017, https://www.axios.com/trump-triumphant-a-consequential-lasting-end-to-2017-1515110718-ea7ba2db-4de6-4e39-8535-e9bde5fdf466.html.

left 107 judgeships vacant, thereby opening the way for Trump to fill them with "originalists" who believe in strict interpretation of what the Constitution originally intended. Trump had 12 appellate judges confirmed in his first year, the most by any new president, and 6 district court judges, the most since Nixon in 1969. With plenty more vacancies to fill, the long-anticipated conservative constitutional counter-revolution may well come about on his watch.[39]

In international affairs, Trump delivered on some of his nationalistic campaign promises in 2017. He withdrew the USA from the Trans-Pacific Partnership (TPP) before negotiations for the creation of this new free-trade bloc were complete, but made slow progress on renegotiating the North America Free Trade Agreement. He also withdrew America from the Paris Climate-Change agreement, but left the door open for its re-entry. Trade war fears initially subsided when he did not follow through his pledge to declare China a currency manipulator and impose tariff penalties on its imports, but one became a reality in mid 2018 when he used his national security prerogative to impose tariffs on China and the European Union. To NATO partners' relief, he reasserted America's commitment to the alliance while demanding that European members contribute more to it. Arguably, Trump's greatest success was to support the coalition that brought about the collapse of so-called Islamic State in the Middle East, but it is unclear if the USA will counter Russian and Iranian ambitions of exploiting the regional power vacuum this created.[40] Nevertheless, the greatest foreign policy problem facing Trump is a relic of the Cold War that Ronald Reagan had largely but not wholly resolved. Unless he can deter communist North Korea from continued development of its nuclear-missile programme, it could soon threaten America's mainland. This might bring about the most dangerous war crisis that the USA has faced since the Able Archer 83 war scare of late 1983. It remains to be seen whether Trump's summit meeting with North Korean leader Kim Jong-un in Singapore in June 2018 leads to substantive progress on this score.

For the present, Trump's make-America-great-again pledge depends on his economic success. Continued employment growth at home and the global economy's uptick combined to make his first-year record look very good. A tight labour market pushed up average hourly wages

[39] Charlie Savage, 'Trump Is Rapidly Reshaping the Judiciary. Here's How," *New York Times*, 11 November 2017, https://www.nytimes.com/2017/11/11/us/politics/trump-judiciary-appeals-courts-conservatives.html? 'Full-Court Press,' *The Economist*, 13 January 2018, p. 34.

[40] Ross Douthat, 'A War Trump Won,' *New York Times*, 16 December 2017, https://www.nytimes.com/2017/12/16/opinion/sunday/war-trump-islamic-state.html.

by nearly 3% in 2017, the highest gains coming at the bottom of the income distribution to the particular benefit of blacks and Hispanics. To keep the good times rolling, Trump and the congressional Republicans promoted a huge tax cut that he signed into law in December 2017. This reduced corporate income taxes from 35% to 21%, required repatriation of $3 trillion that US businesses held abroad but subjected returned income to tax rates of just 8–15% and reduced levies on pass-through income by 10% for commercial realtors (like Trump Enterprises). In contrast to business, individual taxpayers received only temporary rate reductions to keep the bill's 10-year deficit costs within $1.5 trillion. Meanwhile, repeal of Obamacare's individual mandate will mean higher insurance premiums for Americans suffering ill health because healthy ones will likely buy less cover; and low-income families on earned income tax credit could lose $19 billion aggregate over ten years because of changes to how inflation is calculated.[41]

The tax bill is projected to boost the 2.3% GDP growth rate of 2017 by 0.7% in 2018 and 1.5% in 2019, but this stimulus carries risks. Firstly, recovery cycles have lasted 9 years maximum since the Reagan expansion of 1982–1991. Trump is gambling on boosting one now entering its ninth year, so a downturn after an unusually long expansion could be severe. Stimulating an already pacey economy also carries the obvious risk of accelerating inflation unless there is an accompanying growth in productivity. Most significantly, the revenue lost to the US Treasury from the tax cuts will add significantly to the public debt— as will probable increases in defence, social programme and infrastructure spending coming under congressional consideration in 2018. In all likelihood, the deficit will run at 5% GDP in Fiscal 2019, a very high level during peacetime prosperity, compared with 3.5% in Fiscal 2017.[42] What happened in the Reagan years when the deficit averaged 5.2% GDP in Fiscal 1983–1986 offers a stark warning for Trump's America and beyond.

[41] Jesse Drucker and Alan Rappaport, 'The Tax Bill's Winners and Losers,' *New York Times*, 16 December 2017, https://www.nytimes.com/2017/12/16/business/the-winners-and-losers-in-the-tax-bill.html.

[42] 'The Great Experiment,' *The Economist*, 10 February 2018, pp. 37–38; Robert Samuelson, 'America's Prudence Deficit,' *Real Clear Politics*, 12 February 2018, https://www.realclearpolitics.com/articles/2018/02/12/americas_prudence_deficit_136239.html.

Reagan's Fiscal 1982 budget plan over-optimistically assumed that enhanced revenue from the growth-boosting 1981 tax cuts would eliminate the budget deficit within four years. However, the speed with which this was produced resulted in an accountancy error allocating greater than intended increases for defence funding. The plan also contained a so-called magic asterisk of yet-to-be-identified domestic cutbacks in future years, but these were never made. Worst of all, the deep recession that resulted from the Federal Reserve's anti-inflation strategy depressed tax revenues that the 1981 tax cut was supposed to boost. To finance what became record peacetime deficits, the USA borrowed from abroad and kept *real* interest rates (the actual rate minus the inflation rate) high in the post-recession years to facilitate this. Massive infusion of foreign capital met its borrowing needs but pumped up the value of the dollar against other currencies. This produced an import boom as Americans flocked to buy relatively cheaper foreign manufacturers but depressed exports because of the uncompetitive pricing of US goods.[43] The huge capital flows worked to the benefit of the financial sector that came to dominate the US economy, but they were instrumental in manufacturing decline. In July 1979, 19.5 million people were employed in this sector (the historic peak) but numbers declined to 18 million in the 1980s (the first decade this ever happened) and fell again to 17 million in 2000. There followed a steep decline to 13.8 billion by the end of 2007 thanks in part to the strong dollar resulting from George W. Bush's expansion of foreign borrowing to fund his tax cuts and wars.[44]

Manufacturing employment slumped further to 11.5 billion during the Great Recession before undergoing minor improvement under Obama to reach 12.3 million by early 2017. There was a total increase of just 200,000 manufacturing jobs in Trump's first year. It remains to be seen how far he can deliver on his promise to rebuild the prosperity of blue-collar America through an expansion of this sector because renewed deficit growth will run counter to this goal. The USA currently relies

[43]Iwan Morgan, 'Monetary Metamorphosis: The Volcker Fed and Inflation,' *Journal of Policy History*, 24 (October 2012), 546–71.

[44]Federal Reserve Bank of St. Louis, 'All Employees: Manufacturing,' January 2018, https://fred.stlouisfed.org/series/MANEMP.

on foreigners to fund some 40% of its total public debt. The increased capital flows needed to keep borrowing from abroad abreast of this level in the context of growing deficits is likely to affect the balance of trade to the detriment of American goods because of the dollar's resultant increase in value.

CONCLUSION

Despite their evident differences, therefore, there are also significant similarities between the early Reagan and Trump presidencies. Reagan promised to renew America's prosperity but the major beneficiaries of his tax cuts were the very rich (the top rate of income tax declined from 70–28% on his watch) and the deficits these produced in conjunction with his defence expansion ultimately helped Wall Street far more than Main Street. Though an unintended consequence of his economic strategy, his presidency marked what economist James Galbraith called the end of normal. For the first three quarters of the twentieth century, the US economy had performed remarkably well in keeping average income and educational levels mostly rising and economic inequality mostly flat or falling. From the 1980s onwards, however, income inequality soared with the consequence that median family income was not much greater in real terms in 2015 than in 1979.[45] The blue-collar animosities that Trump aroused against Hillary Clinton in 2016 should really have been directed against his Republican predecessor under whom the process of manufacturing decline had taken such a significant turn. Trump now promises to restore the good old days through policies that helped to bring them to an end under Reagan—namely tax cuts skewed towards business and the wealthy, deregulation and massive public borrowing. As such, the so-called Age of Trump looks like nothing more than the continuation of the Age of Reagan.

[45] James Galbraith, *The End of Normal: The Great Crisis and the Future of Growth* (New York: Simon & Schuster, 2014); Nicholas Kristoff, 'Reagan, Obama and Inequality,' *New York Times*, 22 January 2015, https://www.nytimes.com/2015/01/22/opinion/nicholas-kristof-reagan-obama-and-inequality.html.

REFERENCES

Allitt, Patrick. *A Climate of Crisis: America in the Age of Environmentalism*. New York: Penguin, 2014.

Anderson, Martin. *Revolution*. San Diego: Harcourt Brace Jovanovich, 1988.

Baker, James. *Work Hard, Study ... and Keep Out of Politics! Adventures and Lessons from an Unexpected Life*. New York: Putnam's, 2006.

Cohen, David. "From the Fabulous Baker Boys to the Master of Disaster: The White House Chief of Staff in the Reagan and G. H. W. Bush Administrations." *Presidential Studies Quarterly*, 32 (September 2002): 463–83.

Collins, Robert. *More: The Politics of Economic Growth in Postwar America*. New York: Oxford University Press, 2000.

Darman, Richard. *Who's in Control? Polar Politics and the Sensible Center*. New York: Simon & Schuster, 1996.

Ellis, Richard, and Nelson, Michael, eds., *Debating the Presidency: Conflicting Perspectives on the American Presidency*. Washington, DC: CQ Press, 2014.

Evans, Rowland, and Robert Novak. *The Reagan Revolution*. New York: Dutton, 1981.

Farhi, Paul. "Trump's Bizarre Communications Strategy: Constantly Upstaging His Own Agenda." *Washington Post*, 28 July 2017.

Farrell, John. *Tip O'Neill and the American Century*. Boston: Little, Brown, 2001.

Galbraith, James. *The End of Normal: The Great Crisis and the Future of Growth*. New York: Simon & Schuster, 2014.

Gates, Robert. *From the Shadows: The Ultimate Insider's Story of Five Presidents and How They Won the Cold War*. New York: Touchstone, 1996.

Greenstein, Fred. *The Presidential Difference: Leadership Style from FDR to Clinton*. New York: Free Press, 2000.

Heclo, Hugh. "Ronald Reagan and the American Public Philosophy." In W. Elliot Brownlee and Hugh Davis Graham, eds., *The Reagan Presidency: Pragmatic Conservatism and Its Legacy*. Lawrence: University Press of Kansas, 2003.

McCartin, Joseph. *Collision Course: Ronald Reagan, the Air Traffic Controllers, and the Strike That Changed America*. New York: Oxford University Press, 2011.

Meese, Edwin. *With Reagan: The Inside Story*. Washington, DC: Regnery Press, 1993.

Morgan, Iwan. *The Age of Deficits: Presidents and Unbalanced Budgets from Jimmy Carter to George W. Bush*. Lawrence: University Press of Kansas, 2009.

Morgan, Iwan. "Monetary Metamorphosis: The Volcker Fed and Inflation." *Journal of Policy History*, 24 (October 2012): 546–71.

Morgan, Iwan. *Reagan: American Icon*. London: Tauris, 2016.

Neustadt, Richard. *Presidential Power and the Modern Presidents: The Politics of Leadership from Roosevelt to Reagan*. New York: Free Press, 1990.

Pfiffner, James. "The Paradox of President Reagan's Leadership." *Presidential Studies Quarterly*, 43 (March 2013): 81–100.

Pfiffner, James. "The Unusual Presidency of Donald Trump." *Political Insight* (September 2017). http://journals.sagepub.com/doi/abs/10.1177/204190581 7726890.

Reagan, Ronald. *An American Life*. New York: Simon & Schuster, 1990.

Reagan, Ronald. *The Reagan Diaries*, ed. Douglas Brinkley. New York: HarperCollins, 2007.

Schweizer, Peter. *Reagan's War: The Epic Story of His 40-Year Struggle and Final Triumph over Communism*. New York: Doubleday, 2002.

Stockman, David. *The Triumph of Politics: Why the Reagan Revolution Failed*. New York: Harper & Row, 1986.

White House Staff. *Ronald Reagan's Initial Actions Project*. New York: Threshold, 2009.

PART II

Winning at Home

Pushing Back the Obama Legacy: Trump's First Year and the Alt-Right—Evangelical—Catholic Coalition

Lee Marsden

[handwritten annotation: strict father morality]

In the 2016 presidential elections, Donald J. Trump carefully courted an unholy alliance of Alt-Right, conservative evangelicals and Catholics in his successful campaign united around an agenda of pushing back against Obama reforms on LGBTQ, same-sex marriage, health care, reproductive rights, education, environmental policy and foreign policy. This chapter makes use of George Lakoff's understanding of strict father morality to examine the key issues bringing together this coalition and analyses the campaign promises made by Trump, prior to the election, and the extent to which these are being fulfilled over the first year of his presidency. The chapter explores the durability of the coalition across and beyond the first year and how support for Trump's presidency has manifested across key policy issues. The chapter analyses the extent to which Trump has pushed back Barack Obama's legacy. The chapter concludes that the coalition came together around a shared moral framework

L. Marsden (✉)
University of East Anglia, Norwich, UK
e-mail: l.marsden@uea.ac.uk

© The Author(s) 2019
M. Oliva and M. Shanahan (eds.), *The Trump Presidency*,
The Evolving American Presidency,
https://doi.org/10.1007/978-3-319-96325-9_5

that this support was essential to securing Trump's election victory, and although Trump was able to make only incremental changes to the Obama legacy, such changes were consistent with a strict father moral framework, which helped retain support among this key demographic.

Among many remarkable and surprising US presidential results, the 2016 election stands out as almost incomprehensible. An untried and inexperienced non-politician, celebrity real estate developer, was able to comfortably win the Electoral College while losing the popular plebiscite by almost three million votes. As commentators and academics have reflected on a result which few 'experts' predicted, Trump and his campaign are credited with tapping into popular white discontent and presenting himself as one not only who understood and sympathised with their plight but also who would actively work to represent them and restore their economic fortunes in Washington. The reality is that Trump is a New York billionaire businessman interested in tax breaks for corporations and an unlikely champion of the marginalised and forgotten of the flyover states. How can we explain such a phenomenon and how did this play out in his first year in office?

In this chapter, I argue that the Trump campaign tapped into the resentment of those who felt they had been left behind, dissatisfaction with the Obama legacy, which threatened traditional values and a mix of nationalism and racism that coalesces around a coalition of Alt-Right, conservative evangelicals and white Catholics. These were joined by pragmatic conservatives who hitched themselves to Trump's wagon when it looked as though he offered the best chance of success for a Republican candidate. In seeking to explain how such a disparate coalition emerged and was sustained over the first year of the Trump administration, we need to look beyond the rational actor model whereby rational voters vote based on a cost–benefit analysis in terms of their own individual interests. Clearly, voters who voted for Trump did not vote for their own self-interest, for if jobs did return to the 'rust belt', it would be with reduced employee rights and lower taxes for big corporations and businesses. Reduced health care as a result of opposition to the Affordable Care Act or Obamacare was not in the interest of white workers any more than their black and Hispanic co-workers.

It was not in the self-interest of working-class white males or white women to elect a President with a reputation for misogyny and predatory behaviour. And yet white males without a college education voted for Trump by a margin of 67 to 28%, the largest margin in exit polls since 1980, those with one supported Trump 49 to 45%.[1] Fifty-three per cent of white women who cast their votes did so for Donald Trump, including 63% of white women without a college degree.[2] It would seem against the self-interest of conservative evangelicals and white Catholics who described themselves as values voters to throw their lot behind a man who in many ways was the antithesis of those social values. And yet, exit polls undertaken by Pew Forum indicated that white evangelicals and white Catholics had turned out to vote for Trump in greater percentages than even George W. Bush achieved, with 81% of white evangelicals and 60% of white Catholics voting for him.[3]

In order to understand the phenomena of Trump's victory and the continuing resilience of that support, we need to go beyond discussions of the tactical flaws in the Clinton campaign, the impact of celebrity politics, demographics or blatant and unconscious racism and consider what unites those overwhelmingly white voters who delivered Trump's victory. Since the 1990s, Berkeley professor George Lakoff has sought to analyse why Republicans and Democrats vote the way they do and adopt particular policy stances. Through a series of works on the brain and cognitive sciences, Lakoff presents two differing and opposing world views dependent upon competing moralities.[4] He juxtaposes a strict father morality against a nurturant parent morality, arguing that what unites conservatives is a shared world view based on their view of a traditional family model with a strict father who leads, protects, disciplines and controls the family. Other family members accept the strict father's role without protest as the way things are supposed to be. Liberals, on the other hand, adopt a nurturant parent morality based on caring for those less fortunate, putting support mechanisms in place and embracing difference.

[1] Alec Tyson and Shiva Maniam, 'Behind Trump's Victory: Divisions by Race, Gender, Education,' *Pew Research Center*, 9 November 2016.

[2] Katie Rogers, 'White Women Helped Elect Donald Trump,' *The New York Times*, 9 November 2016.

[3] Gregory Smith and Jessica Martínez, 'How the Faithful Voted: A Preliminary 2016 Analysis,' *Pew Forum*, 9 November 2016.

[4] George Lakoff, *Don't Think of an Elephant: Know Your Values and Frame the Debate* (White River Junction, VT: Chelsea Green Publishing, 2016); George Lakoff, *Moral Politics: How Liberals and Conservatives Think* (Chicago and London: University of Chicago Press, 2016); George Lakoff and Elisabeth Wehling, *The Little Blue Book* (New York: Free Press, 2012).

Lakoff was introduced to the concept through reading the bestsell-
ing book *Dare to Discipline* by Christian child psychologist and founder
of Focus on the Family, James Dobson.[5] Dare to Discipline encourages parents to apply corporal punishment to their children because it
is argued children are naturally wilful and will seek what pleases them
and not what is right. They should be punished until they obey instinc-
tively, shaping their will to know right from wrong. The rationale is that
when a child is physically punished for wrongdoing, they learn not to do
it again. For Dobson, the loving parent is the strict father who knows
right from wrong and cares enough about his child to administer punishment to teach invaluable lessons about life. The key lessons or assumptions to be learned are that the world is a dangerous place with evil in it.
The world is competitive and made up of winners and losers, and there
is clarity between what is right and wrong. What is needed in such a
world are clear guidelines, a strict father who is able to protect and support his family in a dangerous world and teach his children right from
wrong. Discipline and self-control, Dobson argues, become internalised
and are necessary in a competitive world where discipline, self-reliance
and the pursuit of self-interest are virtues.[6] For conservative evangelicals,
like Dobson, morality and prosperity are synonymous with the attributes
of 'individual responsibility, and discipline, pursuing your self-interests,
should enable you to prosper'.[7]

Strict father morality is an idealised form of a certain type of American
family that resonates with the experience of many of the voters who
supported Donald Trump's presidency. Strict father morality families
reward obedience and punish disobedience in order to instil self-discipline
and self-reliance, which Lakoff refers to as the Morality of Reward and
Punishment.[8] In practising 'tough love', the child is able to grow into
adulthood equipped for a competitive and dangerous world with a
clear moral compass. Succeeding in such a world requires self-discipline
brought about by obedience to authority, firstly in the home and in

[5] James Dobson, *Dare to Discipline* (New York: Bantam Books, 1977).

[6] Dobson, *Dare to Discipline*.

[7] Lakoff, *Moral Politics*, p. 5.

[8] Lakoff, *Moral Politics*, p. 67.

adulthood through submitting to your own authority. Self-discipline is the key to economic success in a competitive environment, and success has to be earned through your own efforts, and 'handouts' from the state are considered immoral in such thinking because they represent failure and circumvent the necessity for self-discipline and self-reliance. Such a view is consistent with the thrust of conservative thinking that in pursuing self-interest then the rest of society benefits. Rather than taking resources the self-sufficient contribute to rather than detract from societal well-being.

In strict father morality, Moral Strength is a crowning virtue and equips the father to 'support, protect and guide his family'.[9] Moral Strength is contrasted with moral weakness which is seen as immoral. In such thinking, welfare is immoral because it discourages the moral good of work, providing condoms to combat teen pregnancy or clean needles to drug addicts is moral weakness and evil. The self-disciplined can say no to sex and drugs and those who choose not to do so are immoral and deserve to be punished.[10] In a world view with a clear conception of the role of authority, right and wrong, good and evil, there is a sense of how things ought to be. A hierarchical moral order is presented as natural whereby there is an order of dominance in which:

> God [is] above man, man above nature, adults above children, Western culture above non-Western culture, American above other nations. The moral order is all too often extended to men above women, whites above non-whites, Christians above non-Christians, straights above gays.[11]

While it would be wrong to categorise all conservatives as influenced by their own upbringing, or idealised version about how they would have liked to have been brought up, in the way described by Lakoff, there is enough substance to suggest that the metaphors and memes pursued by the Trump campaign resonated, and continues to resonate, with strict father morality.

[9] Lakoff, *Moral Politics*, p. 74.
[10] Lakoff, *Moral Politics*, pp. 73–75.
[11] Lakoff, *Don't Think of an Elephant*, p. 128.

ALT-RIGHT

The influence of the Alternative Right or Alt-Right on the outcome of the presidential elections remains open to conjecture, but the awareness of the movement grew exponentially particularly after Democratic candidate Hillary Clinton chose to make the movement the central part of a key election speech on 25 August 2016, following Trump's decision to appoint Steve Bannon as his campaign chief executive. In a speech lasting approximately half an hour, Clinton sought to demonstrate Trump's unsuitability for office through his association with Alt-Right views, which she characterised as white supremacist.[12] Steve Bannon became Executive Director of Breitbart Media in 2012 and quickly grew the organisation to become the third largest conservative media outlet after Fox News and the Drudge Report. Bannon espoused economic nationalism, and, although not Alt-Right himself, at the Republican Party convention prior to the election, he described Breitbart as a 'platform for the Alt-Right'.

Bannon provided a platform for views which were far beyond the pale for traditional Republicans. The Alt-Right's antecedents can be traced to the evolution of a century of far right thought originating in the fascist movements in Twentieth-Century Europe. In the twenty-first century, the Tea Party and Birther movement, questioning Barack Obama's American citizenship, championed small government and loosely veiled racist tendencies.[13] Breitbart provided a platform for white nationalist views that had been largely confined to far-right websites, chat rooms and social media. This online movement of mainly young white men opposed to multiculturalism, immigration, feminism and political correctness used memes to spread a white nationalist message, which owed much to the teachings of Jared Taylor and Richard Spencer.

Taylor formed the New Century Foundation think tank in 1991 out of which grew the American Renaissance Movement advocating separation of the races. Spencer also opposed interracial marriage, advocating a white nationalism where white and non-whites would live in

---

[12] Hilary Clinton, 'Hilary Clinton Speech on How Donald Trump's Campaign Has Mainstreamed the "Alt-Right" Hate Movement,' 25 August 2016, https://www.youtube.com/watch?v=sYyZX3UW8Qc.

[13] M. Taylor, *What Is the Alt-Right?* (London: Create Space Independent Publishing Platform, 2016); George Hawley, *Making Sense of the Alt-Right* (New York: Colombia University Press, 2017); David Neiwert, *Alt-American: The Rise of the Radical Right in the Age of Trump* (London and New York: Verso, 2017).

separate states and coined the term Alt-Right in 2008. Spencer founded AltRight.com in 2010, and the National Policy Institute, in Arlington, Virginia, the following year. In 2012, he became editor of Radix Journal which advocates a 'peaceful ethnic cleansing' of the non-white population of the USA.[14] Spencer extols the traditional role of women as child bearers and mothers and expresses views which resonate with the strict father model identified by George Lakoff. Spencer and Bannon, dismissed by many in the Alt-Right as being Alt-Lite, quickly identified Trump as the candidate most able to appeal to a constituency which felt let down by politicians, including mainstream Republicans dismissed by the Alt-Right as 'cuckservatives', a pejorative term for race traitors who had surrendered their masculinity.[15]

The Alt-Right's significance lies not in their numerical or organisational strength, which amounts to little more than an active online presence, but rather in their targeted attacks on mainstream Republicanism and their support for the more populist Trump positions on immigration, the perceived threat posed by immigration or travel from Muslim majority countries, opposition to diversity and inclusion, white identity politics and the need to 'drain the swamp' of vested interests in Washington. Steve Bannon's access to Trump towards the end of the campaign trail and during much of the first year in office strengthened Trump's populist impulse around such issues. Bannon gave expression to a world view which resonated with a strict father morality. In 2010, he set out his views in a documentary, Generation Zero.[16]

Generation Zero depicts a world in which an incompetent political class is dominated by global financial elites. The financial crash of 2008 and subsequent government bailouts are represented as a betrayal of working people. Bannon presents an image of an America in decline, which he attributes to an outworking of the counterculture of the 1960s and 1970s. For Bannon, the institutional stability and moral values of the 1950s were overturned by socialism and black power politics and the unfettered greed of a free enterprise system devoid of a moral compass, which eventually led to the financial crisis of 2008. The Clinton presidency is singled out as the epitome of these destabilising trends with a

---

[14] Hawley, *Making Sense of the Alt-Right.*

[15] John Woodrow Cox, 'Let's Party Like It's 1933: Inside the Alt-Right World of Richard Spencer,' *Washington Post*, 22 November 2016.

[16] Stephen Bannon, Documentary Generation Zero, 2010, https://www.youtube.com/watch?v=bsqu9gh6xhk.

capitalism

combination of what Generation Zero refers to as crony capitalism and welfare socialism.[17] America had survived and grown stronger through the crises of the war of independence, the Civil War and the Second World War and now faced a fourth crisis, identified in the generational theory writings of William Strauss and Neil Howe.[18] This fourth crisis was more pronounced than previous crises because of the growth of secularism and break down of Judeo-Christian values essential, in Bannon's world view, for sustaining the American tradition of liberty and free enterprise and restraining its worst impulses to the detriment of ordinary working people.[19]

Bannon's world view is most clearly revealed in a speech via Skype at the Human Dignity Institute in the Vatican in the summer of 2014. The conference on poverty was hosted by conservative Catholics and provided a platform for Bannon to present a global vision, which tapped into popular disquiet in America and Western Europe about a crisis of capitalism and the protection of elites, including bank executives, from the consequences of their actions. Bannon, himself an Irish American Catholic, set out an analysis of a crisis of both capitalism and Judeo-Christian values. He depicts the twentieth century as a time of barbarity as world wars were fought and won by the 'Judeo-Christian West against atheists'.[20] Capitalism generated vast wealth which was distributed to a rising middle class, people who had come from working-class environments and creating a Pax Americana. Over the past few decades, this world had begun to unravel and now America and the West faced crisis:

> I believe we've come partly offtrack in the years since the fall of the Soviet Union and we're starting now in the 21st century, which I believe,

---

[17] Bannon, *Generation Zero*.

[18] Neil Howe and William Strauss, *Generations: The History of America's Future, 1584 to 2069* (New York: William Morrow and Co., 1991); Neil Howe and William Strauss, *The Fourth Turning: What the Cycles of History Tell Us About America's Next Rendezvous with Destiny* (New York: Broadway Books, 1997).

[19] Alexander Livingston, 'The World According to Bannon,' *Jacobin*, 7 February 2017, https://www.jacobinmag.com/2017/02/bannon-trump-muslim-travel-ban-breitbart-generation-zero/.

[20] J. Lester Feder, 'This Is How Steve Bannon Sees the Entire World,' https://www.buzzfeed.com/lesterfeder/this-is-how-steve-bannon-sees-the-entire-world?utm_term=.jaMxrodeMD#.svD3JbdxQ8.

strongly, is a crisis both of our church, a crisis of our faith, a crisis of the West, a crisis of capitalism.[21]

Bannon identifies three converging tendencies. Firstly, he identifies two versions of capitalism, which he finds equally problematic, a state-sponsored crony capitalism of the type seen in China and Russia, where capitalism creates wealth and value for small elites and does not spread value creation across society. The other type of capitalism is identified as 'the Ayn Rand or the Objectivist School of libertarian capitalism', which commodifies and objectifies people in the name of personal freedom, a capitalism that appeals to younger people and yet is far removed from what he describes as the 'enlightened capitalism' of the Judeo-Christian West. The second tendency, which complements the first, is the secularisation of the West with popular culture targeting millennials under 30 to secularise. This converges with the third tendency which is 'outright war against jihadist Islamic fascism'.[22]

The message from Bannon around these three tendencies of capitalism, secularism and jihadism is that there needs to be return to Judeo-Christian values in capitalism with caps on wealth creation and distribution and an imperative to use wealth to create jobs and to protect the West in a civilisational clash with the forces of Islamist jihadism. He identifies a centre right populist movement with the Tea Party, Front National in France and Brexiteers in the UK comprising of 'really the middle class, the working men and women in the world who are just tired of being dictated to by what we call the party of Davos'—a global elite dictating to the rest of the world how it should be run:

I will tell you that the working men and women of Europe and Asia and the United States and Latin America don't believe that. They believe they know what's best for how they will comport their lives. They think they know best about how to raise their families and how to educate their families. So I think you're seeing a global reaction to centralized government, whether that government is in Beijing or that government is in

[21] J. Lester Feder, 'This Is How Steve Bannon Sees the Entire World,' https://www.buzzfeed.com/lesterfeder/this-is-how-steve-bannon-sees-the-entire-world?utm_term=.jaMxrodeMD#.svD3JbdxQ8.

[22] J. Lester Feder, 'This Is How Steve Bannon Sees the Entire World,' 15 November 2016, https://www.buzzfeed.com/lesterfeder/this-is-how-steve-bannon-sees-the-entire-world?utm_term=.jaMxrodeMD#.svD3JbdxQ8.

Washington, DC, or that government is in Brussels. So we are the platform for the voice of that.[23]

In the question and answer session following his talk, Bannon emphasised the Tea Party and Breitbart's role as the representative of working- and middle-class Americans against the crony capitalism prevalent within the Republican Party establishment, the voice of anti-abortion and of traditional marriage. The financial bailout of 2008 is critiqued for rewarding rather than punishing corporations and elites for mismanagement and corporate greed with the associated costs being born by the working and middle classes who were suffering most financial hardship as jobs were outsourced and industry hollowed out.[24]

Bannon's populist instinct chimed with Trump's own and with the strict father morality, which objected to handouts and believed in self-help. What was needed was for there to be a level playing field where a candidate, and later president, would be willing to fight against vested interests and the corporations and 'drain the swamp'. When it looked as though Trump was for electoral defeat, it was to Bannon he turned to rescue the campaign in August 2016.[25] Biographer Joshua Green describes Bannon as 'a brilliant ideologue from the outer fringe of American politics ... whose unlikely path happened to intersect with Trump's at precisely the right moment in history'.[26] Bannon's version of Alt-Right politics also resonated with large swathes of the Christian Right, comprising white conservative evangelicals and Catholics.

White Conservative Evangelicals and Catholics

Since the late 1970s, the Christian Right have proved to be an impressive and well-organised political force. Self-identified white evangelicals comprise 26% of the electorate with white Catholics making up a further 23%.[27] Positioning themselves as values voters concerned with moral

---

[23] Feder, 'How Steve Bannon Sees The Entire World'.

[24] Feder, 'Bannon'.

[25] Keith Koffler, *Bannon: Always the Rebel* (Washington, DC: Regnery Books, 2017).

[26] Joshua Green, *Devil's Bargain: Steve Bannon, Donald Trump, and the Storming of the Presidency* (New York: Penguin Press, 2017), p. 21.

[27] Smith and Martínez, 'How the Faithful Voted'.

character as well as specific social concerns including abortion, same-sex marriage, traditional family values, the right to bear arms, free enterprise, low taxation, strong defence and support for Israel, Trump was hardly a natural choice for them as Republican candidate.

The candidacy of Donald Trump threatened to tear the Christian Right apart as the constituency agonised over issues of supporting an arrogant, boorish, womanising, serial adulterer without political experience yet with the potential to defeat or at least run Clinton close after two successive defeats for the Republican Party. Trump's book *Crippled America: How to Make America Great Again* set out his campaign platform and pitch for white- and blue-collar workers and the marginalised middle classes, ignored by both mainstream political parties in government. Contrary to public perception, Trump sought to position himself as a Christian, influenced by the positive-thinking philosophy of Norman Vincent Peale,[28] albeit one who had never found the need to ask God's forgiveness for anything:

> I think people, are shocked when they find out that I am a Christian, that I am a religious person. They see me with all the surroundings of wealth so that they sometimes don't associate that with being religious. That's not accurate. I go to church. I love God, and I love having a relationship with Him.[29]

Trump's announcement that he was running for office with his designation of some Mexican illegal migrants as murderers and rapists, promising to build a wall on the Mexican border, and calls for a temporary ban on Muslims coming into the USA for a period appalled many but not all evangelicals.[30] Jerry Falwell Junior, son of the Moral Majority founder and president of Liberty University, one of the world's largest Christian Universities, endorsed Trump in January 2016, declaring him to be: 'a man who I believe can lead our country to greatness again'. Tony Perkins, President of the Family Research Council understood Trump's appeal: 'Now they see Donald Trump, who is taking on that

---

[28] Norman Vincent Peale, *The Power of Positive Thinking* (New York: Prentice Hall, 1952).

[29] Donald Trump, *Crippled America: How to Make America Great Again* (New York: Threshold Editions, 2015), p. 130.

[30] Donald Trump, 'Here's Donald Trump's Presidential Announcement Speech,' *Time*, 16 June 2015.

same elitist politically correct mindset and not backing down ... They find common cause in this guy, even though he comes from a completely different world'.[31]

In introducing Trump to his students, Falwell explained that he saw much of his father in Trump that he was a man who could not be bought and, unlike other champions of value voters, would deliver on his promises to protect Christianity:

> For decades, conservatives and evangelicals have chosen the political candidates who have told us what we wanted to hear on social, religious, and political issues only to be betrayed by those same candidates after they were elected.[32]

Michael Horton writing in evangelical magazine *Christianity Today* was less impressed. He considered that Trump epitomised the sorry state of evangelicalism in the USA where the state accords rights rather than God, Jesus becomes a brand, and leadership a 'celebration of narcissism, greed, and deceitfulness in the pursuit of power'.[33]

For those evangelicals and Catholic conservatives who preferred pragmatism to character and who sought to elect a president rather than pastor, they were rewarded by Trump's determination to win them over. Support for Israel has always been a key priority for the Christian Right and Trump's speech to the American Israel Public Affairs Committee in March 2016 did not disappoint. He reaffirmed America's commitment to Israel, promised to dismantle the nuclear agreement with Iran, move the US Embassy to Jerusalem, veto anti-Israeli moves in the UN Security Council and stand shoulder to shoulder with Israel, which would always be a Jewish state.[34] In June, he met with one thousand evangelical leaders and received a standing ovation.[35] He promised to appoint anti-abortion justices to the Supreme Court, working together with evangelicals to overturn the Johnson amendment prohibiting the

[31] Tessa Berenson, 'Jerry Falwell Jr., President of Liberty University and Prominent Evangelical Leader, Has Endorsed Donald Trump for President,' *Time*, 26 January 2016.

[32] Jerry Falwell, 'President Falwell Donald Trump Introduction,' 18 January 2016.

[33] Michael Horton, 'The Theology of Donald Trump—Four Words That Reveal What His Followers Really Believe,' *Christianity Today*, 16 March 2016.

[34] Sarah Begley, 'Read Donald Trump's Speech to AIPAC,' *Time*, 21 March 2016.

[35] Elizabeth Dias, 'Donald Trump Receives Standing Ovation at Evangelical Meeting,' *Time*, 21 June 2016.

endorsement of political candidates by tax-exempt groups, including religious organisations:

> I think maybe that will be my greatest contribution to Christianity — and other religions — is to allow you, when you talk religious liberty, to go and speak openly, and if you like somebody or want somebody to represent you, you should have the right to do it.[36]

The meeting was followed by an announcement of an Evangelical Advisory Board for Trump's campaign consisting of twenty-two prominent figures in the Christian Right, including Tea Party favourite Michele Bachmann; James Dobson, founder of Focus on the Family; Jerry Falwell, Jr.; Richard Land, President of the Southern Evangelical Seminary; Ralph Reed, founder of the Faith and Freedom Coalition; and Paula White, Senior Pastor, New Destiny Christian Center who is credited with being the main spiritual influence on Trump.[37]

The relationship between Christian Right leaders and Trump was based on a shared need—Trump for political power through electoral victory and the conservative evangelicals to be able to exert an influence on society they saw declining. Failure by Trump to win not just the backing but also the votes of the overwhelming majority of white evangelicals would lead to defeat in the polls in November. He steadfastly courted the group throughout the campaign and in July named Mike Pence, Indiana Governor and House Republican, as his running mate. Pence had impeccable conservative evangelical credentials, once describing himself as an evangelical Catholic and more recently as 'a Christian, a conservative and a Republican, in that order'.[38] This appointment reassured those who doubted Trump's commitment to evangelical causes and fitness for office by including an experienced moral values policy-maker with good connections in the House and wider Republican Party. Most importantly for the Christian Right, Trump became increasingly credible in delivering the type of America they desired.

---

[36] Michelle Boorstein and Julie Zauzmer, 'Thrilling Christian Conservative Audience, Trump Vows to Lift Ban on Politicking, Appoint Antiabortion Judges,' *Washington Post*, 22 June 2016.

[37] Donald Trump, 'Trump Campaign Announces Evangelical Executive Advisory Board,' Press Release, 21 June 2016.

[38] Max Perry Mueller, 'The Christian Worldview of Mike Pence,' *Religion and Politics*, 10 October 2016, http://religionandpolitics.org/2016/10/10/the-christian-worldview-of-mike-pence/.

By September, the support of the Christian Right looked assured. Stalwart of the movement Phyllis Schlafly, founder of Eagle Forum, died on the eve of her book *The Conservative Case for Trump*, endorsing Trump was released.[39] Schlafly endorsed Trump before other Christian Right leaders and received initial disapproval for doing so. Trump was invited to speak at her funeral and further strengthened support among this constituency.[40] Earlier in the day he had spoken at the 11th Annual Voters Summit and set out his stall in the opening lines of his speech that conservative evangelicals were back at the heart of the political process:

> A lot of people said: I wonder if Donald will get the evangelicals. I got the evangelicals. I'm going to make it up to you too, you watch. There are no more decent, devoted, or selfless people than our Christian brothers and sisters here in the United States.
> So let me say this right up front: A Trump administration, our Christian heritage will be cherished, protected, defended, like you've never seen before. Believe me. I believe it. And you believe it. And you know it. You know it.[41]

In order to shore up another key constituency, Trump turned his attention to Catholic conservatives and announced a 34-member Catholic Advisory Board. Trump had been wounded at the outset of his campaign by criticism of his immigration policy by Pope Francis and in reaching out to US Catholics hoped to offset the damage caused. The advisory group included two former Ambassadors to the Holy See and leading Christian Right political figures including Senator Rick Santorum, former US Senator and presidential candidate; Richard Viguerie, Chairman of ConservativeHQ; Ed Martin, President of Eagle Forum; Gov. Sam Brownback, Kansas Governor and Senator; and Joseph Cella, Founder of the National Catholic Prayer Breakfast.[42] This was followed by a press release on how Trump would handle issues of importance to Catholics.[43]

---

[39] Phyllis Schlafly, Ed Martin, and Brett Decker, *The Conservative Case for Trump* (Washington, DC: Regnery Publishing, 2016).

[40] Julia Hahn, 'Donald Trump at Phyllis Schlafly's Funeral: A Movement Has Lost Its Hero, Our Country Has Lost a Warrior,' *Breitbart*, 10 September 2016.

[41] Donald Trump, 'Trump Values Voter Summit Remarks,' *POLITICO*, 9 September 2016.

[42] Donald Trump, 'Trump Campaign Announces Catholic Advisory Group,' Press Release, 22 September 2016, https://www.donaldjtrump.com/press-releases/trump-campaign-announces-catholic-advisory-group.

[43] Donald Trump, 'Issues of Importance to Catholics,' Press Release, 22 September 2016.

While discomfort remained among his critics within the Christian Right, exacerbated by the release of the infamous Trump Tape, it appeared that Trump had won over all but the most diehard opponents.

Trump afforded the opportunity to appoint sympathetic Supreme Court justices, repeal Obamacare, uphold traditional marriage, protect religious freedom, increase school choice, support for Israel, overturn the Iranian nuclear deal, and to roll back Obama's liberal agenda.[44] Trump provided a lifeline for a movement which had seen its fortunes wane and for which the prospects of another four to eight years outside the White House were unacceptable. The ends (increased religious influence) would justify the means (of overlooking the indiscretions of a flawed candidate). The Christian Right were able to mobilise their supporters who turned out for Trump in unprecedented numbers with 81% of white evangelicals supporting Trump against only 16% for Clinton and 60% of white Catholics against only 37% for the Democratic candidate.[45]

For the loose coalition of Alt-Right, conservative evangelicals and white Catholics, it would not be enough for Trump to not be Clinton, but he would be expected to deliver on his campaign promises to 'Make America Great Again' by increasing employment, reducing taxes, reducing immigration and refugees, building a wall on the Mexican border, supporting Israel, restricting travel from Muslim majority countries, providing a block grant for parents to have their children educated in faith schools if they wish and appointing pro-life Supreme Court Justices.[46] Trump was also expected to roll back the Obama legacy, which epitomised Lakoff's nurturant parent model of affirmative action, welfare and health care, environmental protection measures at the expense of traditional industry, and increased bureaucracy and regulation, support for abortion and LGBTQ rights over support for the traditional family.

[44] Sarah Pulliam Bailey, 'We're All Sinners': Jerry Falwell Jr Defends Donald Trump After Video of Lewd Remarks,' *Washington Post*, 10 October 2016.

[45] Pew Research Center, 'How the Faithful Voted: A Preliminary 2016 Analysis,' 9 November 2016, http://www.pewresearch.org/fact-tank/2016/11/09/how-the-faithful-voted-a-preliminary-2016-analysis/ft_16-11-09_relig_exitpoll_religrace/.

[46] Sarah Pulliam Bailey, 'We're All Going to Be Saying "Merry Christmas": Here Are Donald Trump's Campaign Promises on Religion,' *Washington Post*, 7 December 2016; Peter Montgomery, 'Trump This Thanksgiving,' Right Wing Watch, 23 November 2016, http://www.rightwingwatch.org/post/religious-right-thankful-for-trump-this-thanksgiving/.

ROLLING BACK THE OBAMA LEGACY

The Trump administration from the outset was qualitatively and quantitatively very different from that of the outgoing Obama administration. The Alt-Right-Evangelical-Catholic coalition was well represented in government with Steve Bannon appointed as Chief Strategist and Senior Counsel with a seat on the principals' committee of the National Security Council, and Michael Flynn appointed National Security Advisor. Conservative evangelicals included Mike Pence as Vice-President; Betsy DeVos as Education Secretary paving the way for public funding to go to faith schools; Rick Perry, Energy Secretary; Tom Price, Head of the Department of Health and Human Services; Scott Pruitt, Administrator of the Environmental Protection Agency; Secretary of State, Rex Tillerson; Attorney General Jeff Session; Chief of Staff, Reince Priebus; CIA Director, Mike Pompeo; and UN Ambassador, Nikki Haley, are all committed Christians and active members of their churches and are in agreement on those issues of most importance to Values Voters.[47]

The conservative coalition needed to govern was somewhat broader than the one necessary to secure victory in the Electoral College. Mainstream Republicans and corporate interests were co-opted and courted as Bannon, Priebus and Jared Kushner the President's son-in-law competed for the president's attention and political strategy in a dysfunctional White House.[48] Key personnel, however, had very little governmental experience, middle-ranking organisational positions remained unfilled, and key personnel resigned or were dismissed in record numbers for the first year of an administration in the post war era.[49] These included Bannon, Priebus, Flynn, Price, two White House Communications Directors, White House Press Secretary and an FBI Director. Bannon is credited with crafting the inaugural address and

[47] Bill Donohue, 'Trump Will Be Religion-Friendly,' *Christian News Service*, 7 December 2016; Emily McFarlan Miller, Adelle Banks, and Kimberley Winston, 'Trump Advisers: The Faith Factor,' *Religion News*, 13 December 2016; Patricia Miller, 'Meet the New Christian Right, Same as the Old Christian Right,' *Religion Dispatches*, 12 December 2016; Jack Noland and Anna Massoglia, 'Betsy DeVos and Her Big-Giving Relatives: Family Qualifies as GOP Royalty,' *Open Secrets*, 1 December 2016.

[48] See Michael Wolff, *Fire and Fury: Inside the Trump White House* (London: Little, Brown, 2018).

[49] Summer Meza, 'Trump Administration Holds Highest Rate of First-Year Staff Turnover,' *Newsweek*, 28 December 2017.

executive orders on immigration and refugees, including the Muslim travel ban, which resonated with the Alt-Christian Right supporters but ran into legislative difficulties, through ineptitude and inexperience from Trump and his Chief Strategist who were unable to secure congressional approval.

The portrayal of Bannon as the driving force behind the Trump victory and governmental programme was increasingly resented by Trump, Kushner and daughter Ivanka.[50] Bannon was featured in two articles in the first month of the new administration including Time Magazine under the title 'The Great Manipulator' and a New York Times op-ed headlined 'President Bannon?'[51] Neither Bannon nor Trump was able to deliver an effective legislative programme without courting and involving Republicans in the House and Senate. Campaign promises to have Mexico pay for a border wall, to halt Muslim travel to the USA and to repeal Obamacare have all fallen short. Although Trump was unable to enact much legislation, he was nonetheless able to govern through a combination of executive actions, cabinet-level agency decision and Congressional Review Acts. In the following sections using the *Washington Post*'s data set on policy implementation, I examine areas where the Trump administration has actually rolled back on the Obama legacy rather than the rhetorical promises which have yet to be realised.[52]

Environment

One of the Obama's most successful policies was to start addressing the issue of climate change and demonstrate US leadership through signing up to the Paris Climate Change Agreement. One of the Trump's first acts was to withdraw from the agreement signalling an intention to prioritise economic development over the environment. The Trump administration has abandoned the restrictions on fracking introduced under the previous administration in 2015 and allowed roads to be built through wildlife refuges. Permission for drilling for oil and gas in the Arctic National Wildlife Refuge was granted along with developing the Access

---

[50]Wolff, *Fire and Fury*; Koffler, *Bannon: Always the Rebel*; Green, *Devil's Bargain*.

[51]David Von Drehle, 'Is Steve Bannon the Second Most Powerful Man in the World?' *Time*, 2 February 2017; 'President Bannon?' *New York Times*, 27 January 2017.

[52]Darla Cameron, 'How Trump Is Rolling Back Obama's Legacy,' *The Washington Post*, 31 January 2018.

and Keystone XL pipelines. Protection for migrating birds against wind turbines and greenhouse emissions from power plants has been overturned. The administration has also overturned the need to take into account climate change and flooding protection when designing and building infrastructure projects.

Although not substantial, such incremental changes resonate with a strict father morality which prioritises humanity over animals and the environment, America over other nations, and reducing bureaucracy to encourage a culture of self-help, discipline and hard work designed to restore personal prosperity through creating employment.

Labour and Finance

The Trump administration withdrew from the Trans-Pacific Partnership (TPP), an initiative designed by the Obama administration to increase America's role and presence in the Asia-Pacific region in response to Chinese influence. Trump presented the agreement as disadvantageous to the USA with the possible loss of American jobs and negative effects on the balance of trade. Such sentiments resonate with an America First approach with a mistrust of foreigners and a self-help philosophy that negates the need to cooperate or work for the common good. This approach extends to a decision to no longer report on pay by race or gender. Strict father morality would identify such bureaucratic regulations as unnecessary state interference in placing obstacles in the way of conducting business. Concerns over gender and race are interpreted as political correctness and a challenge to an order which places man above woman and white over non-white. The administration has sought to reduce bureaucratic burdens on employers by cutting business regulations and safety measures with the principle adopted of cutting two business regulations for every new one introduced. Such measures are in accord with a strict father moral order which places employers above employees.   *work!*

Health Care

One of the first acts of the administration was to reintroduce the Mexico City global gag rule, introduced by Ronald Reagan and reintroduced by George W. Bush. The policy, consistently revoked by Democratic administrations, prohibits US assistance for organisations that advocate, support, participate in or manage coercive abortion or involuntary sterilisation overseas.[53] Moral and religious conscience protection was afforded to individuals and organisations whose conscience precludes providing services or care which offend their sensibilities such as abortion, providing contraception or working with LGBTQ communities. Again, strict father morality conceptions of right and wrong trump political correctness and reaffirm a world view which considers that women should not have control over their bodies and reproduction, and that heterosexuality is the only acceptable form of sexuality.

Obamacare has not been repealed, but the tax penalty for non-compliance with the need to carry insurance cover has been lifted. The Affordable Care Act, in strict father morality, creates a welfare dependency and state involvement rather than encouraging self-help and individual responsibility to provide for their own care. Although many Trump supporters benefit from Affordable Health Care Act, its association with the nurturant parent morality of the Obama administration made this a touchstone issue in the election and first year in office. Although not a matter of legislation the early appointment of Neil Gorsuch, as successor to Antonin Scalia, as Supreme Court Justice with the potential to affect pro-life adjudications represented the single most significant achievement of the first year of the Trump.

Civil Rights

The Obama administration required authorities to justify the demolition of public housing and to protect public housing from the risk of flooding. Courts were instructed not to use fines on the poor as a means of boosting public funds. The Trump administration overturned or rescinded all such moves. Strict father morality posits that individuals are responsible for providing their own housing rather than be reliant on the public authority and that law breaking deserves to be punished.

Worker and Consumer Safety

The Trump administration reduced the number of workplace protections available during its first year in office including for transgender employees. Plans to introduce further food labelling and nutritional information on packaging to help combat obesity were delayed. These measures are

---

[53] Donald Trump, 'Presidential Memorandum Regarding Mexico City Policy,' *White House*, Washington, DC, 23 January 2017.

those advocated by a nurturant parent morality, which seeks to protect citizens from dangers they may not be aware of, as a parent would seek to protect their child. Strict father morality places responsibility on the individual rather than the state or the employer to protect themselves and their own family.

Immigration

Immigration directly feeds into constructions of American identity for many Trump supporters reducing migration and expelling those migrants who overstayed visas or entered the country illegally was a key issue in the election. Trump's proposed travel ban on visitors from six Muslim majority nations is consistent with a rhetoric which posits Muslims as 'other' and a potential security threat. In a strict father morality, the presence of Latino and Hispanic migrants challenges visions of a mainly white America and is a physical reminder of changing demographics which threaten the maintenance of white domination. Trump's commitment to building a wall on the Mexican border extended to signing orders for the deportation of 200,000 Salvadorians, 60,000 Haitians and 2500 Nicaraguans. Where the Obama administration agreed to accept 100,000 refugees each year, the Republican administration reduced this number to 45,000.

Education

Over the course of the first year, federal standards at public schools were eliminated and a National School Choice proclamation made vouchers available to enable parents to pay for a greater choice of education provider, including religious and home schooling, policies advocated by Betsy DeVos.[54] The strict father knows what is best for his child, and in education, that responsibility can be delegated but not handed over to the school. Parental choice aligns with strict father morality enabling parents to move children from schools which teach values at variance with their own to ones where they are in accord.

---

[54]Donald Trump, 'National-School-Choice-Week-Proclamation,' *White House*, Washington, DC, 26 January 2017.

Foreign Policy

Despite the bellicose rhetoric deployed during the campaign castigating Obama's foreign policy-making, changes under Trump were rhetorical rather than practical. The Iranian nuclear deal negotiated by the Permanent 5 members of the UN Security Council and the European Union has been abandoned by Trump, if not the other signatories. Relations with Cuba have remained largely unaltered after Obama's rapprochement, and the North Atlantic Treaty Organisation remains an essential component of US security considerations, despite the president declaring on the campaign trail that it was not fit for purpose. The significant changes have occurred in withdrawing from the TTP and the Paris Agreement and in the relationship with Israel.

Under the Obama presidency, relations between the president and Prime Minister Netanyahu were strained. Although settlement building continued in the Occupied Palestinian Territories, including East Jerusalem, Obama sought to constrain Israel's more provocative policy positions in the Palestinians and adopt a more even handed approach towards Israel/Palestine. Within the first year, Trump visited Israel and fulfilled his campaign promise to recognise Jerusalem as the capital of Israel and move the US Embassy from Tel Aviv to Jerusalem. Support for Israel is consistent with a strict father morality which has a Judeo-Christian God above man; support for Israel is presented as consistent with God's word in conservative evangelical circles and the pioneering spirit of Israel and its unwillingness to compromise on its claim to the land seen as a sign of strength in the face of political correctness.

DURABILITY OF THE ALT-RIGHT, EVANGELICAL, CATHOLIC COALITION

The Alt-Right, evangelical and Catholic coalition was a loose association of like-minded voters rather than a formal coalition. In this chapter, I have suggested that groups of like-minded conservative voters coalesced around the Trump campaign because of a shared strict father morality rather than through rational choice. All sectors of the electorate not only are mainly concerned with the economy and security but also have other key issues that can prove decisive in elections. The Alt-Right were concerned about political correctness, the survival of the white majority and an economic and political system that favoured elites over working- and middle-class Americans. Conservative evangelicals and Catholics were concerned about abortion and challenges to the traditional family. Memes including 'Make America Great Again' and 'America First' resonated and galvanised support, but governing was about taking practical steps to make such memes real.

The US economy performed well during Trump's first year in office with growth rates up to 3.2%, higher than Obama's last year in office. The US stock markets including The Dow Jones Industrial Average, Standard & Poor's 500 Index and the Nasdaq index all reached record levels. Unemployment continued falling to the lowest rate since the financial crash to 4.8%. Average hourly earnings increased by 2.8% over the twelve months. Although job creation has not been significant, Trump supporters could find encouragement in the economic data.[55]

Over the first year, Trump's job approval ratings among Republican voters remained virtually unchanged around 87%, according to a Gallup survey, although Democrats and Independents rated him lower over the course of the year.[56] The Pew Research Center polling suggested that despite fulfilling a number of campaign promises for white evangelicals job approval among the group had slipped for 78–61% and among Catholics from 36 to 26%.[57] PRRI research over the first year still revealed strong white evangelical and Catholic support for Trump with 49% of Catholics and 72% of white evangelicals approving of the job he was doing and thirty per cent agreeing that there was almost nothing that Trump could do to lose their support. 13% of white evangelicals, however, strongly opposed Trump.[58]

Trump's character and behaviour had alienated and continued to alienate those evangelicals who put moral character ahead of political expediency. Russell Moore, President of the Ethics and Religious Liberty Commission of the Southern Baptist Convention,[59] and Andrew

[55] Daniele Palumbo, 'Donald Trump and the US Economy in Six Charts,' BBC Online, 20 January 2018.

[56] Gallup, 'Presidential Approval Ratings—Donald Trump,' *Gallup*, January 2018.

[57] Pew Research Center, 'Stark Partisan Divisions over Russia Probe, Including Its Importance to the Nation,' 7 December 2017.

[58] PRRI, 'One Nation, Divided, Under Trump: Findings from the 2017 American Values Survey,' *Public Religion Research Institute*, 5 December 2017.

[59] Russell Moore, 'If Donald Trump Has Done Anything, He Has Snuffed Out the Religious Right,' *Washington Post*, 9 October 2016.

Crouch, editor of Christianity Today, led the charge of Trump's unsuitability as the choice of evangelicals.[60] Still others, including prominent Christian ethicist David Gushee[61] and Mark Labberton,[62] President of Fuller Theological Seminary, have questioned whether to continue defining themselves as evangelicals. Overall though, evangelical support remained steadfast throughout the first year.

The Alt-Right lost their champion when Steve Bannon was dismissed from the White House. However, the Alt-Right was never an effective force in mobilising electoral support, but the candidacy and election of Trump were sufficient to elevate the Alt-Right from the fringe of American politics to prominence by giving expressions to views that would not otherwise attract attention. Although Trump was never part of the Alt-Right in retweeting comments from people who were he raised the profile of Alt-Right politics. Trump's candidacy and election dealt the 'organized conservative movement a devastating blow, creating an opening for right-wing alternatives'.[63] Not being a member of the Alt-Right, Trump would inevitably disappoint as president while still remaining the mainstream political leader most closely attuned to their aspirations.

CONCLUSION

In this chapter, I have argued that a loose coalition of white Alt-Right, Evangelical and Catholic voters endorsed Trump's candidacy and subsequent election, even though he represented the antithesis of the character values traditionally upheld by the Christian Right. This disparate coalition was able to coalesce around a world view which ascribes to a strict father morality in which strong leadership, discipline, self-control and self-help are seen essential qualities in a country where the working and middle class in the flyover states have disproportionately suffered economic hardship following the financial crisis of 2008. Trump was

[60] Andy Crouch, 'Speak Truth to Trump—Evangelicals, of All People, Should Not Be Silent About Donald Trump's Blatant Immorality,' *Christianity Today*, 10 October 2016.

[61] David Gushee, *Still Christian: Following Jesus Out of American Evangelicalism* (Louisville, KY: Westminster John Knox Press, 2017).

[62] Mark Labberton, ed., *Still Evangelical? Insiders Reconsider Political, Social, and Theological Meaning* (Downers Grove, IL: Inter Varsity Press, 2018).

[63] Hawley, *Making Sense of the Alt-Right*, p. 116.

able to articulate a narrative in accord with a strict father morality where corporate interests, immigration, crony capitalism, attacks on traditional family values, political correctness and Islamist terrorism were preventing America from being Great Again. A narrative endorsed by Steve Bannon and the Alt-Right and Christian Right leaders. The support of 81% of conservative evangelicals and 60% of white Catholics helped deliver the Electoral College for Trump.

The first year of the Trump administration was characterised by political ineptitude with numerous key administrative posts unfilled and little progress made in terms of new legislation. However, the appointment of Neil Gorsuch to the Supreme Court and tax cuts delivered some of the promises made in the election campaign and helped sustain support from Trump voters. Through the use of executive actions, cabinet-level agency decision and Congressional Review Acts, Trump was able to slowly and incrementally roll back some of the Obama legacy around the environment, labour and finance, health care, civil rights, worker and consumer safety, immigration and education. The measures taken and change implemented are in accord with a strict father moral framework, which gradually erodes the role of the state in protecting rights and providing safety nets and encourages individual responsibility.

REFERENCES

Dobson, James. *Dare to Discipline.* New York: Bantam Books, 1977.

Green, Joshua. *Devil's Bargain: Steve Bannon, Donald Trump, and the Storming of the Presidency.* New York: Penguin Press, 2017.

Gushee, David. *Still Christian: Following Jesus Out of American Evangelicalism.* Louisville, KY: Westminster John Knox Press, 2017.

Hawley, George. *Making Sense of the Alt-Right.* New York: Colombia University Press, 2017.

Howe, Neil, and William Strauss. *Generations: The History of America's Future, 1584 to 2069.* New York: William Morrow and Co., 1991.

Howe, Neil, and William Strauss. *The Fourth Turning: What the Cycles of History Tell Us About America's Next Rendezvous with Destiny.* New York: Broadway Books, 1997.

Koffler, Keith. *Bannon: Always the Rebel.* Washington, DC: Regnery Books, 2017.

Labberton, Mark, ed. *Still Evangelical? Insiders Reconsider Political, Social, and Theological Meaning.* Downers Grove, IL: Inter Varsity Press, 2018.

Lakoff, George. *Don't Think of an Elephant: Know Your Values and Frame the Debate*. White River Junction, VT: Chelsea Green Publishing, 2016.

Lakoff, George. *Moral Politics: How Liberals and Conservatives Think*. Chicago and London: University of Chicago Press, 2016.

Lakoff, George, and Elisabeth Wehling. *The Little Blue Book*. New York: Free Press, 2012.

Neiwert, David. *Alt-American: The Rise of the Radical Right in the Age of Trump*. London and New York: Verso, 2017.

Peale, Norman Vincent. *The Power of Positive Thinking*. New York: Prentice Hall, 1952.

Schlafly, Phyllis, Ed Martin, and Brett Decker. *The Conservative Case for Trump*. Washington, DC: Regnery Publishing, 2016.

Taylor, M. *What Is the Alt-Right?* London: Create Space Independent Publishing Platform, 2016.

Trump, Donald. *Crippled America: How to Make America Great Again*. New York: Threshold Editions, 2015.

Wolff, Michael. *Fire and Fury: Inside the Trump White House*. London: Little, Brown, 2018.

CHAPTER 6

Racial Policy Under Trump

Richard Johnson

This chapter takes stock of the Trump administration's approach to racial policy compared to that of the Obama administration. The racial symbolism of Donald J. Trump's election as president stood in sharp contrast to Barack Obama's election and re-election victories. Trump spent the years prior to his election questioning Obama's citizenship, nationality and legitimacy. Trump's campaign rhetoric contained more outwardly racial content than from any recent presidential candidate. In addition, following the Supreme Court's ruling in *Shelby County v Holder* (2013), Trump was elected in the first presidential election in half a century which lacked the full protections of the Voting Rights Act.

Given these factors, commentators expected to see a dramatic shift in racial policy between the Obama and Trump administrations. Because most of Barack Obama's racial policy initiatives were conducted through the administrative powers of the executive branch, they were vulnerable to easy reversal by his successor. Obama was particularly aggressive in pursuing racial policy initiatives through the powerful Department of Justice (DoJ). President Trump appointed new personnel to reorient the

R. Johnson (✉)
Lancaster University, Lancaster, UK
e-mail: r.johnson10@lancaster.ac.uk

© The Author(s) 2019
M. Oliva and M. Shanahan (eds.), *The Trump Presidency*,
The Evolving American Presidency,
https://doi.org/10.1007/978-3-319-96325-9_6

priorities of the DoJ, diverging from his predecessor on policing, incarceration and voting rights.

This chapter will examine the sharpest areas of contrast between Donald Trump and Barack Obama on racial policy. The first section looks at President Trump's redirection of the Justice Department's agenda by appointing personnel who have long been opponents of the department's traditional initiatives. The second section will chart the policy shifts undertaken by the Trump administration on voting rights. These federal, executive-led policy changes will be situated within the wider context of state-level efforts to alter the franchise and the retreat of the federal courts from providing protection to ethnic minority voters. The final section will examine the Trump administration's sharp turn on matters of policing and criminal justice. Activists in the Black Lives Matter (BLM) group have seen a cautiously supportive administration led by the first African American president be replaced by an administration which has defined itself politically against the BLM movement in favour of groups which promote 'law and order', irrespective of the racially disparate impact of their actions.

THE DEPARTMENT OF JUSTICE

In the field of civil rights, no other federal department compares in importance to the Department of Justice. The DoJ consists of over 100,000 employees and an annual budget of over $30 billion. Historically, the DoJ has been the mainstay for civil rights activists and provided them with a sympathetic ear and a seat at the table of administrations of differing political hues.

The Department of Justice was founded in 1870 as one of the radical reforms of the Reconstruction period following the American Civil War. The department was created a month after the passage of the Civil Rights Act of 1870. To head this new department, Republican President Ulysses Grant appointed Amos Akerman, who used his role as attorney general to prosecute Ku Klux Klan members across the South. Akerman wrote in 1871 that 'extraordinary means' were needed to suppress the Klan. 'These combinations', he warned, 'amount to war and cannot be effectually crushed on any other theory' (White 2016: 526). Under Akerman's direction, over 3,000 Klansmen were arrested, with the worst offenders placed on trial before majority-black juries, who sentenced them to prison (Foner 1988: 457–58). Within a few years, the Justice

Department, as Robert Kaczorowski puts it, 'succeeded in destroying the Klan' (Kaczorowski 2005: 79). It was a first lesson in the profound role that the DoJ could play in the delivery of political power to African Americans.

During the 'Second Reconstruction', C. Vann Woodward's term for the civil rights movement of the 1950s and 1960s, the Justice Department was once more a pivotal player in enforcing the civil rights of African Americans (Woodward 1966: 9). The most significant institutional legacy from that period was the creation of the Department of Justice's Civil Rights Division (CRD). The CRD was a product of the Civil Rights Act of 1957, the first civil rights bill to pass Congress since 1875 and subject to the longest filibuster in Senate history. The CRD has a staff of about seven hundred, a budget of over $160 million, and been the engine of federal civil rights enforcement since its creation. The CRD is tasked with the enforcement of all major civil rights laws, including the centrepieces of the Second Reconstruction's legislative reforms: the Civil Rights Act of 1964, the Voting Rights Act of 1965 and the Fair Housing Act of 1968. Barack Obama's first Attorney General Eric Holder described the CRD as the DoJ's 'crown jewel'.

President Obama entrusted the leadership of the DoJ to two reform-minded African American attorneys general, Eric Holder (2009–2015) and Loretta Lynch (2015–2017), who arguably delivered more visible gains to African Americans than from any other executive department during Obama's presidency. When commentators criticised the first black president for failing to deliver to loyal African American supporters, the Obama administration could point to the work of the Justice Department. For example, under the Obama administration, the DoJ sued two of the main culprits of predatory lending practices during the housing boom. The DoJ argued that African American and Hispanic mortgage borrowers who qualified for loans were charged higher fees or placed incorrectly into subprime loans. The Department secured a $335 million settlement from Bank of America in the largest residential fair-lending settlement in history. In a similar case, the DoJ secured a $175 million compensation settlement for black and Hispanic home-owners from Wells Fargo. Neither case addressed the underlying systemic issues surrounding housing segregation in the USA, but they demonstrated the willingness of the Obama administration to use the DoJ's prosecutorial powers to win concessions for African Americans and Hispanics (Johnson 2018).

Under the Trump administration, the continued commitment of the DoJ to racial equality measures is less apparent. President Trump replaced Barack Obama's outgoing Attorney General Loretta Lynch, the first black woman to hold the position, with Alabama Senator Jefferson 'Jeff' Beauregard Sessions. Sessions has long had a fraught relationship with the civil rights community. As a US attorney, Sessions was rebuked for maliciously prosecuting African Americans who tried to register to vote in rural Perry County, Alabama. Albert Turner, a local civil rights activist who was a pall-bearer at Martin Luther King's funeral, and two colleagues were charged by Sessions on 29 counts of vote fraud for allegedly tampering with ballots during the 1984 Democratic primary. Known as the 'Marion Three', these civil rights activists were found not guilty by a federal grand jury. Corretta Scott King later wrote, 'Mr Sessions has used the awesome powers of his office in a shabby attempt to intimidate and frighten elderly black voters'.[1]

In 1986, the Senate Judiciary Committee blocked Sessions's nomination to a federal judgeship. According to testimony from senior DoJ trial attorney Gerald Hebert, Sessions had described civil rights groups, such as the NAACP, as 'un-American', 'communist-inspired' organisations, which 'force civil rights down the throats of people'. Sessions admitted describing a white civil rights lawyer as 'a disgrace to his race'.[2] He described the Voting Rights Act as 'a piece of intrusive legislation'.[3] Two Republicans sided with eight Democrats on the committee to vote against his appointment. Democratic Senator Ted Kennedy described Sessions as 'a throwback to a disgraceful era' and that his nomination for the minor judgeship was 'a disgrace to the Justice Department'.[4] Twenty-one years later, Republicans on the Judiciary Committee unanimously voted to confirm Sessions as the head of the Justice Department. While Loretta Lynch's confirmation took a lengthy five months, a record in recent history, Sessions was confirmed in less than a month.

---

[1] https://www.documentcloud.org/documents/3259988-Scott-King-1986-Letter-and-Testimony-Signed.html#document/p1.

[2] http://njlaw.rutgers.edu/collections/gdoc/hearings/8/87601234/87601234_1.pdf.

[3] Sarah Wildmna, 'Closed Sessions,' *New Republic*, 30 December 2002.

[4] Howard Kurtz, 'Federal Court Nominee Attacked Rights Groups,' *Washington Post*, 1986.

President Trump has made other senior appointments within the Justice Department which clash with the agency's historic aims. Trump designated the lawyer John Gore as the acting Assistant Attorney General for Civil Rights, the office in charge of leading the CRD. Before his nomination, one of Gore's main areas of expertise had been to defend state governments against allegations of civil rights violations in voting law. Gore, for example, defended the state of Florida against charges that its process of purging voters from the electoral roll disproportionately targeted ethnic minorities. A federal court found that Florida had violated the National Voter Registration Act, a statute which Gore is now tasked with defending in the CRD.

In 2016, Gore signed an *amicus curiae* brief in support of a Virginia voter ID law which was challenged in federal courts (*Lee v Virginia State Board of Elections* (2016)). Gore and colleagues wrote that lower levels of minority turnout following the passage of such laws were attributed to the possibility that 'members of minority races may disproportionately choose, for socio-economic or other reasons, not to take advantage of this equal opportunity [to vote]'.[5] Gore's *amicus* brief did not draw the connection between the economic costs of acquiring voter identification paperwork, travelling to official state ID offices, and the cost of the ID with the 'socio-economic' reasons for not voting. In fact, they posited the opposite, 'Wealthier individuals are less able or willing to expend time that could be put to other uses because of their higher hourly wages and less likely to take time off from demanding work schedules', suggesting that, if anything, wealthier Americans were disproportionately affected by the requirement to have a state-issued photo ID to vote.

VOTING RIGHTS

One of the most crucial areas of civil rights enforcement pursued by the DoJ is in voting rights. Donald Trump's election followed one of the most serious reversals in voting rights enforcement since the collapse of the First Reconstruction in the late nineteenth century. For the first time in over a century, the Supreme Court in 2013 struck down a major piece of civil rights legislation. It marks a declarative finale to the high court's spasmodic commitment to protecting civil and voting rights.

[5] http://moritzlaw.osu.edu/electionlaw/litigation/documents/TRIALBRIEF foramicicuriae021716.pdf.

In the 2013 case *Shelby County v Holder*, the Supreme Court rendered the most powerful element of the Voting Rights Act of 1965 (VRA) inoperable. Between 1965 and 2013, Section 5 of VRA forced jurisdictions with a history of voting rights violations to seek approval from the federal government before bringing any changes in election law or practice. Jurisdictions under 'preclearance' were forced to submit even the most minor changes for review by the Justice Department or the Circuit Court of the District of Columbia. It was a turning point in the struggle against attempts by municipal and state legislatures to dilute the voting power of newly enfranchised African Americans. Making the VRA stronger than nearly any other piece of American civil rights law, Section 5 recognised pervasive patterns of institutional racism rather than merely placed the burden of civil rights enforcement on the individual victims of racism (see also Frymer 2005).

The evisceration of the Voting Rights Act in 2013 empowered state-level actors to implement changes to election law which would have previously been rejected by the preclearance procedure. In some cases, Republican-dominated state legislatures proposed changes which were nearly identical to those which the Justice Department had blocked under Section 5 months earlier. On the other hand, voting rights laws are being liberalised in states under Democratic control. This contestation over the expansion and restriction of the franchise for the purposes of partisan and racial advantage has been a long-standing feature of American politics (Valelly 2016).

The USA has experienced an intensification of racially polarised partisanship, where racial identity and party support have become increasingly aligned. In 2012, Barack Obama was elected with the lowest share of the white two-party vote of any president in US history, while simultaneously benefiting from turnout and support from African Americans not seen since Ulysses Grants elections during Reconstruction (Johnson 2017). Class support is strongly racially bifurcated. Donald Trump won two-thirds of the vote of working-class whites, a record of any Republican, while Hillary Clinton won three-quarters of the vote of working-class non-whites. Clinton won only 2 out of the 660 mostly white counties with incomes below the national median, while she won 96 out of 98 majority-black counties.

Given the strong correspondence between race and partisanship, efforts to restrict partisan opponents' access to the ballot are inseparable from efforts to restrict racial groups' voting rights. Efforts to depress the turnout of Democratic voters will necessarily disparately impact ethnic minority voters.

Voter ID Laws

The most common tool used to restrict the franchise in recent years has been laws which require a narrow set of official photo identification cards in order to vote in person. States have made certain licences which are more likely to be owned by whites (e.g. gun licences, passports) permissible while not permitting state IDs which are more likely to be used by non-whites (e.g. food stamp cards, community college IDs).

During the Obama presidency, the Justice Department filed suits on behalf of plaintiffs in several states (Texas, North Carolina, Wisconsin) to oppose efforts by Republican state legislatures to make voting more difficult through restrictive ID laws. Civil rights groups, such as the NAACP, argue that hundreds of thousands of voters, especially those who are poor and ethnic minority, are rendered unable to vote because they lack the required ID card. In Alabama alone, the NAACP believes that over 100,000 citizens lack the ID necessary to vote, the majority being African American.

In a dramatic shift in policy in February 2017, Attorney General Jeff Sessions reversed the DoJ's opposition to Texas's strict voter identification law, known as SB 15. The law attracted public attention by allowing Texas gun-owner permits as valid voter ID but not identification cards issued by Texas public universities and community colleges. The law was originally blocked in 2012 under Section 5 of the Voting Rights Act; however, after the *Shelby County* decision, the state of Texas quickly acted to reintroduce the restrictions.

Left without the advantages of Section 5 preclearance, the Obama administration's Department of Justice was forced to use the pre-VRA tactic of joining with civil rights groups to sue the state of Texas over the law. The suit pointed out that over 600,000 adult citizens in the state would be barred from voting because they lacked the requisite identification cards. African Americans were three times as likely as whites not to have the correct identification, and Hispanics were twice as likely. For example, while 96.2% of white adult citizens in Texas have drivers' licences, only 86.9% of African Americans do (*Veasey v Abbott* (2016)).

Under President Trump, the Justice Department announced that it would no longer side with the black and Hispanic defendants in the case. In spite of the DoJ's recusal, a federal judge ruled in April 2017 that the voter ID law was discriminatory. In June 2017, the Texas state legislature passed a new bill, labelled SB 5, which Republican officials argued remedied the discriminatory features identified by the court in April. In July

2017, the Justice Department issued a statement to the federal courts embracing Texas's new voter ID law, claiming that 'As amended by SB 5, Texas's voter ID law both guarantees to Texas voters the opportunity to cast an in-person ballot and protects the integrity of Texas's elections'. The DoJ added, 'SB 5 fully remedies any discriminatory effect in Texas's voter ID law'.[6]

A month later, the federal courts disagreed with the Department of Justice. Judge Nelva Gonzales Ramos of the Southern District of Texas invalidated the law on the grounds that SB 5 fell 'far short of mitigating the discriminatory provisions of SB 14'. Judge Ramos added, 'SB 5 perpetuates the selection of types of ID most likely to be possessed by Anglo voters and, disproportionately, not possessed by Hispanics and African-Americans'. During the Trump presidency, the DoJ has shifted from being on the side of the victims of a racially discriminatory voting law to the side of the perpetrators.

Voter Purges

The zealous removal of 'inactive' voters from the electoral register has been another way in which states have attempted to limit the franchise for partisan-racial gain. Opponents of these practices argue that states have wantonly removed 'inactive' or 'ineligible' voters in areas with high Democratic—and, therefore, minority—electorates. The result is that legally registered voters are removed from the electoral rolls without their knowledge or consent. Defenders argue that the policy is necessary to maintain accurate voting records. Some have also argued that higher barriers to registration prevent the indolent from voting. Alabama's Secretary of State John Merrill, who is in charge of the state's election laws, stated in 2016, 'If you're too sorry or lazy to get up off of your rear and to go register to vote, or to register electronically, and then to go vote, then you don't deserve that privilege. As long as I'm Secretary of State of Alabama, you're going to have to show some initiative to become a registered voter in this state'.

In June 2017, the CRD requested extensive details from state governments about how they maintain their electoral registers. The request coincided with President Trump's controversial 'Commission on

---

[6]http://projects.statesman.com/documents/?doc=3889129-Voter-ID-Remedies-USA.

Electoral Integrity' which stems from the president's view, with little evidence, that 'millions of people voted illegally' in 2016.[7] The Trump administration has reversed the federal government's position on vote purging methods, a change from not only the Obama administration but also the previous Bush and Clinton administrations.

The National Voter Registration Act of 1993, passed by President William J. Clinton, and the Help American Vote Act of 2002, passed by President George W. Bush, provided safeguards for American citizens in an effort to facilitate the ease of voting. Since their passage, administrations have interpreted these laws as prohibiting states from using voter inactivity as a trigger for removing a voter from the electoral register. In other words, failure to vote should itself not be a reason in itself to invalidate someone's voter registration. *republican majority*

The state of Ohio, however, has pursued legislation, which does precisely this, removing voters from the electoral register if they fail to vote in two consecutive election cycles. If someone voted for Obama or McCain in 2008 but sat out the 2012 presidential election, under the Ohio law, by the time of the 2016 election, that voter would be de-registered from voting unless new action was taken. In 2016, the Sixth Circuit Court blocked the measure from taking full effect before the presidential election, and the case (*Husted v A Philip Randolph Institute* (2018)) reached the Supreme Court shortly after President Trump placed Neil Gorsuch on the Supreme Court.

The Trump Justice Department defended the state of Ohio, rather than the civil rights group which contested the state law. During oral arguments in January 2018, Justice Sonia Sotomayor pressed the Solicitor General, Noel Francisco, who represents the White House's position, to explain the sudden change. Sotomoyor stated,

> There's a 24-year history of solicitor generals of both political parties... who have taken a position contrary to yours... [It] seems quite unusual that your office would change its position so dramatically... After that many Presidents, that many solicitor generals, this many years – the vast majority of states...who read it the way your opponents read it, most people read it that way – how did the solicitor general change its mind?.

[7]https://twitter.com/realDonaldTrump/status/802972944532209664?ref_src=tws-rc%5Etfw.

Adding to Sotomayor's query, Justice Ruth Bader Ginsberg puzzled during oral argument, 'I thought that the United States was taking the position, consistently, that non-voting was not a reliable indicator of residence change'. Francisco confirmed that indeed 'our prior position was based on an understanding of the statute that read into it a reliable evidence requirement, and we said that non-voting was not that kind of reliable evidence'. But, Francisco added that, in spite of the interpretations of the previous administrations, the Trump administration had re-read the relevant legislation and concluded that the previous administrations were wrong.

In spite of Sotomayor's and Ginsberg's challenges, the federal judiciary has increasingly retreated from protecting voting rights. During Trump's first year in office, the federal judiciary lifted a decades-old consent decree which had sharply limited the Republican Party from challenging citizens' voting qualifications in an effort to purge them from the electoral register.

The decree stemmed from a lawsuit following the 1981 gubernatorial election in New Jersey. Republicans had sent intimidating messages which threatened people with fines and prison time if they voted illegally. In the case *Democratic National Committee v Republican National Committee* (1982), the court ordered that the Republican Party 'refrain from undertaking any ballot security activities...where a purpose or significant effect of such activities is to deter qualified voters from voting and the conduct of such activities [is] disproportionately in or directed towards districts that have a substantial proportion of racial or ethnic [minority] populations'. This consent decree was left in effect for thirty-five years. On 1 December 2017, the consent decree expired.

While in place, the decree was occasionally violated, prompting Justice Department intervention. One famous incident occurred in North Carolina during the 1990 US Senate election. Incumbent Republican senator Jesse Helms was facing former Charlotte mayor Harvey Gantt, who was the first ever African American nominated by the Democratic Party for the Senate. The Republican Party sent 150,000 postcards to African American voters in the state warning them about the penalties of voting improperly (see Fig. 6.1).[8]

---

[8] D. Drummond Ayres, 'Judge Assails GOP Mailing in North Carolina,' *New York Times*, 6 November 1990.

> **Voter Registration Bulletin**
>
> If you moved from your old precinct over 30 days ago, contact the County Board Of Elections for instructions for voting on Election day.
>
> When you enter the voting enclosure, you will be asked to state your name, residence, and period of residence in that precinct. You must have lived in that precinct for at least the previous 30 days, or you will not be allowed to vote.
>
> It is a Federal crime, punishable by up to five years in jail, to knowingly give false information about your name, residence, or period of residence to an Election Official.
>
> PAID FOR BY THE N.C REPUBLICAN PARTY

Fig. 6.1 North Carolina Ballot Security Leaflet (Republican Party, 1990 Mid-Term Elections) *Source* North Carolina Collection, UNC Chapel Hill

I interviewed Carter Wrenn, who was the director of Jesse Helms's campaign. Wrenn explained to me that the campaign's main strategy was to disqualify African American voters who were registered improperly but, due to an oversight, the campaign overstepped what was legally permissible in the written content of the postcards.

> I was the one responsible for that screw up. Yeah we did that... We knew Gantt's big push was African American turnout. So, we said we'll try to determine whether black African Americans [sic] register properly. Did you live in the home where you were registered in? And the theory was that if you mailed them and the letter came back... and says you don't live there, then you're challengeable.[9]

According to Wrenn, this tactic was in itself legal. The content of the letter, however, violated the 1982 court order because intimidating ballot security messages contravened the Voting Rights Act. Wrenn explained the process which led to their issuance:

> The problem was that the wording of the postcards was intimidating...I approved the idea, approved the mailing, budgeted the money for

[9] Author interview with Carter Wrenn, 22 July 2015 (Raleigh, North Carolina).

it, handed it to a guy. And he got the thing all done up. And never run it by the attorney. And he brought it into me and said here's the copy; approve this. And I was busy, and I said put it over there. Two or three weeks went by, and I never even looked at it. Finally, he came in one day and said, if you don't approve it today, it's not going to get mailed. And I just said, mail it. And then the thing came up – I don't remember if it was during the election or after – that it violated the Voting Rights Act. I had to talk to the lawyer [chuckles]. And he said, yeah you've got a problem. And it did violate the Voting Rights Act. It was just a screw up. And so after the election, we had the Justice Department sat down with these two lawyers. They were investigating and interviewing everybody. And basically we just said, it was a screw up.[10]

In 2016, officials in three North Carolina counties deployed similar 'vote caging' techniques, using undelivered post as a way of removing voters from the electoral register. As many as 4,500 voters, who were disproportionately African American, were removed from the electoral register in Beaufort (138 voters), Cumberland (approximately 4,000 voters) and Moore (approximately 400 voters) counties.

The NAACP filed a lawsuit on behalf of voters who had been improperly removed, including a 100-year-old African American woman. A federal judge, Loretta Biggs, who was appointed by Barack Obama to the District Court for mid-North Carolina, intervened to prevent the purges, stating that they were a violation of the 1982 order. It was one of the last uses of the order before it expired in 2017.

Biggs told lawyers for the state that she was 'horrified' by the purging process, which she described as 'insane'. She added, 'this sounds like something that was put together in 1901', a reference to when North Carolina's pro-civil rights constitution was torn up in favour of a new state constitution which deprived African Americans of the political rights. In her court opinion, Biggs wrote, 'Voter enfranchisement cannot be sacrificed when citizens through no fault of their own have been removed from the voter rolls... Moreover, electoral integrity is enhanced, not diminished, when all citizens who are eligible to vote are allowed to exercise that right free from interference and burden unnecessarily imposed by others'.[11] With the *DNC v RNC* (1982) consent

[10]Ibid.
[11]*North Carolina NAACP v State Board of Elections* (2016).

decree now expired, it is easier for actors to engage in 'ballot security' processes which result in reducing turnout and purging qualified voters from the electoral register, thus limiting the franchise for partisan-racial gain.

Felon Disenfranchisement

Punitive voter ID laws and de-registration drives are relatively new innovations in efforts to restrict access to the ballot box. Most of the methods which were used to disenfranchise African Americans during the Jim Crow era—poll taxes, literacy tests, grandfather clauses, all-white primaries—have been banned through civil rights law or overturned in the courts. One of the last racial disenfranchisement tools of the Jim Crow period which remain legally in effect in numerous American states and even at the federal level is the lifetime deprival of voting and other civil rights from those who have committed a crime.

During the Jim Crow era, 'felon disenfranchisement' laws were introduced as a means of depriving the vote from, especially, African Americans through a facially race-neutral method (see Uggen and Manza 2002; Behrens et al. 2003; Manza and Uggen 2006; Lerman and Weaver 2014). As Michelle Alexander (2012) writes in the *New Jim Crow*, once an American is given 'felon' status, old forms of discrimination become legal: the denial of social housing, welfare benefits, jury service, the right to vote, access to jobs and educational opportunities. Over 5 million Americans are 'felons', disproportionately African Americans.

In 1998, a federal court embraced the constitutionality of Mississippi's felon disenfranchisement law, which barred 28% of African American men in the state from voting for life (Chin 2002: 422). The court acknowledged the obvious historical evidence that the law had been introduced into Mississippi's post-Reconstruction constitution for racist purposes. In 1896, the state Supreme Court described felon disenfranchisement as designed 'to obstruct the exercise of the franchise by the Negro race' (*Ratliff v. Beale*, 20 So. 865, 868 (Miss. 1896)). But, in 1998, the federal court was satisfied that the law was no longer used in a racially discriminatory way, in spite of its indisputably racist origins (*Cotton v. Fordice*, 157 F.3d 388 (5th Cir. 1998)).

Former felons can experience a deprival of equal citizenship even after they have completed their sentence. Thirty-one states and the federal government impose lifetime bans on felons serving on juries, which has resulted in nearly one-third of black men being ineligible from jury service in the USA (Alexander 2012: 121). In four states (Florida, Virginia, Kentucky and Iowa), all ex-felons experience lifetime bans on voting. Six more states (Mississippi, Alabama, Tennessee, Arizona, Nevada and Wyoming) ban most ex-felons from voting for life. For example, in Mississippi, people who have served a jail sentence for theft receive a lifetime ban on voting. Mississippi's felon disenfranchisement provisions bar 166,000 citizens who have completed their prison sentences from voting for the rest of their lives (Uggen et al. 2016: 15).

The state which has the most ex-felons who are barred from voting is Florida, which Christopher Uggens and colleagues estimate deprives voting rights from 1.4 million adults who have completed their prison sentences (Uggens et al. 2016: 15). These non-voting American citizens are disproportionately African American, and their votes could have been decisive in recent presidential elections where Florida was a pivotal state. Florida voters will be given the chance to expand the franchise by a popular referendum in November 2018 which proposes to restore voting rights to all ex-felons who have completed their sentences, except for those convicted of murder or a sexual offence. The provision, known as the Voting Restoration Amendment, is a constitutional amendment which requires 60% approval from participating voters.

States with Democratic leadership have taken more proactive action. Virginia's felon disenfranchisement provision was codified in its 1902 segregationist constitution, which barred the right to vote from any Virginian who had been convicted of 'any felony, bribery, petit larceny, obtaining money or property under false pretenses, embezzlement, forgery, or perjury' for the rest of their lives. At the constitution convention in 1901, delegate R. L. Gordon made clear that the provision's purpose was 'to disenfranchise every negro that I could disenfranchise under the Constitution of the United States, and as few white people as possible' (Bodenhamer 2012: 153).

Governor Terry McAuliffe (2014–2018) promised to return voting rights to those who had completed their sentences, but he was blocked from changing the state constitution by the Republican-controlled legislature. The office of governor in Virginia, however, has a number of robust reserved powers. One of McAuliffe's predecessors, Douglas Wilder (1990–1994), was the first African American elected to a governorship in US history. Wilder explained in an interview with me, 'The governor of Virginia is a powerful constitutional office.

Very powerful...The reason in Virginia we don't have two terms for the governor is because the governor not only has 4000 appointments. We have a line item veto; we have amending authority of any bill that comes before the governor. Any bill. So, it's just—we know our power'.[12] One of these powers is the governor's ability to grant pardons and clemencies, which can restore individuals' voting rights.

In an executive order in April 2016, McAuliffe announced that all people who had felonies but had completed parole would have their voting rights restored to them. However, the Virginia Supreme Court ruled that McAuliffe could not grant across-the-board clemency. He would need to restore each ex-felon's right to vote individually after reviewing his or her particular case. McAuliffe set about 'reviewing' each individual case and signed thousands of clemency orders. By the time he left office in January 2018, McAuliffe had signed over 172,000 individual clemency orders which restored the voting rights to Virginians who had long completed their sentences. A study by McAuliffe's office showed that 46% of the newly restored voters were African Americans, while only 19% of Virginia's overall population is black.[13]

Because the underlying felon disenfranchisement law has not changed, a less-supportive governor in the future could end the practice of returning voting rights to those who have completed their sentences. McAuliffe's successor is a Democrat, Ralph Northam, who supports the clemency action. Northam won his election in November 2017 with 54% of the vote. An estimated 454,885 African Americans voted for Northam; his majority over his Republican opponent Ed Gillespie was 233,444. African American turnout surpassed white turnout, delivering Northam his victory.

Other State Level Actions

As the example in Virginia shows, the move towards restricting the franchise is not uniform. In 2018, Democrats controlled the state legislature and governor's office in eight states, compared to twenty-six which have total Republican control. In the few states with Democratic control, state

---

[12] Author interview with L. Douglas Wilder (18 July 2015, Richmond, VA).
[13] http://governor.virginia.gov/newsroom/newsarticle?articleId=15207.

governments have been exploring ways of expanding the eligible electorate and making voting easier.

In 2015, the Democratic New Jersey state legislature passed the New Jersey Democracy Act, which sought to make voting easier. The law would automatically register eligible citizens to vote when they applied for a driver's licence; early voting would be implemented for a fortnight before elections; voters could register to vote online; 17-year-olds could register to vote if they would be 18 by the next election; the postal voting process was simplified; and foreign-language voting materials would be made more accessible. Republican Governor Chris Christie vetoed the bill saying, 'This bill should be called the "Voter Fraud Enhancement and Permission Act"'. In November 2017, with Christie retiring due to term limits, Democrats gained the governor's seat from the Republicans. Democratic governor Phil Murphy has indicated his willingness to support measures similar to those in the 2015 Democracy Act.

Criminal Justice

In 2016, 1.45 million Americans were in prison, a number which has increased fivefold in the last 40 years, compared to only a doubling of the overall US population in the same period. Although African Americans only make up 13% of the US population, they constitute the biggest single major ethnic group in American prisons (see Fig. 6.2). Barack Obama wrote in a 2017 *Harvard Law Review* article that 'our criminal justice system exacerbates inequality', a reality which he first witnessed as a community organiser in Chicago in the 1980s (Obama 2017).

The Obama administration made steps to address the racial imbalance in the American carceral system. During Obama's presidency, the number of African Americans in prisons declined modestly from 499,900 in 2008 to 439,800 in 2016. The proportion of prisoners who were African American declined from 38.3 to 33.4% during the period.

First, during the brief period when the Democrats had unified control of the House, Senate and White House, Congress passed the Fair Sentencing Act of 2010 which reduced the sentencing disparity for crack cocaine compared to powder cocaine. Crack, which is more commonly used by African Americans, had been weighted for sentencing purposes as 100 times more serious than powder cocaine usage by the

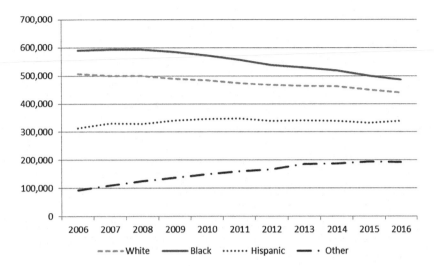

Fig. 6.2 Racial composition of prisoners in US state and federal correctional facilities. Based on data from https://www.bjs.gov/content/pub/pdf/p16.pdf (Table 3)

Anti-Drug Abuse Act of 1986. The Fair Sentencing Act reduced the ratio to 18:1. Because this reform was made through statute, a rarity of Obama-era racial policy, it is more difficult for the Trump administration to reverse.

Second, the Justice Department revised sentencing for non-violent offenders. The DoJ encouraged federal prosecutors not to seek the most serious punishment in these cases, which were usually drug related. However, early in his tenure, Attorney General Jeff Sessions revoked the memo and, instead, ordered US attorneys to pursue the most serious punishment possible. This change in course will lead to more and longer prison terms for those arrested for drug charges. While African Americans and whites use drugs at similar rates to their proportion of the overall population, African Americans are much more likely to serve prison sentences for drug possession: 12.5% of illicit drug users are black, but 33% of those in US prisons for drug-related offences are African American.[14]

[14]www.naacp.org/criminal-justice-fact-sheet/.

Access to Justice

The Obama administration sought to expand legal services for the poor, disproportionately benefiting racial minorities. In 2010, the Obama administration created the Office for Access to Justice (ATJ) within the Department of Justice. The ATJ attracted several prominent members, including Harvard Law professor Laurence Tribe, and was led by Lisa Foster, who for ten years had served as a California Superior Court judge. During the Obama administration, the ATJ participated in dozens of lawsuits where it had identified poor clients who had been given inadequate legal support. It took action against the states of Washington and New York when it was revealed that they did not provide sufficient legal aid to poor defendants. The ATJ has been effectively closed by the Trump administration. In February 2018, its acting director stood down and was not replaced. As the agency's small staff have departed, new staff have not been hired.

The Trump Justice Department has taken other steps which will impose greater burdens on poor criminal defendants. In February 2016 under the Obama administration, a letter from the ATJ's Lisa Foster, the CRD's director Vanita Gupta and Assistant Attorney General Karol Mason urged local courts not to impose excessive fines on poor defendants. The Obama administration was concerned that men and women were being imprisoned not on the basis of their original crime but because they were too poor to pay the harsh fines placed on them for petty offences. In the letter, the DoJ offered $2.5 million in grants to localities which demonstrated efforts to reduce the use of excessive fines and fees on indigent defendants. In December 2017, Attorney General Jeff Sessions revoked the letter and ended the grant scheme.

Labour Market

In spite of modest improvements made during the Obama administration, the American carceral system continues to impact African Americans disproportionately. Black men are imprisoned six times the rate of white men. One in nine black children in America has a parent in prison. The racial imbalance in incarceration distorts the labour market. According to Bruce Western and Becky Pettit (2010), more young African American men without a high school degree are in prison (37%) than in work (26%).

During his 2018 State of the Union address, Donald Trump congratulated himself for delivering the lowest unemployment rate for African Americans since records began in the 1970s. However, one of the biggest contributors to the African American unemployment rate is the number of African Americans who are taken out of the labour market (and, therefore, unemployment statistics) due to incarceration. While 1.6% of white men aged between 25 and 54 are incarcerated, 7.7% of black men in the same age range are in prison. If they were counted as unemployed, the unemployment rate for black men of working age would jump from 11 to 19%, while the unemployment rate for their white equivalents would increase from 5 to 6%.[15]

Police Department Consent Decrees

During the Obama administration, the Department of Justice reacted to high-profile incidents of police brutality by investigating twenty-five departments for the use of excessive force, unlawful arrest and discriminatory policing. The power to conduct special investigations into local police departments for racial discrimination has belonged to the Justice Department since 1994 when the Democratic Congress acted in the wake of the beating of Rodney King by the Los Angeles Police Department. Both presidents Clinton and Bush used these powers on a similar number of police departments as to Barack Obama. Where Obama differed, however, was in his willingness to take on high-profile and politically influential departments such as Chicago, as well as those which have been the sites of civil rights protests by the Black Lives Matter (BLM) movement, such as Ferguson (Missouri), Cleveland, North Charleston and Baltimore.

These reports were unflinching in their criticism of the police and explicitly identified racial bias in police practices. The DoJ report on Ferguson, for example, found that in the two-year period before the killing of unarmed teenager Michael Brown by a police officer, African Americans had experienced 'disparate impact in nearly every aspect of Ferguson's law enforcement system', comprising 90% of police citations, 93% of arrests and 100% of incidents in which police dogs were used on citizens. Ferguson is two-thirds African American and one-third white.

---

[15] Jeff Guo, 'America Has Locked Up so Many Black People It Has Warped Our Sense of Reality,' *Washington Post*, 26 February 2016.

The DoJ investigators found 'substantial evidence of racial bias among police and court staff in Ferguson'. The report includes a litany of disturbing incidents, based on interviews with residents, of police using physical violence against unarmed residents, abusive language and regular stops of law-abiding residents for ID to see if they had any warrants outstanding. After the report, Attorney General Eric Holder paid tribute to the Black Lives Matter movement by acknowledging, 'Some of those protestors were right'.

At the end of the Obama presidency, the Department of Justice under Attorney General Loretta Lynch entered into a 'consent decree' with the City of Baltimore, the site of rioting after a 25-year-old, unarmed black man was killed when police broke his spinal cord in their custody. The DoJ found that Baltimore City Police Department had 'engaged in a pattern or practice of conduct that violated the Constitution and federal laws by making unconstitutional stops, searches, and arrests... [and] using enforcement strategies that disproportionately impact African Americans, in violation of Title VI of the 1964 Civil Rights Act'. The consent decree would implement a wide set of reforms to the city's police department at the instruction of the Department of Justice.

The decree created community oversight of the police, introduced stricter procedures for investigations of police wrongdoing, emphasised de-escalation techniques between police and suspects and required that Baltimore police undergo training about 'the specific history and racial challenges in the City of Baltimore'. These reforms would be mandatory and would cost the city millions of dollars. However, Baltimore's elected leadership, including its African American mayor Catherine Pugh and Police Commissioner Kevin Davis, supported the consent decree.

In April 2017, shortly before the Baltimore consent decree was due to go into effect, the Justice Department under Attorney General Jeff Sessions ordered a 90-day delay to review whether the decree was consistent with President Trump's 9 February 2017 executive order on policing. The DoJ stated, 'we have grave concerns this consent decree will reduce the lawful powers of the police department and result in a less safe city'. Days later, Judge James Bredar of the US District Court of Maryland and appointed by Barack Obama ruled the DoJ pause invalid and ordered the consent decree to move forward. Not convinced that the DoJ would oversee the consent decree faithfully, in October 2017 Judge Bredar appointed Kenneth Thompson, an African American lawyer from Baltimore, to act as the monitor of both the city of Baltimore and the DoJ in ensuring the full implementation of the decree.

In September 2017, the Justice Department announced that it would be ending *all* of its reviews of local law enforcement agencies. In a statement, Attorney General Sessions declared that he would be putting an end to 'expensive wide-ranging investigative assessments that go beyond the scope of technical assistance and support'. This volte-face has left months-long investigations prematurely suspended in fifteen major police departments across the country.

The North Charleston Police Department was one of the police departments whose Obama-era review was suspended under the Trump administration. In April 2015, an unarmed, fifty-year-old black, forklift truck driver was shot dead (in the back) by a police officer after fleeing from him at a traffic stop. The shooting was filmed on a passer-by's phone. A year later, the Justice Department under Loretta Lynch launched a review of policing in North Charleston through a Community Oriented Policing Services (COPS) programme. North Charleston is 47% African American, but only 18% of police officers in the city are black (Patton 2017: 71). An independent report by the College of Charleston's Race and Social Justice Initiative found that 65% of 122,818 traffic stops without arrest or citation which occurred in the city between 2011 and 2015 involved African American drivers (Patton 2017: 72).

In September 2017, after eighteen months of investigations, the Justice Department under Jeff Sessions brought the review of North Charleston police to a sudden halt.[16] Sessions not only ended the planned two-year review six months early, but he suppressed its 601-page report. On 18 October 2017, South Carolina Senator Tim Scott, the US Senate's lone black Republican, wrote to Attorney General Sessions 'to urge you [Sessions] to release any final or near final findings'. Scott, who was raised in poverty in North Charleston, informed Sessions, 'North Charleston residents and elected officials continue to be very interested in receiving the results of the COPS Office's already conducted assessment of the police department'.[17]

---

[16] https://www.justice.gov/opa/pr/department-justice-announces-changes-collaborative-reform-initiative.

[17] https://bloximages.newyork1.vip.townnews.com/postandcourier.com/content/tncms/assets/v3/editorial/0/c6/0c6123d0-b4fb-11e7-9b7d-bbbf3180ac63/59e8eeb66b47f.pdf.pdf.

Other Reversals in Criminal Justice

The Department of Justice has undertaken further reversals in criminal justice policy under the Trump presidency.

During the Obama presidency, the federal government did not execute a single prisoner. Attorney General Eric Holder was personally opposed to the death penalty. Attorney General Jeff Sessions, however, has been a strong advocate for the death penalty. As attorney general of Alabama, Sessions supported the use of the death penalty against the mentally disabled (e.g. Holly Woods, who was defined by a federal court as 'mentally retarded') and those who had not committed a capital crime, such as drug dealers.[18] Within the first year of Trump's presidency, the Justice Department sought the death penalty in two federal cases.

In August 2016, President Obama's deputy Attorney General Sally Yates announced that the Bureau of Prisons (BOP) would phase out the use of private prisons, following a damning inspector general report. The report revealed that private prisons had higher rates of inter-prisoner assault and use of force by prison staff against inmates. Audits from the Justice Department in 2016 also found that private prisons lacked necessary medical staff. Yates wrote, 'They simply do not provide the same level of correctional services, programs and resources; they do not save substantially on costs; and … they do not maintain the same level of safety and security'. Under Obama, the BOP declined to renew its contract for 1,200 beds in a private prison facility and vowed to end their use entirely by 2021. However, in February 2017, Attorney General Jeff Sessions revoked the order.

Finally, in the wake of the DoJ's investigation into the Ferguson Police Department, President Obama placed restrictions on the '1033 program', which allows police departments to request surplus military equipment from the Department of Defense (DoD) for police officers. After the revelations about the use of inappropriate military-grade weaponry in many of America's local police departments, President Obama banned departments from using the programme to acquire armed vehicles, grenade launchers or bayonets. In August 2017, President Trump removed his predecessor's restrictions on the programme.

---

[18]John Donohue and Max Shoening, 'Jeff Sessions: The Grim Reaper of Alabama', *New York Times*, 8 January 2017.

Conclusion

The expansion of the franchise to ethnic minority voters, especially African Americans, was a key development in the democratisation of the USA. For this reason, Göran Therborn (1977), Robert Mickey (2015), and Edward Gibson and Desmond King (2016) have all argued that comparative political scientists should not regard the USA as fitting in the category of a 'democracy' until after the Voting Rights Act of 1965 came into full effect. Given the intimate linkage between racial minorities' access to the ballot box and the vitality of American democracy, backsliding on voting rights protections by the federal judiciary, federal executive branch and state-level governments provoke serious cause for concern. As Robert Mickey and colleagues (2017) have written, democratic reversal in the USA is unlikely to take the form of a dramatic coup d'état, a declaration of martial law, or the imposition of single-party rule. Instead, reversal is likely to resemble the processes of the American state itself, which are diffuse and incremental but ultimately hugely consequential. When race and party so closely align, efforts to rewrite the rules of the political game to advantage a particular party inescapably also rewrite the rules to advantage a particular race. Steps which appear individually to be minor, colourblind, or innocuous have the aggregate effect of tilting the playing field away from historically marginalised groups, reasserting historic imbalances in racial power.

References

Alexander, Michelle. *The New Jim Crow.* New York: The New Press, 2012.

Behrens, Angela, Christopher Uggen, and Jeff Manza. "Ballot Manipulation and the Menace of Negro Domination: Racial Threat and Felon Disenfranchisement in the United States, 1850–2002." *American Journal of Sociology*, 109 (2003): 559–605.

Bodenhamer, David. *The Revolutionary Constitution.* Oxford: Oxford University Press, 2012.

Chin, Gabriel. "Rehabilitating Unconstitutional Statutes: An Analysis of Cotton v Fordice." *University of Cincinnati Law Review*, 71 (2002): 421–55.

Foner, Eric. *Reconstruction: America's Unfinished Revolution, 1863–1877.* New York: Harper & Row, 1988.

Frymer, Paul. "Racism Revisited: Courts, Labor Law, and the Institutional Construction of Racial Animus." *American Political Science Review*, 99 (2005): 3, 373–87.

Gibson, Edward, and Desmond King. "Federalism and Subnational Democratization: The South in the Nineteenth and Twentieth Centuries." In J. Behrend and L. Whitehead, eds., *Illiberal Practices*. Baltimore, MD: Johns Hopkins University Press, 2016.

Johnson, Richard. "Racially Polarised Partisanship and the Obama Presidency." In E. Ashbee and J. Dumbrell, eds., *The Obama Presidency and the Politics of Change*. London: Palgrave Macmillan, 2017.

Johnson, Richard. "Race, Ethnicity, and Immigration." In G. Peele, C. Bailey, J. Herbert, J. Cain, and B. G. Peters, eds., *Developments in American Politics 8*. London: Palgrave Macmillan, 2018.

Kaczorowski, Robert. *The Politics of Judicial Interpretation: The Federal Courts, the Department of Justice, and Civil Rights, 1866–1876*. New York: Fordham University Press, 2005.

Lerman, Amy, and Vesla Weaver. *Arresting Citizenship: The Democratic Consequences of American Crime Control*. Chicago and London: University of Chicago Press, 2014.

Manza, Jeff, and Christopher Uggen. *Locked Out: Felon Disenfranchisement and American Democracy*. Oxford: Oxford University Press, 2006.

Mickey, Robert. *Paths Out of Dixie: The Democratization of Authoritarian Enclaves in America's Deep South*. Princeton: Princeton University Press, 2015.

Mickey, Robert, Steven Levitsky, and Lucan Way. "Is America Still Safe for Democracy?" *Foreign Affairs*, May 2017.

Morrow, Helen. *New Destination Dreaming: Immigration, Race, and Legal Status in the Rural American South*. Redwood City, CA: Stanford University Press, 2011.

Obama, Barack. "The President's Role in Advancing Criminal Justice Reform." *Harvard Law Review*, 130 (2017): 811.

Patton, Stacey. *The State of Racial Disparities in Charleston County, South Carolina*. Charleston, SC: Avery Research Center for African American History and Culture, 2017.

Therborn, Göran. "The Rule of Capital and the Rise of Democracy." *New Left Review*, 103 (May/June 1977): 3–41.

Uggen, Christopher, and Jeff Manza. "Democratic Contraction? Political Consequences of Felon Disenfranchisement in the United States." *American Sociological Review*, 67 (2002): 777–803.

Uggens, Christopher, Ryan Larson, and Sarah Shannon. *6 Million Lost Voters: State-Level Estimates of Felony Disenfranchisement, 2016*. Washington, DC: The Sentencing Project, 2016.

Valelly, Richard. "How Suffrage Politics Made and Makes America." In R. Vallely, S. Mettler, and R. Lieberman, eds., *Oxford Handbook of American Political Development*. Oxford: Oxford University Press, 2016.

Western, Bruce, and Becky Pettit. *Collateral Costs: Incarceration's Effect on Economic Mobility*. Philadelphia: Pew Charitable Trusts, 2010.

White, Ronald. *American Ulysses: A Life of Ulysses S Grant*. New York: Random House, 2016.

Woodward, C. Vann. *The Strange Career of Jim Crow*. Oxford: Oxford University Press, 1966.

CHAPTER 7

Bad Hombres: The Trump Administration, Mexican Immigration and the Border Wall

Kevern Verney

INTRODUCTION

Announcing his candidacy for the presidency of the USA in 2015, Donald J. Trump outlined the issues that he saw as central to his campaign—'illegal immigration, underemployment, a shrinking gross domestic product, an aging nuclear arsenal, and Islamic terrorism'. In respect to unauthorized migrants from America's southern neighbour he noted 'When Mexico sends its people, they're not sending their best'. More specifically, 'they're sending people that have lots of problems, and they're bringing those problems to us. They're bringing drugs. They're bringing crime. They're rapists. And some, I assume, are good people'. His solution was simple. 'I would build a great wall, and nobody builds walls better than me, believe me, and I'll build them very inexpensively, I will build a great, great, wall on our southern border. And I will have Mexico pay for that wall'.[1]

[1] *Washington Post* staff, 'Full Text: Donald Trump Announces a Presidential Bid,' *Washington Post*, 16 June 2015, https://www.washingtonpost.com/news/post-politics/wp/2015/06/16/full-text-donald-trump-announces-a-presidential-bid.

K. Verney (✉)
Edge Hill University, Ormskirk, UK
e-mail: verneyk@edgehill.ac.uk

© The Author(s) 2019
M. Oliva and M. Shanahan (eds.), *The Trump Presidency*,
The Evolving American Presidency,
https://doi.org/10.1007/978-3-319-96325-9_7

Reflecting on his relationship with the mainstream media, the New York billionaire lamented that the 'dishonest' press coverage of his speech focused on these remarks and neglected other aspects of his speech. Notwithstanding this sense of injustice, in the subsequent campaign Trump used every opportunity to remind voters of his resolve to build a border wall and make Mexico pay for it. He repeated the pledge in the book published to promote his campaign; it became a mantra at his political rallies and featured in the presidential debates with his Democratic opponent, Hillary R. Clinton. In short, it became one of the best-known policy commitments associated with his candidacy.[2]

Although dismissed by Clinton as a campaign stunt, in office President Trump took every opportunity to reaffirm his commitment to build a wall. 'We will soon begin the construction of a great wall along our southern border. It will be started ahead of schedule', he promised in his first address to a joint session of Congress on 28 February 2017. The wall was a recurring theme in his twitter account. 'The Wall is the Wall', he tweeted on 18 January 2018, 'it has never changed or evolved from the first day I conceived of it' and 'will be paid for, directly or indirectly, or through longer term reimbursement, by Mexico'. In December 2017, and in his first State of the Union address in January 2018, the president highlighted 'building a wall on the Southern border' as one of the four key 'pillars' of his administration's plans for national security and for immigration reform.[3]

Given the importance he attached to it, Trump was vague on points of detail, such as the precise form the wall would take, the time it would take to construct and at what cost. This reticence can be attributed to a number of factors. During the 2016 campaign, a border wall could be seen as the

[2] Donald J. Trump, *Crippled America: How to Make America Great Again* (New York: Threshold Editions, 2015), pp. 13–14, 19–20; Presidential Debate at the University of Nevada in Las Vegas, 19 October 2016, http://www.presidency.ucsb.edu/ws/index.php?pid=119039.

[3] 'Trump Speech to Congress; Full Transcript,' 1 March 2017, http://www.bbc.co.uk/news/world-us-canada-39124596; https://twitter.com/realDonaldTrump/status/953948941674078208; https://twitter.com/realDonaldTrump/status/953951365532876800; *National Security Strategy of the United States of America, December 2017*, pp. 9–10, https://www.whitehouse.gov/wp-content/uploads/2017/12/NSS-Final-12-18-2017-0905.pdf; 'The Full Speech—Trump's State of the Union Address,' 31 January 2018, https://www.theguardian.com/us-news/2018/jan/30/the-full-text-of-trumps-state-of-the-union-address.

kind of promise candidates make to win voter approval, but which they are unlikely to implement if elected. In the words of Hillary Clinton, it was a 'rallying cry more than it was a creditable policy proposal'. Moreover, for most of the campaign a Trump victory seemed unlikely. Opinion pollsters, including those working for the Trump campaign, placed him well behind, at one point in August trailing Clinton by 12–17 percentage points. On election night, 8 November, even Kellyanne Conway, Trump's campaign manager, and the candidate himself were reportedly resigned to the inevitability of defeat. The perception of unpreparedness was subsequently reinforced by John Kelly, White House Chief of Staff, who in January 2018 did not deny press reports that he had described the president as 'uninformed' when he made campaign promises about a wall.[4]

Another reason for Trump's reluctance to provide more detail is the practical problems associated with building a wall. In the first instance, there is the enormity of the task. The US border with Mexico is nearly 2000 miles (3200 kilometres) in length. It passes through a variety of landscapes, much of which is remote and hostile, ranging from 9000-ft mountain peaks in New Mexico to uninhabited forest land in southeast Arizona and arid desert in Arizona and California. The Algodones, or Imperial Sand Dunes, in eastern California, stretching over 1000 square miles, is the largest sand dune ecosystem in the USA and would require wall engineers to overcome the problem of constantly shifting sands. Two-thirds of the border runs along rivers, most notably the Rio Grande in Texas, presenting challenges of a different kind. In addition to constructing the wall itself, food and shelter would need to be provided for at least 1000 workers and access roads built to transport equipment, workers and supplies, including at least 339 million cubic feet of concrete—three times more than that required for the Hoover Dam—that would need to be manufactured in specially constructed plants nearby.[5]

[4] Hillary Rodham Clinton, *What Happened* (London: Simon & Schuster, 2017), p. 225; Michael Wolff, *Fire and Fury: Inside the Trump White House* (London: Little, Brown, 2018), pp. 9–12, 18; 'Trump Wall: President Denies Changing View on Mexico Border Plan,' 18 January 2018, http://www.bbc.co.uk/news/world-us-canada-42724380.

[5] 'What Would It Take for Donald Trump to Deport 11 Million and Build a Wall?' *New York Times*, 19 May 2016, https://www.nytimes.com/2016/05/20/us/politics/donald-trump-immigration.html; 'Donald Trump's Mexico Wall: Who Is Going to Pay for It?' *BBC News*, 6 February, 2017, http://www.bbc.co.uk/news/world-us-canada-37243269; Lucy Rodgers and Nassos Stylianou, '6 Things That Could Topple Donald Trump's Border Wall,' *BBC News*, 16 June 2017, http://www.bbc.co.uk/news/resources/idt-d60acebe-2076-4bab-90b4-0e9a5f62ab12.

Seeking to turn a negative into a positive, Trump has tried to portray the harsh environment as an advantage. Qualifying his initial position, that the wall run the entire length of the border, he argued it would only need to be 'about 1,000 miles' long. In other areas, security would be provided by natural 'physical barriers' or 'the terrain is too difficult for people to cross'. Even if this claim is valid, and modern technology could overcome the challenges of construction, the financial cost would be considerable.[6]

Writing in 2006, the then Arizona Congressman J. D. Hayworth estimated the cost of a 'modern border security fence' 'from the Pacific Ocean to the Gulf of Mexico', as being 'four to eight billion dollars'. Even allowing for inflation, this would appear to be a considerable underestimate. Moreover, the physical barrier envisaged by President Trump is not a 'security fence', but a concrete wall between 30-feet and 55-feet high and foundations up to 20-feet deep. In March 2017, the Department of Homeland Security published a notice inviting companies to submit designs for a wall. The specifications provided were for 'procuring concrete wall structures, nominally 30 feet tall, that will meet requirements for aesthetics, anti-climbing, and resistance to tampering or damage'. The companies selected to build eight prototypes in September were allocated a budget of up to $450,000 for a section of wall just 30-feet high by 30-feet long.[7]

During the election, Trump's initial costing for the wall was $12 billion. By January 2018, he had revised the estimate up to $20 billion. Other forecasts have been more costly, ranging from up to $25 billion by Wall Street research and brokerage firm Bernstein Research, to $31 billion by construction consultants Gleeds and $40 billion by Konstantin Kakaes, an international security fellow with the New America Foundation. A report by Senate Democrats went so far as to predict construction costs of $70 billion.[8]

---

[6] Trump, *Crippled America*, pp. 23–24.

[7] J. D. Hayworth with Joseph J. Eule, *Whatever It Takes: Illegal Immigration, Border Security, and the War on Terror* (Washington, DC: Regnery Publishing, Inc., 2006), p. 178; 'Design Build Structure—Federal Business Opportunities,' Update: 9 March 2017, https://www.fbo.gov/index?s=opportunity&mode=form&tab=core&id=f61a-85538f383ec3ed9cac3c9e21d6f1&_cview=0; '100 Days: What Might Trump's Border Wall Look Like?' *BBC News*, 27 April 2017, http://www.bbc.co.uk/news/world-us-canada-39727705; 'US-Mexico Border Wall Prototype Construction Starts,' *BBC News*, 27 September 2017, http://www.bbc.co.uk/news/world-us-canada-41407194.

[8] '6 Things That Could Topple Donald Trump's Border Wall'; 'Trump Wall: President Denies Changing View on Mexico Border Plan.'

Past experience suggests that initial costings are likely to understate the funding required. In 2006, the Secure Fence Act authorized the construction of a 700-mile fence along the Mexican border at a projected cost of $2.2 million to $3 million a mile. By the time, the fence was completed in 2013 this had risen to $3.9 million a mile, at a total cost of more than $7 billion. This for a barrier much less substantial than the structure envisaged by Trump.[9]

The border patrols needed to man it, and the regular repair and upkeep costs, will constitute a financial burden on top of the expenditure needed to construct a wall. Projections of the maintenance costs for the existing 700-mile fence over a 20- to 25-year period range from $6.5 billion to $42 billion. Since 2000, the number of US border agents has more than doubled, to 20,000, and by 2013 the annual budget for the US Border Patrol exceeded $3 billion. Projected maintenance costs for Trump's wall have been estimated at $150 million a year.[10]

Given the construction and maintenance costs, it is easy to understand Trump's insistence that funding for the wall will be met by Mexico. Fulfilling this aspiration is problematic, notwithstanding Trump's suggestion that he 'simply make it clear to the Mexican government that it is to the benefit of their very profitable – for them – relationship with the United States to pay for it'. Mexican President Enrique Pena Nieto has publicly rejected any such possibility. In January 2017, he cancelled a visit to the White House following a tweet by Trump that if Mexico was 'unwilling to pay for the badly needed wall' it would be better for the meeting not to go ahead.[11]

Pre-empting such non-cooperation, Trump has put forward a number of proposals to enforce Mexican compliance. None would be easy to implement. One proposal is to 'cut foreign aid to Mexico' and use the

maybe useful for inner Horner discuss. [handwritten annotation]

[9] Michael Dear, *Why Walls Won't Work: Repairing the U.S.-Mexico Divide* (Oxford: Oxford University Press, 2013), pp. 107–8; 'Your Questions on Trump's Wall Answered by Anthony Zurcher,' *BBC News*, 26 January 2017, http://www.bbc.co.uk/news/world-us-canada-38755757; 'Donald Trump's Mexico Wall; Who Is Going to Pay for It?'

[10] Dear, *Why Walls Won't Work*, pp. 107–8; Shannon K. O'Neil, *Two Nations Indivisible: Mexico, the United States, and the Road Ahead* (Oxford: Oxford University Press, 2013), p. 36; U.S. Army Command and General Staff College, *Building the Wall: The Efficacy of a U.S.-Mexico Border Fence* (2014), p. 3; '6 Things That Could Topple Donald Trump's Border Wall.'

[11] Trump, *Crippled America*, p. 25; 'Donald Trump's Mexico Wall'; Wolff, *Fire and Fury*, pp. 77–78.

funding saved to construct the wall. Strictly speaking, this would mean the USA was financing the wall, as it had provided the aid in the first place. More importantly, it is an idea based on a misconception. 'A lot of people are under the mis-impression that we give foreign aid to Mexico', Jeff Flake, the junior US Senator from Arizona, has noted. In reality, American 'aid to Mexico is the form of drug interdiction and cooperation and other things'. Cutting off funding would curtail investment in programmes that benefitted the USA, such as the 2008 Merida initiative by which the USA pledged $1.3–$1.5 billion to work with the Mexican government to crack down on drugs cartels.[12]

Taxing remittances sent by Mexican workers in the USA to their families in Mexico is an oft-discussed possibility, not least because such transfers amount to some $25 billion a year. Simple to grasp, and thus attractive in appeal, the enforcement of such a measure is problematic. Mexican communities affected could seek alternative, undocumented, means to send home their earnings. This is particularly the case in an age when Internet technology provides an ever-increasing number of ways to accommodate credit transfers.[13]

Another option would be to levy tariffs on Mexican imports. However, Forbes has estimated that existing duties on Mexican goods would need to be quadrupled to raise sufficient funding, and then it would take ten years to recoup the costs of the wall at present-day trade levels. In practice, a tariff hike on the scale required would be a strong incentive for US companies to source products elsewhere, with a corresponding reduction in tax revenue. The Mexican government could also respond by ending tax benefits for US investors, worth an estimated $101 billion in 2013.[14]

Alternatively, the USA could levy a border adjustment tax on goods from overseas at the place of consumption. However, for Mexico to fund the wall this would require exporters from America's

[12] Trump, *Crippled America*, p. 25; *Money, Guns and Drugs: Are U.S. Inputs Fuelling Violence on the U.S.-Mexico Border?* Hearing Before the Subcommittee on National Security and Foreign Affairs of the Committee on Oversight and Government Reform, House of Representatives, One Hundred Eleventh Congress, first session, 12 March 2009 (Washington, DC: U.S. Government Printing Office, 2010), pp. 37, 71; O'Neill, *Two Nations Indivisible*, p. 135.

[13] Trump, *Crippled America*, p. 25; Paul Ganster with David E. Lorey, *The U.S.-Mexican Border Today: Conflict and Cooperation in Historical Perspective*, Third Edition (Lanham: Rowman & Littlefield, 2016); p. 156; 'Donald Trump's Mexico Wall.'

[14] Ibid.

southern neighbour to absorb the extra costs. If they passed them on, by raising prices, then American consumers could end up footing the bill.[15]

Raising travel visa and border crossing fees would be a popular move with many Republicans, but is unlikely to raise the amount of revenue required to fund the construction of a wall. It could have a negative impact on trade, particularly if the Mexican government responded with tariffs on American goods. It would hit US citizens who travelled across the border, including an estimated one million Americans living in Mexico.[16]

In June 2017, the president advanced another solution, arguing a border wall could be made self-funding by incorporating solar panels into its construction. 'We're thinking of something that's unique, we're talking about the southern border, lots of sun, lots of heat', he explained at a rally in Iowa. 'We're thinking about building the wall as a solar wall, so it creates energy and pays for itself. And this way, Mexico will have to pay much less money'. He implied that the plan was of his own devising, 'an idea that nobody has heard of yet'. In reality, it originated with the Gleason construction company, one of the more than 200 contractors who submitted a wall design in response to the Department of Homeland Security invite three months earlier.[17]

Gleason was not one of the companies selected to build prototypes for the wall, none of which included plans for solar panels. An omission that reflects the problems in incorporating solar technology into the wall in a way that would be economically viable. For power collected to be utilized, it would have to be connected to the mains grid in border towns and cities, most located at least 40 miles away. This would require significant expenditure. President Pena Nieto has rejected the possibility of Mexico making any contribution to such a project.[18]

[15] Ibid.

[16] Trump, *Crippled America*, p. 25; 'Donald Trump's Mexico Wall'; O'Neil, *Two Nations Indivisible*, p. 6.

[17] 'Donald Trump Talks up Solar Panel Plan for Mexico Wall,' *BBC News*, 22 June 2017, http://www.bbc.co.uk/news/world-us-canada-39767844.

[18] Kendra Pierre-Louis, 'A Border Wall Made of Solar Panels Wouldn't Actually Be Good for the Environment,' *Popular Science*, 23 June 2017, https://www.pop-sci.com/border-wall-solar-panels; Tracy Jan, 'Trump's Proposal for a "Solar" Border Wall Now Appears Dead,' *The Washington Post*, 26 October 2017, https://www.washingtonpost.com/news/wonk/wp/2017/10/26/trumps-proposal-for-a-solar-border-wall-now-appears-dead/?utm_term=.5ea4b879c6b1.

Moreover, even if a solar wall could be made self-sustaining it would require a long time before the initial outlay could be offset by lower energy costs. 'The most popular source of green energy is solar panels. They work, but they don't make economic sense', as Trump himself previously observed. 'Some estimates claim it takes as long as several decades after installing solar panels to get your money back. That's not exactly what I would call a sound investment'.[19]

Notwithstanding his pledge to make 'Mexico pay for that wall', in office Trump has acknowledged the difficulties in achieving this goal, at least in the short to medium term. He has accepted that the initial cost of constructing the wall will have to be funded by the American taxpayer and recouped from Mexico at a later date. This objective is equally fraught with problems.

Even if Mexico could ultimately be made to pay for the wall, the timescale needed to secure reimbursement could be a decade or longer. In the interim, the USA would have to bear the construction costs. These would be considerable. Moreover, they would be in addition to major increases in public expenditure needed to meet other policy commitments made by the Trump administration.

In February 2018, Congress approved $500 billion in budget spending. This included an additional outlay of $165 billion for the military, raising total projected expenditure on the armed forces in 2018 to more than $700 billion. Within days, the president outlined a further funding request for Congress to approve $200 billion investment over a decade for infrastructure projects, such as roads, highways, ports and airports. In December 2017, Congress approved a series of major tax cuts. Fulfilling another Trump campaign pledge, this reduced levels of federal government income needed to meet the subsequent hikes in expenditure. The result was an annual budget deficit of more than $1 trillion, at a time when the total indebtedness of the USA was already more than $20 trillion.[20]

There are political difficulties in securing federal funding for a wall. Democratic leaders in Congress remain opposed to the wall, notwithstanding efforts by Trump to link expenditure on it with approval for

---

[19] Trump, *Crippled America*, p. 65.

[20] Anthony Zurcher, 'Seven Things Trump's $500 bn Spending Splurge Tells Us,' *BBC News*, 9 February 2018, http://www.bbc.co.uk/news/world-us-canada-43008311; 'Trump's Infrastructure Blueprint "a Scam",' *BBC News*, 12 February 2018, http://www.bbc.co.uk/news/world-us-canada-43034786.

other measures favoured by the party, such as protected status for the so-called DACA Dreamers, unauthorized immigrants brought into the USA illegally as children. There is also opposition to the wall from Republicans, concerned at the financial outlay, or with electoral districts along the border containing Hispanic voters hostile to the project. Tacitly acknowledging such difficulties, the president omitted expenditure on the wall from his spending plans submitted to Congress in April 2017. Although Congress authorized an additional $1.5 billion in spending for border security in May, this could only be used for the repair and maintenance of existing fencing, infrastructure and surveillance.[21]

In addition to financial and political concerns, the construction of a border wall would have environmental consequences. The border includes long stretches of unspoilt wilderness, such as the Big Bend National Park in Texas. Aesthetically, it is difficult to see how a 30-feet high wall could blend in naturally in such an environment, let alone be 'beautiful'. The border region is a finely balanced ecosystem that is home to a rich variety of animal and plant wildlife. This includes endangered species like black bears, cougars, desert bighorn sheep, the North American jaguar, ocelots and the Sonoran pronghorn, a desert subspecies unique to the region that the US government has been working to conserve for more than a decade. A border wall could have catastrophic consequences for these animals, limiting freedom of movement to forage and restricting genetic diversity. There is already evidence that the 700 hundred miles of border fencing constructed since 2006 has had a harmful impact on wildlife.[22]

[21] 'Immigration Effort to Protect Dreamers Collapses in U.S. Senate,' *BBC News*, 16 February 2018, http://www.bbc.co.uk/news/world-us-canada-43079903; 'Trump Backs Down on Border Wall Funding,' *BBC News*, 26 April 2017, http://www.bbc.co.uk/news/world-us-canada-39708768; 'U.S. Budget: No Cash for Trump's Wall in Budget Deal,' *BBC News*, 1 May 2017, http://www.bbc.co.uk/news/world-us-canada-39767844.

[22] Jonathan Sullivan, 'What Would Trump's Wall Mean for Wildlife?' *BBC News*, 1 September 2016, http://www.bbc.co.uk/news/science-environment-37200583; 'Donald Trump's Mexico Wall'; '6 Things That Could Topple Donald Trump's Border Wall'; Victoria Gill, 'Trump's Divided Desert: Wildlife at the Border Wall,' *BBC News*, 18 June 2017, http://www.bbc.co.uk/news/science-environment-39888754; Ganster and Lorey, *The U.S.-Mexican Border Today*, p. 183.

Admittedly, Trump's campaign statements on green issues suggest he has limited concern for the environment. This view is reinforced by initiatives during his first year in office. In early 2017, his administration approved the construction of ecologically controversial oil pipelines in Alaska and South Dakota. In June, he withdrew American support for the Paris Climate Change Agreement. In December, he authorized increased development in the federally protected Bears Ears and Grand Staircase national monument territory in Utah.[23]

The potentially damaging economic and environmental impact of a wall on the human inhabitants of the border region will be less easy to dismiss. In Texas, a wall could deny ranchers access to fertile grazing land for their livestock along the Rio Grande. Fourteen so-called twin cities, like San Diego in the USA and its counterpart, Tijuana, in Mexico, exist on the border. Transnational in character, they have considerable social and economic interdependence. Many inhabitants live in one country but commute to work across the border. Key health and environmental issues, like tackling air pollution, maintaining access to fresh water and providing for sewage disposal, can only be addressed by cooperation between political authorities on both sides of the border.[24]

Opposition from border residents to a wall, because of the impact it could have on their lives, is a further problem for the Trump administration. The 2006 Secure Fence Act met with a series of legal challenges from border residents. Given that an estimated 66% of land on the border is owned by private citizens, Trump's more ambitious project will, inevitably, meet with resistance from property owners.[25]

[23]'Dakota Pipeline: What's Behind the Controversy?' *BBC News*, 7 February 2017, http://www.bbc.co.uk/news/world-us-canada-37863955; 'Paris Climate Deal: Trump Pulls U.S. Out of 2015 Accord,' *BBC News*, 1 June 2017, http://www.bbc.co.uk/news/world-us-canada-40127326; Julie Turkewitz, 'Trump Slashes Size of Bears Ears and Grand Staircase Monuments,' *The New York Times*, 4 December 2017, https://www.nytimes.com/2017/12/04/us/trump-bears-ears.html; Anthony Zurcher, '10 Ways Trump Has Changed America,' *BBC News*, 12 January 2018, http://www.bbc.co.uk/news/world-us-canada-42653793.

[24]James Cook, 'Border Town Divided on Trump's Wall,' *BBC News*, 23 February 2017, http://www.bbc.co.uk/news/world-us-canada-39047830; *U.S.-Mexico Border: Issues and Challenges Confronting the United States and Mexico* (Washington, DC: U.S. Government Accounting Office, 2011), pp. 11, 16, 35.

[25]Dear, *Why Walls Won't Work*, p. 148; Gerald S. Dickinson, 'The Biggest Problem for Trump's Border Wall Isn't Money: It's Getting the Land,' *The Washington Post*, 3 March 2017, https://www.washingtonpost.com/posteverything/wp/2017/03/03/the-biggest-problem-with-trumps-border-wall-isnt-money-its-getting-the-land/?utm_term=.9adc047ee779.

Although the courts are likely to uphold the right of the federal government to enforce compulsory purchase orders, under the doctrine of eminent domain, the process would be lengthy and likely to extend beyond the duration of Trump's tenure of office, even if he was re-elected in 2020. Success in the courts would also come at a price. In addition to the legal costs, property owners would have to be given reasonable compensation for their land, with the amount awarded in each case likely to be the subject of debate.[26]

In some areas, the wall would need to cross land on Native American reservations, such as the 62-mile stretch of borderland owned by the Tohono O'odham Nation in Arizona. This would present even greater legal difficulties as such lands have property rights protected by the US Constitution and federal statutes. The acquisition of this territory would require the passage of federal legislation. It would be politically sensitive, involving the rights of indigenous peoples, and the compulsory purchase of land they hold to be sacred.[27]

If that was not problem enough, a 1970 treaty signed by the USA with Mexico prohibits the construction of structures on the border that interfere with the flow of the Rio Grande and other waterways. Although this challenge could be overcome by constructing the wall on US territory, away from the river, this would bring complications, such as American citizens being trapped into living the 'wrong' side of the wall.[28]

Much of the public and media debate on Trump's wall has focused on the practical difficulties involved in its construction. This is understandable. The problems are considerable. At the same time, there are serious

[26] Dickinson, 'The Biggest Problem for Trump's Border Wall'; 'Border Town Divided on Trump's Wall'; James Cook, '100 Days: What Might Trump's Border Wall Look Like?' *BBC News*, 27 April 2017, http://www.bbc.co.uk/news/world-us-canada-39727705.

[27] Dickinson, 'The Biggest Problem for Trump's Border Wall'; Charlotte England, 'Native American Tribe Vows to Stop Donald Trump Building Mexican Border Wall on Their Arizona Reservation,' *The Independent*, 27 January 2017, http://www.independent.co.uk/news/world/americas/native-american-tribe-stop-donald-trump-us-mexican-border-wall-arizona-reservation-land-tohono-o-a7549841.html.

[28] 'Border Town Divided on Trump's Wall'; 'Treaty to Resolve Pending Boundary Differences and Maintain the Rio Grande and Colorado River as the International Boundary Between the United States of America and Mexico,' 23 November 1970, https://www.state.gov/documents/organization/125390.pdf; '100 Days: What Might Trump's Border Wall Look Like?'; '6 Things That Could Topple Trump's Border Wall'; Dear, *Why Walls Won't Work*, p. 149.

questions about the validity of the arguments that have been advanced to justify it being built. It is by no means certain that a border wall would be an effective barrier to illegal immigration. From 2006 to 2009, there were over three thousand reported breaches of existing fencing that cost $4.4 million to repair. The new land barriers erected as a result of the 2006 Secure Fence Act also led to a rise in the number of attempts to enter the USA by other means. San Diego experienced a doubling in the number of undocumented seaborne migrants and a 700% increase in drugs seizures.[29]

Others opted for a different route. Since 1990, federal law enforcement officers have uncovered more than 200 tunnels under existing border fencing. Some of these were over half a mile in length and equipped with lighting, drainage, ventilation, rail tracks and elevators. This level of sophistication reflects that fact that illicit entry into the USA has become increasingly controlled by criminal gangs. Demanding $3000 or more per head, illegal immigration is a lucrative source of income for Mexican drug cartels seeking to diversify their sources of revenue. One unfortunate consequence of the 2006 Act is that it has turned people smuggling from being an amateur undertaking to a form of organized criminal activity.[30]

Increasingly, migrants seeking to enter the USA without authorization come not just from Mexico but Central and South America. Fleeing from poverty, political instability and high crime levels, they are prepared to risk any dangers, endure any hardships. Some 500 migrants die every year attempting to bypass existing border fencing by walking through hostile mountainous terrain and desert, a tally that does not include those who perish in the wilderness and whose bodies are never found. Despite such perils, it has been estimated that 75% of migrants seeking covert entry into the USA ultimately succeed in their objective.[31]

---

[29] Dear, *Why Walls Won't Work*, p. 174.

[30] 'Your Questions on Trump's Wall Answered'; Dear, *Why Walls Won't Work*, p. 174; Peter Eichstaedt, *The Dangerous Divide: Peril and Promise on the U.S.-Mexico Border* (Chicago: Lawrence Hill Books, 2014), pp. 26, 39; Filiz Garip, *On the Move: Changing Mechanisms of Mexico-U.S. Migration* (Princeton: Princeton University Press, 2017), p. 159.

[31] Jens Manuel Krogstad, '5 Facts About Mexico and Immigration to the U.S.,' Pew Research Center, 11 February 2016, http://www.pewresearch.org/fact-tank/2016/02/11/mexico-and-immigration-to-us/; 'Border Town Divided on Trump's Wall'; 'U.S. Border Arrests at Lowest Since 1971—Trump Administration,' *BBC News*, 5 December 2017, http://www.bbc.co.uk/news/world-us-canada-42241671; 'Mexico Finds Nearly 200m

This statistic raises doubts about Trump's claim that a wall is only needed to cover 1000 miles, as in the remaining 900-mile stretch of border security would be provided by 'natural protection such as mountains, wastelands or tough rivers or water'. It is equally testimony to human ingenuity. Ironically, although a wall could have devastating consequences for the wildlife of the border region it is unlikely to prove an effective barrier for the one species it is designed to exclude, the human animal.[32]

The need to safeguard the USA from not just illegal immigration but the greater threat of Islamic terrorism is an argument that has been advanced by advocates of a border wall since the 9/11 attacks of 2001. 'Unless we act soon, we could be facing another catastrophe on the order of September 11', predicted Sean Hannity in 2006. Continuing in apocalyptic vein, he warned that in 'allowing people to cross our border unchecked, we invite a security risk into our homeland. There is no way of knowing if any – or how many – terrorists have already slipped across our border'. Referencing the southern boundary with Mexico, he noted that there were already 'eight million illegal immigrants' in the USA who 'continue to slip through our borders unchecked at an alarming rate. We cannot deny that it would be terribly easy for any terrorist with a modicum of training to cross the border just as easily'.[33]

Donald Trump evoked like fears in announcing his candidacy for the presidency. It was not just criminals, drug dealers and rapists from Mexico who illegally crossed the border, he argued. The unwanted influx was 'coming from all over South and Latin America' and 'probably – probably – from the Middle East. But we don't know. Because we have no protection and we have no competence, we don't know what's happening'. Similarly, the National Security Strategy document issued by the

Migrants Hidden in Cramped Lorry,' *BBC News*, 4 February 2018, http://www.bbc.co.uk/news/world-latin-america-42935071; '6 Things That Could Topple Donald Trump's Border Wall'; Garip, *On the Move*, pp. 2, 179; Rachel St. John, *Line in the Sand: A History of the Western U.S.-Mexico Border* (Princeton: Princeton University Press, 2011), p. 200; Eichstaedt, *The Dangerous Divide*, p. 230; Hayworth with Eule, *Whatever It Takes*, p. 1.

[32] Trump, *Crippled America*, pp. 23–24; 'Donald Trump's Mexico Wall: Who Is Going to Pay for It?'; 'Trump Wall: President Denies Changing View on Mexico Border Plan.'

[33] Sean Hannity, 'Introduction to Hayworth with Eule,' *Whatever It Takes*, pp. ix–x; Ed Ashurst, *Alligators in the Moat: Politics and the Mexican Border* (No place: Ed Ashurst Publishing Company, 2016), p. 192; S. Deborah Kang, *The INS on the Line: Making Immigration Law on the U.S.-Mexico Border, 1917–1954* (Oxford: Oxford University Press, 2017), p. 170.

Trump administration in December 2017 warned that 'Terrorists, drug traffickers, and criminal cartels exploit porous borders and threaten U.S. security and public safety'.[34]

Such claims are questionable. None of the 9/11 attackers illegally crossed the border. They entered the USA under legitimate visas. A report by the US Army Command and General Staff College in 2014 noted that in almost all documented cases of terrorists located in the USA the perpetrators had entered the country legally. There was no documented case of a terrorist gaining entry to the USA from Mexico. The threat posed by Islamic terrorist groups entering the USA from Mexico was minimal. Such conspirators would need assistance from radicalized members of the Muslim community, yet the Muslim population of Mexico was 'only a couple of thousand'.[35]

If border security did represent a terrorist threat, it was more likely to come from the north. Canada had a Muslim population of around 750,000, concentrated largely in Toronto and Montreal. In 2006, a failed Al Qaeda bomb plot was discovered in Toronto that resulted in the arrest of 17 suspects. Most of the 3400-mile-long US border with Canada had little or no security measures in place. Inhospitable during the winter, in the summer it provided easier opportunities for illegal border crossings than the mountainous and desert terrains of Mexico.[36]

American anxieties over illegal Mexican immigration are easy to understand. Between 1965 and 2015, more than 16 million Mexicans went to live and work in the USA in one of the greatest mass migrations of the twentieth century. The pace of migration intensified over time, with over 2 million Mexicans relocating north of the border between 2001 and 2006. In 1970, less than a million Mexicans lived in the USA. By 2000, this had risen to 9.4 million, and 12.8 million by 2007. By 2014, Mexicans made up 28% of the nation's 42.4 million foreign-born population, a much higher proportion than for any other nationality. The same year, Mexicans comprised 52%, or 5.8 million, of the estimated 11.1 unauthorized immigrants living in the USA. More than half of all Mexican immigrants settled in just two states, 37% in California and 21%

[34] 'Full Text: Donald Trump Announces a Presidential Bid'; Trump, *Crippled America*, pp. 19–20; *National Security Strategy of the United States of America*, p. 9.

[35] *Building the Wall*, pp. 4, 13, 18–23, 57–58, 62.

[36] *Building the Wall*, pp. 18, 23, 68–69.

in Texas, reinforcing the impression of a mass exodus from America's southern neighbour.[37] This perception, developed over more than half a century, is difficult to shift. It does not, however, take account of changes in migration patterns in more recent years. Since the economic crisis of 2008, there has been negative net migration from Mexico. Between 2009 and 2014, 870,000 Mexicans moved north of the border, but this was more than offset by the one million Mexican migrants who left the USA. Unauthorized Mexican immigrants in the USA peaked at an estimated 6.9 million in 2007, but fell to 5.8 million by 2014. Over a ten-year period, there has been a trend of declining levels of Mexican immigration to the USA, with the majority of Mexican immigrants moving in the opposite direction.[38]

In December 2017, Trump hailed the 25% fall in the number of illegal migrants arrested at the border over the previous 12 months as proof of improved security. Tougher border controls from 2006, combined with the increased deportation of illegal immigrants under the George W. Bush and Obama administrations, did have an impact. At the same time, the long-term decline in illegal immigration can be attributed to a variety of factors.[39]

[37] Jens Manuel Krogstad, '5 Facts About Mexico and Immigration to the U.S.'; Ana Gonzalez-Barrera, 'More Mexicans Leaving Than Coming to the U.S.,' Pew Research Center, 19 November 2016, http://www.pewhispanic.org/2015/11/19/more-mexicans-leaving-than-coming-to-the-u-s/; Jie Zong and Jeanne Batalova, 'Mexican Immigrants in the United States,' Migration Policy Institute, 17 March 2016, https://www.migrationpolicy.org/article/mexican-immigrants-united-states; Jens Manuel Krogstad, Jeffrey S. Passel, and D'Vera Cohn, '5 Facts About Illegal Immigration in the U.S.,' Pew Research Center, 3 November 2016, http://www.pewresearch.org/fact-tank/2017/04/27/5-facts-about-illegal-immigration-in-the-u-s/.

[38] Gonzalez-Barrera, 'More Mexicans Leaving Than Coming to the U.S.'; Jeffrey S. Passel and D'Vera Cohn, 'Overall Number of U.S. Unauthorized Immigrants Holds Steady Since 2009,' Pew Research Center, 20 September 2016, http://www.pewhispanic.org/2016/09/20/overall-number-of-u-s-unauthorized-immigrants-holds-steady-since-2009/.

[39] 'U.S. Border Arrests at Lowest Since 1971—Trump Administration'; Gonzalez-Barrera, 'More Mexicans Leaving Than Coming to the U.S.'; From 2009–2014 two million unauthorized migrants were deported from the United States, 'The Highest Level Ever Recorded'; Dear, *Why Walls Won't Work*, pp. 181–82.

The slow economic recovery in the USA after 2008 meant fewer job opportunities for migrants. By 2012, the Mexican economy was growing at twice the rate of the USA, leading to greater optimism about the country's future. Although a 2015 survey found that 48% of Mexican adults still believed prospects were better in the USA, 33% of respondents believed the quality of life was the same in both countries, an increase of 10 percentage points since 2007.[40]

Demographic change also played a part. In the 1960s and 1970s, Mexican women had an average of six children, a figure that dropped to just over two children by 2013. By 2020, there will be 100,000–200,000 fewer Mexicans coming of age every year compared to 2010, leading to less competition for jobs for young workers. Non-economic factors are another factor. In a survey undertaken by the Mexican government 61% of returning migrants between 2009 and 2014 cited family as the main reason for coming home.[41]

Another change in recent years has been the rise in the number of illegal immigrants from Central American countries using Mexico as a highway to enter the USA. In 2014, the Mexican government committed to heightened security measures at its southern border. In 2015, Mexico deported around 150,000 unauthorized immigrants, mostly from the 'northern triangle' states of El Salvador, Guatemala and Honduras. This development creates a further dilemma for the USA. The construction of a border wall risks alienating Mexico at a time when it would arguably make more sense to work with the Mexican government to prevent unlawful immigration at its perimeter with Central America, which is only around one-third the length of the US–Mexico border.[42]

---

[40]Gonzalez-Barrera, 'More Mexicans Leaving Than Coming to the U.S.'; Dear, *Why Walls Won't Work*, p. 185.

[41]O'Neil, *Two Nations Indivisible*, pp. 33, 57; Gonzalez-Barrera, 'More Mexicans Leaving Than Coming to the U.S.'

[42]Filip, *On the Move*, p. 179; Carl Meacham and Michael Graybeal, *Diminishing Mexican Immigration to the United States: A Report of the Center for Strategic and International Studies (C.S.I.S.) Program* (Lanham: Rowan & Littlefield, July 2013), pp. 12–17; Passell and D'Vera Cohn, 'Overall Numbers of U.S. Unauthorized Immigrants Holds Steady Since 2009'; 'U.S. Border Arrests at Lowest Since 1971—Trump Administration'; 'Mexico Finds Nearly 200 Migrants Hidden in Cramped Lorry'; Krogstad, '5 Facts About Mexico and Immigration to the U.S.'

The desire for both confrontation and cooperation is a paradox at the heart of US relations with Mexico. Since the 1980s, successive administrations have introduced increasingly stringent border security. At the same time, they have sought ever closer economic ties with Mexico. The North American Free Trade Agreement (NAFTA) between Canada, the USA and Mexico in 1994 has brought increasing economic interdependence between the three countries resulting in a $19 trillion economic market with some 470 million consumers.[43]

By 2012, Mexico was the number two trading partner for the USA behind Canada. In 2013, Mexico purchased more US exports than the whole of Latin America. It brought more American goods than France, Germany, the Netherlands and the UK combined, accounting for around 14% of all US exports. Some American states are even more dependent on trade with Mexico. Every month, Texas exports more than $7 billion in products south of the border and California a further $2 billion. Even more geographically far removed states, like South Dakota, Nebraska and New Hampshire, rely on Mexico for a quarter of their exports. Mexico is the first or second most important export market for 22 US states. In all, it has been estimated that some 5 million to 6 million jobs in the USA are dependent upon trade with Mexico.[44]

Admittedly, President Trump has been a harsh critic of NAFTA, describing it as 'perhaps the greatest disaster trade deal in the history of the world'. However, the reason for this opposition is his perception that the agreement favours Mexico at the expense of the USA. He has been a strong advocate of free trade in principle, acknowledging that the USA accounted for just '5 percent of the world's population' and had 'to trade with the other 95 percent'. He has pursued a renegotiation of NAFTA rather than its outright abandonment. Similarly, he has accepted that a border wall 'needs beautiful doors' to allow for legal immigration and the free transit of goods and services.[45]

[43]Carla A. Hills, 'NAFTA's Economic Upsides: The View from the United States,' *Foreign Affairs* (January/February 2014), p. 2, https://www.foreignaffairs.com/articles/canada/2013-12-06/naftas-economic-upsides.

[44]'6 Things That Could Topple Donald Trump's Border Wall'; Hills, 'NAFTA's Economic Upsides,' pp. 2, 4; O'Neil, *Two Nations Indivisible*, pp. 6, 9, 113.

[45]'Presidential Debate at Washington University in St Louis, Missouri,' 9 October 2016, http://www.presidency.ucsb.edu/ws/index.php?pid=119038; 'Presidential Debate at Hofstra University in Hempstead, New York,' 26 September 2016, http://www.presidency.ucsb.edu/ws/index.php?pid=118971; 'What's at Stake as Nafta Talks Begin?'

The 'beautiful doors' would get a lot of use. Every day, almost one million people cross the US–Mexico border. During the same time, nearly $1 billion in goods and services cross the border. An estimated 5.5 million commercial trucks cross the border every year, and that doesn't take account of people commuting to work, travelling as tourists, going to shop or to visit family and friends. There are also less welcome visitors. Up to 80% of the illegal drugs that enter the USA from Mexico do so in trucks or cars that pass through lawful ports of entry, as do the majority of unauthorized immigrants. In fact, more than half of immigrants living illegally in the USA entered the country legally and then outstayed their visas.[46]

The dilemma for the Trump administration is how to prevent illegal immigration and unlawful commerce without bringing catastrophic results for legitimate commerce and freedom of movement. US–Mexico ports of entry are among the busiest border crossings in the world. On a normal day, some commuters to the USA leave home at 3.00 am to get to work on time. The US Commerce Department has estimated that a one-minute delay at the border could cost the USA $100 million in income and over 500 jobs. In 2007, increased border security measures bringing delays of two to three hours were estimated to have an economic cost for both countries of $7.2 billion at the San Diego–Tijuana crossing alone.[47]

Trump's focus on a border wall reflects a further longstanding limitation in US border policy. Efforts to counter unauthorized immigration and the rise of Mexican drug cartels since the 1980s have been one-sided, focused on supply whilst doing comparatively little to address the

BBC News, 16 August 2017, http://www.bbc.co.uk/news/business-40943041; 'US Calls for "Major" Nafta Overhaul,' *BBC News*, 17 August 2017, http://www.bbc.co.uk/news/business-40952823; Trump, *Crippled America*, p. 164.

[46] O'Neill, *Two Nations Indivisible*, pp. 117–18; Hills, 'NAFTA's Economic Upsides,' p. 3; 'Your Questions on Trump's Wall Answered'; Douglas S. Massey, Jorge Durand, and Nolan J. Malone, *Beyond Smoke and Mirrors: Mexican Immigration in an Era of Economic Integration* (New York: Russell Sage Foundation, 2003), p. 99; Eichstaedt, *The Dangerous Divide*, p. 83; Robert Lee Maril, *The Fence: National Security, Public Safety, and Illegal Immigration Along the U.S.-Mexico Border* (Lubbock, TX: Texas Tech University Press, 2012), p. 287.

[47] Raoul Lowery Contreras, *The Mexican Border: Immigration, War and a Trillion Dollars in Trade* (Moorpark, CA: Floricanto Press, 2015), p. 19; O'Neill, *Two Nations Indivisible*, p. 119; Ganster and Lorey, *The U.S.-Mexico Border Today*, p. 212.

problem of demand. Between 1973 and 2013, the USA spent an estimated $.2.5 trillion in trying to prevent illicit drugs from entering the country. Over the same period, the estimated number of chronic drug users in the USA rose to more than 20 million, and the street value of hard drugs like cocaine fell by more than 70%. The USA is the largest drugs market in the world, worth an estimated $320 billion a year, with US authorities spending $40 billion a year in their efforts to reduce the influx of drugs.[48]

Rather than allocating extra resources to stop the supply of drugs, it would be more logical to invest in reducing demand, through more treatment centres for drug addicts, and public information campaigns on the dangers of drug use, of the kind that have been effective in driving down cigarette sales. Successive administrations have put 'far too little emphasis on prevention, like good education, after school programming', 2016 Democratic presidential candidate Bernie Sanders noted, along with 'meaningful job opportunities that give young people healthy alternatives to drifting into a life of drug use'.[49]

Moreover, the violent rise of Mexican drug cartels has been fuelled by the easy availability of high-calibre military-style firearms north of the border. In 2010, there were an estimated 107,000 gun shops in the USA, of which 12,000 were located in close proximity to Mexico, enjoying sales 'much higher than average'. An estimated 90–95% of the guns used by cartels come from the USA. Robust enforcement of existing checks against gun shops that knowingly sell to drug dealers could have a significant impact on cartel activity. Equally, US border security is focussed almost exclusively on traffic entering the USA from Mexico rather than targeting drugs money and illegal firearms smuggled south.[50]

---

[48] Eichstaedt, *The Dangerous Divide*, pp. 62–64; *Money, Guns and Drugs*, p. 2.

[49] *Money, Guns and Drugs*, pp. 20–21; Eichstaedt, *The Dangerous Divide*, pp. 64–65; Maril, *The Fence*, p. 289; Bernie Sanders, *Our Revolution: A Future to Believe In* (London: Profile Books Ltd., 2017), p. 380.

[50] *Money, Guns and Drugs*, pp. 2–3, 22, 38, 46, 52–53; Edward S. Casey and Mary Watkins, *Up Against the Wall: Re-Imagining the U.S.-Mexico Border* (Austin: University of Texas Press, 2014), p. 23.

The persistence of unauthorized immigration reflects not just the aspirations of migrants but the desire of American employers for cheap labour. If effective legislation were introduced to check this demand, with jail sentences and punitive fines for employers who hired illegal immigrants, then the scale of such migration could be greatly reduced.[51]

The practical difficulties in building a border wall are formidable. The arguments advanced for its construction are not persuasive. This raises the obvious question of why the wall was so central to Trump's election campaign. In a time of political and economic uncertainty, there is, as one commentator has observed, 'a natural human tendency to revert to tribalism', blaming foreign influences and minority groups for complex problems. This explanation is endorsed by leading figures in both main political parties. 'When people feel left out, left behind, and left without options, the deep void will be filled by anger and resentment', reflected Hillary Clinton, 'depression and despair about those who supposedly took away their livelihoods or cut in line'. Jeff Flake lamented the 'recent season of scapegoating', resulting in 'the dehumanization of vast groups of people based on nationality or ethnicity'. George W. Bush publicly noted that the nation had 'seen nationalism distorted into nativism' and 'forgotten the dynamism that immigration has always brought to America'.[52]

Albeit depressing, this outlook is supported by historical experience. Nativism, 'a deep-seated antipathy' towards foreigners 'based upon emotions of fear and hated', has been a recurring phenomenon in the American past at times of national uncertainty and self-doubt. In 1856, one congressional committee complained that European countries were turning the USA into a 'receptacle for the dregs and off-scourings of

---

[51] Massey, Durand, and Malone, *Beyond Smoke and Mirrors*, p. 105; Hayworth and Eule, *Whatever It Takes*, pp. 175, 179–80; U.S. Army War College, *The Dark Side of Illegal Immigration: Cause for National Concern* (No place: CreateSpace Independent Publishing Platform, July 2014), p. 5; 'Your Questions on Trump's Wall Answered'; King, *The INS on the Line*, p. 170.

[52] M. D. Allen Frances, *Twilight of American Sanity: A Psychiatrist Analyses the Age of Trump* (New York: William Morrow, 2017), pp. 122–23; Clinton, *What Happened*, p. 277; Jeff Flake, *Conscience of a Conservative: A Rejection of Destructive Politics and a Return to Principle* (New York: Random House, 2017), p. 48; 'Decoding Bush's Thinly Veiled Trump Speech,' *BBC News*, 20 October 2017, http://www.bbc.co.uk/news/world-us-canada-41689272.

their population', thereby 'relieving themselves of the burden of pauperism and crime'. In 1907, the congressional Dillingham Committee condemned the inferior quality of 'new' immigrants entering the USA since the 1880s. Popular nativist authors of the day reinforced these perceptions. In 1916, Madison Grant claimed the USA was becoming home to 'the least desirable classes and types from each European nation now exporting men', and in 1921 T. Lothrop Stoddard warned of 'the dangerous foreign races' advancing in the 'insidious guise of beggars at our gates, pleading for admittance to share our prosperity'. Ironically, it was during this period of mass immigration, that President Trump's paternal grandfather migrated to the USA from Germany, in 1885, followed by his mother, who emigrated from Scotland in 1918.[53]

His immigrant heritage notwithstanding, Trump's demonization of Mexican immigrants as drug dealers, rapists and criminals echoes nativist sentiments of the past. At a time of painful economic adjustments at home, global political uncertainty and heightened fears of terrorism, such sentiments have popular appeal. No matter that nearly all economists believe that immigration provides net economic benefits for the USA, and that newly arrived immigrants are nearly half as likely to commit crimes as native-born Americans.[54]

[53] Maldwyn Jones, *American Immigration* (Chicago: University of Chicago Press, 1992), pp. 126, 130, 152–57; Madison Grant, *The Passing of the Great Race: Or, the Racial Basis of European History*, Fourth Revised Edition (New York: Charles Scribner's Sons, 1936, first published 1916), p. 211; T. Lothrop Stoddard, *The Rising Tide of Color Against White World Supremacy* (Burlington, IA: Ostara Publications, 2011, first published 1921), p. xiv; Trump, *Crippled America*, p. 21.

[54] 'Donald Trump and the Politics of Paranoia,' *BBC News*, 24 January 2016, http://www.bbc.co.uk/news/magazine-35382599; 'Trump's Speech to Congress'; 'Kate Steinle: Trump Outrage over Murder Case Acquittal,' *BBC News*, 1 December 2017, http://www.bbc.co.uk/news/world-us-canada-42190455; 'Indianapolis Colts' Edwin Jackson "Killed by Illegal Immigrant",' *BBC News*, 5 February 2018, http://www.bbc.co.uk/news/world-us-canada-42952519; O'Neil, *Two Nations Indivisible*, pp. 43, 51.

158   K. VERNEY

REFERENCES

Casey, Edward S., and Mary Watkins. *Up Against the Wall: Re-Imagining the U.S.-Mexico Border*. Austin: University of Texas Press, 2014.

Contreras, Raoul Lowery. *The Mexican Border: Immigration, War and a Trillion Dollars in Trade*. Moorpark, CA: Floricanto Press, 2015.

Dear, Michael. *Why Walls Won't Work: Repairing the U.S.-Mexico Divide*. Oxford: Oxford University Press, 2013.

Eichstaedt, Peter. *The Dangerous Divide: Peril and Promise on the U.S.-Mexico Border*. Chicago: Lawrence Hill Books, 2014.

Frances, M. D. Allen. *Twilight of American Sanity: A Psychiatrist Analyses the Age of Trump*. New York: William Morrow, 2017.

Ganster, Paul, with David E. Lorey. *The U.S.-Mexican Border Today: Conflict and Cooperation in Historical Perspective*. Third Edition. Lanham: Rowman & Littlefield, 2016.

Garip, Filiz. *On the Move: Changing Mechanisms of Mexico-U.S. Migration*. Princeton: Princeton University Press, 2017.

Hayworth, J. D., with Joseph J. Eule. *Whatever It Takes: Illegal Immigration, Border Security and the War on Terror*. Washington, DC: Regnery Publishing, Inc., 2006.

John, Rachel St. *Line in the Sand: A History of the Western U.S.-Mexico Border*. Princeton: Princeton University Press, 2011.

Jones, Maldwyn. *American Immigration*. Chicago: University of Chicago Press, 1992.

Kang, S. Deborah. *The INS on the Line: Making Immigration Law on the U.S.-Mexico Border, 1917–1954*. Oxford: Oxford University Press, 2017.

Maril, Robert Lee. *The Fence: National Security, Public Safety, and Illegal Immigration Along the U.S.-Mexico Border*. Lubbock, TX: Texas Tech University Press, 2012.

Massey, Douglas S., Jorge Durand, and Nolan J. Malone. *Beyond Smoke and Mirrors: Mexican Immigration in an Era of Economic Integration*. New York: Russell Sage Foundation, 2003.

Meacham, Carl, and Michael Graybeal. *Diminishing Mexican Immigration to the United States: A Report of the Center for Strategic and International Studies (C.S.I.S.) Program*. Lanham: Rowan & Littlefield, July 2013.

O'Neil, Shannon K. *Two Nations Indivisible: Mexico, the United States, and the Road Ahead*. Oxford: Oxford University Press, 2013.

CHAPTER 8

Grab 'Em by the Legacy: Rolling Back the Years with President Trump

Clodagh Harrington

On election night 2016, the US Ambassador to the United Nations, Samantha Power, hosted a party at her New York apartment for 37 female diplomats. Guests including former Secretary of State Madeline Albright and Gloria Steinem wore brooches made of shattered glass to celebrate the seemingly inevitable victory of the first woman president of the USA.[1] When asked to later reflect on her decision to host the gathering, Power stated 'Well, I've had a lot of bad ideas in my life, but none as immortalized as this one.'[2] As this potential moment of enormous gain on behalf of women and girls everywhere ended dramatically, two realities became starkly apparent. The first, in the words of a post-election *Newsweek* headline was that, 'the presidential election was a referendum

---

[1] 'The Final Year,' Greg Baker (HBO 2018).
[2] 'Susan Glasser interview with Samantha Power,' *Politico*, 15 January 2018.

C. Harrington (✉)
De Montfort University, Leicester, UK
e-mail: cmharrington@dmu.ac.uk

© The Author(s) 2019
M. Oliva and M. Shanahan (eds.), *The Trump Presidency*,
The Evolving American Presidency,
https://doi.org/10.1007/978-3-319-96325-9_8

on gender, and women lost.'[3] The second was that the maverick victor was no champion of women's rights. The response to Donald J. Trump's stunning 30-state electoral college victory from all sides was one of disbelief.

This chapter will focus on some aspects of women's rights in the context of the Trump agenda. The content will examine the tone and rhetoric used on the campaign trail in relation to women. Specific issues around reproductive and parental leave rights along with the responses from those on various points of the political spectrum will be scrutinized. Some consideration will be given to the fact that whilst Trump was not the candidate of choice for conservative Christians, by 8 November 2016, he had sufficiently convinced them to put their faith in him. In addition, the chapter will consider how the Trump administration actively sought to undo various gender-related achievements by its liberal predecessor, as well as unpicking some longer term progress specifically around reproductive rights. Suitable acknowledgement will be given to the ongoing media frenzy around these divisive topics, and the challenges faced by observers to push past online spats and political hyperbole in order to map out which aspects of the Obama era legacy were ripe for unravelling by a conservative successor. Liberals continuously accused Trump of holding women in contempt, and it is easy to draw this conclusion based on his words and previous personal history. On the campaign trail, his supporters were quick to dismiss the distasteful rhetoric as harmless banter. The reality, however, is that a candidate's words do carry weight, and the words of a president are laden with consequence. In the cyclical whirl of controversial comments, liberal backlash, conservative justification and Trump's own two cents worth via Twitter, it is necessary to divorce words from deeds to measure potential manifestations of misogyny. The chapter will begin with an attempt to locate and interpret Donald Trump's policy views relating to women and reproductive rights.

MAN V POLICY

The rhetoric of individuals seeking and gaining the highest office in the land is inevitably laden with significance. It sets expectation and invites imitation. Presidential candidates are invariably prone to hyperbole as

[3] Nine Burleigh, 'The Presidential Election Was a Referendum on Gender and Women Lost,' *Newsweek*, 14 November 2016.

they vie for public attention, column inches and airtime. They may over-state their case or create headline-grabbing sound bites in order to push ahead of the competition, particularly during the primary campaigning period. Nonetheless, they are running for the most high-profile job in the world, hence their every word will be relentlessly scrutinised. As a result of his often incendiary language on the campaign trail, Donald Trump received billions of dollars' worth of free airtime and column inches, not least from liberal media outlets apoplectic with rage at his utterances.[4] Trump engaged in continuous word-battles with a range of women, from Fox anchor Megan Kelly to Republican rival Carly Fiorina. Clearly, his style was divisive as responses ranged from shock and offence to glee at the candidate's overt disdain for what he perceived as political correctness.

However, whilst the content of the verbal spats suggested a clear lack of respect for women on a personal level, it was not a given that they were reflective of candidate Trump's policy positions around women's rights in general. In the context of the wider Republican Party gen-der agenda, it was evident that this candidate without previous political experience had little or no ideological or policy position when it came to such issues. In order to create some context, a look back through the public utterances of Donald Trump through his decades as a real estate mogul and later a reality television star offered some insight. The *Daily Telegraph* collated a 'sexism tracker' in which it gathered key quotes relating to a range of women, including his three wives, staff members and female public figures of the day.[5]

With the obvious caveat that a high-profile celebrity with no public office has the freedom to speak to the press as he pleases, even his most ardent supporter would concede that Donald Trump is no feminist. This is hardly an exception to the majority of his Republican peers or prede-cessors and therefore not necessarily problematic from a GOP voter per-spective. In fact, many voters would consider a 'feminist' president to be a cause for concern. The modern Republican Party has successfully tai-lored its appeal to certain types of women, and this strategy has worked well. For the past three decades, a majority of white women have voted

---

[4] Niv Sultan, 'Election 2016: Trump's Free Media Helped Keep Cost Down, But Fewer Donors Provided More of the Cash,' OpenSecrets.org, 13 April 2017.

[5] Claire Cohen, 'Donald Trump Sexism Tracker: Every Offensive Comment in One Place,' *Daily Telegraph*, 14 July 2017.

for the GOP presidential candidate. However, it is not the case that white women consist of a homogenous voting block. In reality, their voting patterns relate to a number of factors. As a rule, married heterosexual religious women without university degrees are the most likely group to vote Republican.[6]

As a benchmark, one 2015 survey shows that female Democrat voters were twice as likely as Republicans to identify as feminist, whilst their male counterparts were three times more inclined.[7] Not coincidentally, the GOP has offered few female presidential candidates in its history. In 2016, the only GOP female presidential candidate was doubtless an inspiration to women on a professional level, as she had been the first women to head a top 20 *Fortune* company. On the hot-button issues, Fiorina stated that she was opposed to same-sex marriage and abortion, but in general her comments were more nuanced than those of her recent candidate predecessors Bachmann and Palin. For example, she supported abortion in cases of rape or incest. She was also not afraid to embrace the 'f' word, arguing that conservatives should stop backing away from the idea of feminism, as it can have so many meanings. In 2015, when Donald Trump was asking Twitter 'if Hillary Clinton is unable to satisfy her husband, what makes her think she can satisfy America?'[8] Fiorina was declaring that 'Feminism begins as a rallying cry to empower women' she stated at a June 2015 event in Washington DC.[9]

After withdrawing from the 2016 race, Fiorina signed up for the vice-presidential ticket of Ted Cruz. The Texan senator held very clear views on 'moral values' issues and spoke out against abortion in all cases except when the mother's life was in danger. As well as being against same-sex marriage and civil unions, he supported cutting federal funding to Planned Parenthood and was not in favour of federally mandated parental leave. So, by anyone's measure, Cruz was unlikely to draw the feminist vote. Perhaps inviting former Hewlett-Packard CEO Fiorina

---

[6] Julie Kohler, 'The Reason Why White Women Vote Republican and What to Do About It,' *The Nation*, 1 February 2018.

[7] Public Religion Research Institute, Millennials, Sexuality and Reproductive Health Survey, March 2015.

[8] @realdonaldtrump, Twitter, 16 April 2015.

[9] Tessa Berenson, 'Here's How Carly Fiorina Wants to Redefine Feminism,' *Time*, 11 June 2015.

on board, as a relative but not hard-line conservative, Cruz aimed to broaden his appeal. In the end, the plan did not work, and Cruz withdrew his nomination for the presidency.

Hence, whoever clinched the Republican nomination, it was clear that there was going to be some consistency with regard to women's rights issues. The matter of women's health is a perennial partisan flashpoint and in those early campaign trail days, the chasm between the Democrat view of what government should offer women diverged sharply with that of Ted Cruz, Marco Rubio and the majority of their fellow Republican rivals. In contrast, maverick GOP candidate Trump had no history of strong views on issues such as reproductive rights or maternity pay. In fact, he had stated publicly in the past that he was 'very pro-choice' but by 2015 had come out as 'pro-life.'[10]

Any worries that potential supporters may have had about this inconsistency were allayed, in part at least, by Trump's choice for the vice-presidential ticket. There was no questioning the pro-life commitment of Indiana Governor Mike Pence.

THE SECOND TELEVISION DEBATE

When the recording of Trump's vulgar comments about women appeared in October 2016, for a moment it cast doubt on the candidate's ability to swagger through this damaging moment. Even the value-neutral *Reuters* news agency ran a headline 'Trump in crisis after lewd remarks about women come to light.' It would be difficult to spin this story out of the headlines. High-profile Republicans lined up to criticize their candidate's 2005 remarks. Paul Ryan claimed to be 'sickened' whilst Mitch McConnell found the words to be 'repugnant.' Others, including Utah Governor Gary Herbert, called for Trump to step aside, stating that 'tonight, millions of Republicans are facing a moment of truth.'[11]

Demonstrating not for the last time, his canny skills for managing negative press and controlling the narrative, Trump swiftly turned the

---

[10] Donald Trump on 'Meet the Press,' *NBC*, 24 October 1999; Donald Trump at the Iowa Freedom Summit, 24 January 2015.

[11] Emily Stephenson and Roberta Rampton, 'Trump in Crisis as Lewd Remarks About Women Come to Light,' *Reuters*, 7 October 2016.

story on its head. Eschewing remorse, he dismissed his words from eleven years earlier as 'locker room banter, a private conversation that took place many years ago' and apologised 'if anyone was offended.'[12] He later claimed that the tapes were fake. Many conservatives were put off their candidate after the tape's release. For a moment, it appeared that Trump's unprecedented roll was slowing to a halt. Gallup polls showed his support from US adults at around 30% in the second week of October 2016, compared to 40% in favour of Clinton. Among Republicans, his support was steady at around 64%. By the end of the month, his overall support had crept back up to 35%.[13]

In his 1987 book, *The Art of the Deal*, Trump outlined his strategy whenever he perceived himself to be under attack. He would fight back twice as hard and overwhelm his opponent.[14] More than thirty years on, his approach remained consistent. Negative campaign tactics are a perennial factor in US elections but this time, the psychological warfare contained a new Trump twist, perhaps amplified by the gender of his opponent. At the second presidential television debate on 9 October 2016 at Washington University in St. Louis, Trump went to full attack mode, digging up four women from Bill Clinton's past that had made allegations of sexual harassment or worse against him. The plan was to seat the women near Bill and Chelsea Clinton during the debate, and clearly send a message, which conflated the forty-second president's personal indiscretions with candidate Clinton's ability to run the country.

When Clinton was speaking, Trump circled around behind her, and at one point referred to her as 'the devil,' and someone with 'tremendous hate in her heart.'[15] He declared that should he win the election, he would send his opponent to prison. A *CNN* snap poll afterwards showed that 57% thought that Clinton won, against 34% who decided Trump had. In an interaction characterised by personal abuse and vicious accusations, commentators observed that the key losers on the night included

---

[12] Stephenson and Rampton, 'Trump in Crisis.'

[13] Presidential Election 2016, Key Indicators: Candidate Image, Gallup November 2016

[14] Donald Trump, *The Art of the Deal*, Ballantine, 1987.

[15] Steve Holland and Emily Stephenson, 'Trump Vs Clinton: He Calls Her a Devil, She Says He Abuses Woman,' *Reuters*, 10 October 2016.

personal integrity and any focus on policy detail; 64% of female voters polled stated that they disapproved of Trump's personal attacks on Clinton and her husband.[16]

Come election time, expediency may have won the day. Influential Trump supporter Jentezen Franklin, pastor of the Free Chapel megachurch in Georgia explained to journalists, 'Until Jesus runs for office, it will always be the lesser of two evils.'[17] Franklin and many of his peers were pragmatic enough to accept that if Trump was their only option, then they may as well get behind his candidacy. Clearly, support for Hillary Clinton was out of the question. The traditional Religious Right default setting on election day to stay home if there was not a suitable candidate was no longer acceptable. In addition, Trump was politically savvy enough to realise that if he was going to meaningfully woo conservative Evangelicals and Catholics, he would need to at least listen to their concerns if not faithfully align with them all. By mid-2016, the candidate from New York had conducted a closed-door meeting with 900 evangelical leaders and had created an Evangelical Executive Advisory Board of 25 individuals who could offer advice on matters of a spiritual nature.[18] The board included high-profile conservatives such as former congresswoman Michelle Bachmann, political operative Robert Reed and pastor Jerry Falwell, Jr. Whatever the thrice married known philanderer was personally lacking in religious credentials, he was clearly demonstrating his willingness to listen to those with a more direct line to God.

Speaking at Ralph Reed's Faith and Freedom Coalition 'Road to Majority' conference in June 2017, Trump quoted the bible and reassured those present that he was protecting their religious freedoms. His executive order dated May 4 promoting free speech and religious liberty was a comfort to those present. Trump thanked the Coalition for its continuous work on his campaign behalf, sharing references to the millions of emails, phone calls and door-to-door visits its members had

---

[16]CNN/ORC poll, 9 October 2016.

[17]Economist, 'Absalom's Revenge,' 13 October 2016.

[18]Jack Jenkins, 'Meet Donald Trump's New Evangelical Advisory Board,' ThinkProgress.org, 22 June 2016.

made in the run-up to November 2016. In addition, he listed out his progress in relation to matching his campaign promises to their presidential to-do list.[19]

DELIVERING ON CAMPAIGN PROMISES

With his political ear attuned, and mindful of the social conservatives among his voting base, on the 2016 campaign trail Trump offered staunchly anti-abortion rhetoric, including that crucially important promise to appoint a like-minded Supreme Court judge to replace the late Antonin Scalia. Historically, Donald Trump's position on women's reproductive rights has not been particularly clear.[20] From the available evidence, it was difficult for any observers to deduce the extent to which he had personally switched from his earlier pro-choice position to one of anti-abortion, or perhaps he was simply pro-birth, or merely anti-women. Another explanation was perhaps none of the above, but instead that he was highly politically astute, capable of reading the public mood, massaging it and offering solutions, however superficial, for conservative America's 'moral values' agenda.

On the campaign trail, he was inconsistent on these matters which meant so much to so many voters. Possibly, the most memorable moment was at a town hall meeting aired on MSNBC. Speaking to Chris Matthews about abortion, he declared 'I want to ban it.' He had stated the Republican Party line on the topic but did not commit himself personally until pressed by the interviewer. He then conceded that 'there should be some form of punishment' for the woman.[21] Whilst Trump did not sound particularly convinced by his own words, liberals took him at his word and the inevitable social media storm ensued.

The conventional GOP line on this topic does not include 'punishing' the women. The party platform language speaks of a compassionate, rather than punitive, approach. The Republican Party position in relation to reproductive issues and abortion is outlined on its website and

[19] Donald Trump, 'Remarks at the Faith and Freedom Coalition Road to Majority Conference,' 8 June 2017; Donald Trump, 'Promoting Free Speech and Religious Liberty Executive Order 13798,' 4 May 2017.

[20] See Rewire News for a timeline of Donald Trump's shifting position on abortion up to 22 August 2016.

[21] Chris Matthews Town Hall session with Donal Trump, MSNBC, 30 March 2016.

includes promotion of abstinence, tax incentives for adoption and generous funding for fostering. Constitutionally, the GOP line on the role and rights of a foetus are that they would like to see a human life amendment added to the constitution and endorse legislation to make clear that the Fourteenth Amendment's protections apply to unborn children.[22] Hence, Trump quickly walked back on his punishment comments in 2016, and in further interviews, aligned himself with a reliable voice on the topic. As he told the *New York Times*, 'Like Ronald Reagan, I am pro-life, with exceptions.'[23]

PRESIDENT TRUMP AND MEXICO CITY/ GLOBAL GAG RULING

The Mexico City presidential memorandum was one of three executive actions signed by the president on 23 January 2017. Trump was following a long-standing White House tradition dating back to President Reagan. In 1984, Reagan had also been mindful of cementing his pro-life platform. He was obliged to display his commitment, as Evangelical and Catholic conservatives were displeased at his appointment of the moderate Republican Sandra Day O'Connor to the Supreme Court during his first term.[24]

Ever since, it had become tradition for a new president of the opposing party to rescind or reinstate the Mexico City ruling. In Obama's case, he overturned the ruling, also known as the Global Gag, on 23 January 2009, thereby restoring US federal funding for overseas NGOs whose services include abortion provision. Clearly, this was not well received by opponents of the liberal administration. However, there were further developments on his watch, not all of which were straightforwardly pro-abortion. In March 2010, President Obama signed Executive Order 13535.[25] This action reinforced the Hyde Amendment, which was a legislative provision dating back to 1976, banning federal

[22] Republican Party Platform 2016, https://www.gop.com/platform/we-the-people/.

[23] Donald Trump interview, *New York Times*, 18 May 2016.

[24] Daisy Fleming, 'The Mexico City Policy and the Trump Transition,' *Foreign Affairs Review*, 17 February 2017.

[25] Barack Obama, 'Ensuring Enforcement and Implementation of Abortion Restrictions in the Patient Protection and Affordable Care Act,' Executive Order 13535, 29 March 2010.

funding for abortion in the USA. It makes an exception for cases of rape, incest or when the life of the mother is in danger. Here, the president was reaching out to pro-life Democrats whose support he needed in the lead up to the signing of the Affordable Care Act. Responses to the move were predictably mixed. Social conservatives were concerned about the flimsiness of an executive order, whilst progressives lambasted the president for tightening up existing abortion provision.

The Mexico City decision does not directly affect women in America. However, this memorandum sent a clear message to supporters and critics alike with regard to the Trump administration priorities. Here was a nod to his base, who were eagerly awaiting signs of campaign words being translated into presidential deeds. The Order was signed on 23 January 2017, President Trump's first day behind his new desk.[26] So, concerned observers would have seen this was a direct act to revoke the 22 January 2009 memorandum signed by President Obama. The original Reagan era policy stripped US family planning funds from groups involved with abortion. So, the ebb and flow continued with what is an ostensibly International Development issue, but is clearly loaded with meaning for those keeping an eye on a new administration and their gender agenda.

The Trump memorandum took the policy further than that of his conservative predecessors. The figure in question was something in the region of $500 million, so this was a win-win move for the president in relation to pleasing his socially conservative supporters, as well as voters who took issue with the US government undertaking what they viewed as inappropriate forms of foreign policy. Not only were overseas NGOs obliged to disavow any involvement with abortion to receive US family planning funding, but Trump expanded this to refer to *all* funding. The president of the global reproductive health organisation Population Action International (PAI) described it as the global gag rule 'on steroids.'[27] A 2015 PAI report stated that in the aftermath of George W Bush's reinstatement of the global gag rule, shipments of contraceptives were stopped to 16 countries.[28] A 2011

---

[26] Donald Trump, 'Presidential Memorandum Regarding the Mexico City Policy,' 23 January 2017.

[27] Michelle Goldberg, 'Trump Didn't Just Reinstate the Global Gag Rule: He Massively Expanded It,' Slate.com, 24 January 2017.

[28] Population Action International, 'How the Global Gag Ruling Undermines US Foreign Policy and Harms Women's Health (PAI 2015 Report).'

WHO report found that abortions in sub-Saharan Africa increased after the 2001 rule, most likely as a result of the lack of contraceptives.[29] Trump's decision aligned with his wider Jacksonian move away from the liberal international order, and back towards a more inward looking approach, which chimed with his populist 'America First' rhetoric.

Federal Funding for Planned Parenthood

During the 2016 campaign, Trump wrote a letter to anti-abortion leaders, inviting them to join his 'Pro-Life Coalition.'[30] One of the pledges, oft-repeated in his election speeches, was to end funding for Planned Parenthood, the US-based and international non-profit organisation which focuses on reproductive health care and rights (including birth control, pregnancy tests and STD screening). Planned Parenthood receives about one-third of its funding from government, and it is prohibited from using federal funding for abortions.[31] However, opponents of the $500 million + that government provides argue that this funding allows the organisation to use some of its other resources to fund abortion. The funding of Planned Parenthood was a continuously contentious issue between President Obama and the Republican dominated Congress. Towards the end of his presidency, Obama offered what many viewed as his 'parting gift' to reproductive health care provider Planned Parenthood.[32] The December 2016 Health and Human Services regulation protecting federally funded grants for women's health programmes had, in the words of Cecile Richards, president of Planned Parenthood, 'cemented his legacy as a champion of women's rights.'[33] The durability of this legacy was soon called into question. President Trump's 2019

---

[29] Eran Bendavid, Patrick Avila, and Grant Miller, 'United States Aid Policy and Induced Abortion in Sub-Saharan Africa,' *Bulletin of the World Health Organisation*, 27 September 2011.

[30] Donald Trump's 'Pro-Life Coalition' letter, September 2016.

[31] Miriam Berg, 'How Federal Funding Works at Planned Parenthood,' Plannedparenthoodaction.org, 5 January 2017.

[32] Health and Human Services Department proposed rule on Title X Compliance Requirements, see Federal Register link for background, 7 September 2016.

[33] Cecile Richards, Planned Parenthood press release, 14 December 2016.

budget included provisions prohibiting 'certain abortion providers' from receiving federal funds, including 'those that receive funding under the Title X Family Programme.'[34]

MIKE PENCE AND REPRODUCTIVE RIGHTS

Socially conservative voters unnerved by Trump's often inconstant or incoherent position on the thorny issue of reproductive rights could take great solace from the choice of Mike Pence for vice-president. The evangelical Pence, a self-confessed Tea Party supporter, has repeatedly described himself as a Christian, a conservative and a Republican, in that order. The former Governor of Indiana (2013–2017), and Congressman for Eastern Indiana (2001–2013), also spent time as a regional radio show host, on which he described himself as 'Rush Limbaugh on decaf.'[35]

In 2015, Governor Pence signed the Religious Freedom Restoration Act (RFRA) into law. The RFRA was introduced in a private ceremony 'to prevent laws that substantially burden a person's free exercise of religion.'[36] It received nationwide criticism as concerns were raised with regard to the potential for businesses to refuse service to gay and lesbian patrons. A number of businesses and NGOs declared their intent to take their custom elsewhere in the light of the state's position. The Republican Mayor of Indianapolis claimed that the bill sent the 'wrong signal' for the city. Pence defended the legislation by pointing out that 'many people of faith feel their religious liberty is under attack by government action.'[37] Nonetheless, an amendment to the bill was passed in April 2015, with the intention to protect LGBTQ rights.

An examination of Pence's past positions on a range of issues such as LGBTQ rights demonstrates his continuous and consistent conservative stance.[38] As Governor, he ended funding for Planned Parenthood in Indiana, which provided HIV screening. In addition, he opposed

[34]Budget of the US Government, Office of Management and Budget, Fiscal Year 2019, p. 56.

[35]The Rush Limbaugh Show, 'Trump Chooses Rush Limbaugh on Decaf for VP,' 18 July 2016.

[36]Religious Freedom Restoration, Indiana General Assembly, Senate Enrolled Act No 101, 1 July 2015.

[37]Mike Pence statement on RFRA signing, 26 March 2015.

[38]Mike Pence for Congress 2000 website.

needle-sharing schemes and was consistently more socially conservative than many in his party. On the subject of reproductive issues, his positions are not in line with those of moderate Republicans. In March 2016, he introduced a bill, which restricted certain abortion procedures and placed new restrictions on providers. The bill included a ban on abortions in the case of foetal abnormality (including Downs Syndrome) and funeral requirements for foetal remains from abortions or miscarriages (at any stage of pregnancy).[39]

It, therefore, came as a surprise to many when Mike Pence won the 2017 Independent Women's Forum 'Working for Women' award. The conservative think tank aims to 'improve the lives of Americans by increasing the number of women who value free markets and personal liberty.'[40] According to the group, Pence's work embodied their philosophy. Vice-President Pence's name was at the top of the list given his track record of advocating for free markets and limited government including rolling back heavy taxation and regulation, IWF spokeswoman Victoria Coley said in an email. 'These policy positions help create the conditions for more women to thrive professionally and personally and pursue their vision of the American Dream.'[41]

In an interview with Karen Pence, readers were reminded of a 2002 interview in which her husband had stated that he does not dine alone with women who are not his wife and does not attend events where alcohol is served unless his wife is present.[42] Once again, for religious conservatives uncomfortable with a president who bragged about his infidelities, Pence's way was far more in line with their mode of thinking. Clearly, Pence speaks authentically to and for Christian conservatives in a way that Trump simply cannot. There is no meaningful evidence to offer insights into what the vice-president thinks of his boss. Perhaps, like pastor Franklin, he is motivated by pragmatism. As the only sitting vice-president to have set up his own Political Action Committee, he may have his eye on a future presidential run himself.

---

[39] Indiana General Assembly, House Bill 1337, Abortion, 1 July 2016.

[40] Independent Women's Forum website, www.iwf.org/about.

[41] Victoria Coley (IWF) email to *Washington Post*, quoted in Amy Wang, 'Vice President Pence Is Receiving a "Working for Women" Award: Here's a Dive into His Record on Women,' 22 March 2017.

[42] Aaron Blake, 'Mike Pence Doesn't Dine Alone with Other Women,' *Washington Post*, 30 March 2017.

APPOINTMENT OF NEIL GORSUCH
TO THE SUPREME COURT

When Supreme Court justice Antonin Scalia died in February 2016, President Obama's best effort to get his chosen successor Merrick Garland past Senate approval came to nothing. The court seat remained empty for over a year. On the campaign trail, Trump promised to appoint a social conservative to the bench if he won the presidency. He even told audiences that if they didn't like him, they should vote for him anyway, and he would fulfil their Supreme Court requirement.[43] This reinforced the idea that however the Religious Right felt about Trump as an individual, overall they were pragmatic enough to realise that he would deliver for them on one of their most significant issues. According to research conducted by Pew in 2016, 77% of conservative Republicans polled said that Supreme Court appointments were 'very important' to them in their 2016 voting choice.[44] As the nation faced an unprecedented situation where a Supreme Court seat was left vacant for eight months, Republicans saw a win that for some transcended the victory of getting their candidate to the White House. President Trump may only last four to eight years in the White House. A youthful Supreme Court appointee could sit on the bench for decades. In addition, the health of some of the aging justices did not go unnoticed. As Trump ran for the presidency, three judges had already or were about to enter their eighties. The prospect of conservative replacements for the progressive Ruth Bader Ginsberg and Stephen Breyer along with the hugely influential swing voter Anthony Kennedy was deeply appealing to those whose socially conservative agenda could realistically be promoted via the court. This was attractive not least at a time when Congress appeared gridlocked and action via alternative branches of government became ever more attractive. In the words of John Boehner, no fan of Trump, 'the biggest impact any president can have on American society and on the American economy is who's on that court.'[45]

In April 2017, Neil Gorsuch, Trump's choice of successor for Scalia, was sworn in. This was an enormous relief for conservatives across the

---

[43] Donald Trump campaign speech, Cedar Rapids, Iowa, 28 July 2016.

[44] Pew Research Center, 'Top Voting Issues in 2016 Election,' 7 July 2016.

[45] John Boehner interview with Brit Hume, Fox News, 12 October 2016.

nation. Whatever the fate of the Trump presidency, this 49-year-old Catholic known to attend Protestant church was likely to remain in place for decades. He described himself as a constitutional originalist and a textualist. Like many Tea Party supporters, Gorsuch interpreted the constitution as it was meant to be when it was written and believed that the constitutional statutes should be interpreted literally. Such declarations inevitably resulted in progressives pondering the perennial supreme court-related question: could *Roe V Wade* be overturned? In any direct sense, such a development appears deeply unlikely. The issue is more likely to rear its head in the lower courts. There are a range of ways in which Republican controlled legislatures and courts around the country could chip away at *Roe V Wade* and undermine it piecemeal via such means as access restrictions, restriction on health insurance provision and geographical distance to clinics. Examples from the Guttmacher Institute for 2017 include:

- Oklahoma state legislature proposed that there should be written permission from the father before a doctor may carry out a termination.
- Arkansas signed and passed a law (to go into effect in 2018) which includes a clause allowing a husband to sue a doctor who carries out certain types of terminations.
- Other states with conservative lawmakers, such as Ohio, passed strict new abortion laws banning abortion after 20 weeks of pregnancy.

Whilst there is no doubt that the pro-life movement in the USA has been emboldened by the Trump-Pence victory, ongoing change was already taking place, with 338 new restrictions on abortion rights since 2010.[46]

This move towards tightening access was in place long before Donald Trump came to power. As the 45th president moved increasingly closer to the agenda of the Religious Right on key 'moral values' issues, he nonetheless maintained the capacity to offer the unexpected. An example of this was his stance on paid parental leave, which did not conform to conventional GOP wisdom.

---

[46] Guttmacher Institute, Policy Trends in the States 2017, 2 January 2018.

PAID PARENTAL LEAVE

In 2015, at a time when only 12% of American workers were entitled to paid family leave, Barack Obama became the first president to call for paid family leave in his State of the Union address.[47] As other industrialised nations had moved towards such measures throughout the late twentieth century, the USA lagged noticeably behind. Aside from Papua New Guinea, only the USA offered no formal paid parental leave to new parents. The 1993 Family Medical Leave Act allowed up to 12 weeks of unpaid leave to most government and private-sector employees on the birth or adoption of a child. The standard argument was that offering paid family leave would compromise American businesses and lower their capacity for competitiveness. Evidence from other developed nations does not bear this out.[48] Whilst the move was long championed by women's rights activists, their position was strengthened by the fact that paid parental leave could, in fact, assist in strengthening a nation's economy rather than weakening it. The president's plan was pushed via the fiscal 2016 budget and through executive order and memoranda. On Mother's Day 2016, President Obama made the case for paid maternity and paternity leave, calling it a step towards 'the equality that women deserve.'[49]

In the run-up to the 2016 election, a poll conducted by the National Partnership for Women and Families found that 76% of respondents supported the idea of a federal fund created for paid family and medical leave.[50] Despite this notable level of backing, the issue did not rate as a priority among voters who ranked their concerns for Gallup relating to 'the most important issues facing the nation today.'[51] In her 2017 motivational tome 'Women Who Work,' Ivanka Trump mentions the need for affordable childcare and paid parental leave.[52] For women who were concerned about what her father's campaign rhetoric and surprise electoral college win would mean for their rights, there was a strand of

---

[47] Barack Obama, State of the Union address, 20 January 2015.

[48] Steven Pressman, 'Beast of Burden: The Weight of Inequality and the Second Obama Administration,' in Clodagh Harrington, ed., *Obama's Washington: Political Leadership in a Partisan Era* (ISA, 2015).

[49] Barack Obama, Presidential Proclamation, Mother's Day, 6 May 2016.

[50] National Partnership for Women and Families poll, 28–31 January 2016.

[51] 'Most Important Problems,' Gallup ongoing poll.

[52] Ivanka Trump, *Women Who Work: Rewriting the Rules for Success* (Portfolio, 2017).

optimism that the president's favourite daughter may have his ear on matters she prioritised. The presence at the 2016 Republican National Convention of this thirty-something bi-lingual recent convert to Judaism and mother of three offered a powerful extension of Brand Trump. The soft power of the First Daughter reached beyond her father's specific and limited appeal. Taking the podium prior to her father's nomination acceptance speech, she stated 'As a mother myself, of three young children, I know how hard it is to work while raising a family. And I also know that I'm far more fortunate than most.'[53]

At an event in Aston, Pennsylvania on 13 September 2016, with Ivanka the tempering presence at his side, Donald Trump laid out his plans for paid parental leave, which included the prospect of six weeks of paid maternity leave. The plan would be funded by decreasing the cost of insurance fraud.[54] Responses from critics and Democrats were suitably dismissive (not least because the plan only mentioned mothers), but others gave the Republican candidate credit for engaging with an issue that his party predecessors had avoided or rejected outright. Even the most optimistic observers may have wondered how Trump would square his plan with such influential colleagues as Mike Pence, who had previously voted against a proposal to offer four weeks paid maternity leave to federal employees. In addition, Steve Bannon's *Breitbart* had penned an article in 2015 which overtly criticised Obama's mandatory paid maternity leave plans. Nonetheless, Trump was at least talking about a plan and offering some specifics. Trump's fact sheet stated that the plan 'will rewrite the tax code to allow working parents to deduct from their income taxes childcare expenses for up to four children and elderly dependents.' The Trump proposal also included additional spending rebates through the Earned Income Tax Credit making if more feasible for stay-at-home parents to deduct their expenses. The offer would not apply to those earning more than $250,000, or households of more than $500,000.[55]

In May 2017, the administration released a budget, which called for a paid parental leave programme set in the existing unemployment insurance system. According to the budget, states would be required to implement six-week paid parental leave policies, with scope to decide

---

[53] Ivanka Trump speech, Republican National Convention, 21 July 2016.

[54] Donald Trump Childcare speech, Aston, Pennsylvania, 13 September 2016.

[55] Fact Sheet: Donald J Trump's New Childcare Plan (undated).

how they would administer proceedings.[56] From that point onwards, observers noted that the administration fell silent on the matter. However, it received a brief mention in the 2018 State of the Union speech in the same breath as workforce development and utilising worker potential, stating, 'let us support working families by supporting paid family leave.'[57] As a result, the topic was back in the news, as reports circulated of working plans between Ivanka and Marco Rubio. In an interview, Rubio told *Politico* that he was in favour of supporting the plan.[58] There is little doubt that owning this topic would allow the GOP to score a win in a traditionally Democrat realm. The party of social conservatism could have confidence in gaining a majority of the white female vote. However, for many of those women who voted against Trump, the election was a unifying moment. If the GOP was to woo potential future votes beyond the non-college educated white married demographic, they would need to revisit their women's rights agenda.

THE WOMEN'S MARCH

On 21 January 2017, the biggest march on Washington since the Vietnam War took place.[59] This was one of hundreds of such events across the nation, alongside more than 80 worldwide. Previous presidents have witnessed protests against their inauguration, most recently that of George W. Bush. However, the scale of the anti-Trump gatherings was significant. The organisers laid out their principles in relation to the protection of a range of rights and their concerns about what the rhetoric an agenda of the new administration may mean for women and girls across America. Activist Naomi Klein voiced her worry with regard to the new administration's 'drive to denigrate women.'[60] Although the international days of protest were dubbed 'women's march,' they consisted not only of female protesters and estimated numbers were 4 to

---

[56] Lauren Carroll, 'Guarantee 6-Week Paid Leave,' Politifact.com, 16 January 2017.

[57] Donald Trump, State of the Union address, 30 January 2018.

[58] Seung Min Kim, 'Ivanka, Rubio Find a New Project: Paid Family Leave,' Politifact. com, 4 February 2018.

[59] Jeremy Pressman and Erica Chenowith, University of Connecticut, University of Denver, figures for 500 women's marches compiled (2017).

[60] The Women's March: Principles, https://www.womensmarch.com/principles/; Naomi Klein interview, 20 January 2017, www.democracynow.org.

5 million approximately.[61] The message pertaining to rights was a broad and inclusive one, spanning immigration and health care, gay rights and climate change, worker's rights and religious freedom, with placards reminding onlookers that women's rights were human rights.

In January 2018, the anniversary women's march had a more focused theme of 'Look Back, March Forward.' If the 2017 gatherings were to protest what might be, the following year, attention was firmly on calling out the administration's actions in relation to issues such as immigration, healthcare and Planned Parenthood funding cuts. In addition, the 2018 mid-terms and associated lining up of female candidates were paramount. The same week, Donald Trump addressed the 'March for Life' which has taken place in Washington DC annually since the Supreme Court ruled on *Roe V Wade* in 1973. Unlike his Oval Office predecessors, Trump made his remarks live via satellite from the White House rose garden.[62] Much was made of this unprecedented show of support for the anti-abortion movement. In 2017, Mike Pence and Kellyanne Conway had attended but this was a new level of executive engagement. Marjorie Dannenfelser, president of the Susan B. Anthony List, the country's largest anti-abortion political action committee declared that 'President Trump's video address to the March for Life is a crowning moment in a partnership that began before he was elected.'[63]

CONCLUSION

The history of civil rights progress in the USA has continuously demonstrated that when achievements are won, an ensuing period of acceptance or even complacency is far from inevitable. Like democracy itself, social progress can be undermined or unravelled, hence care must be taken to maintain and sustain whatever hard-won gains are made. The 2016 election starkly disproved any assumptions that women voters would universally line up to support the nation's first female presidential nominee. For many, issues of class and culture eclipsed those of gender. Through his words and deeds, President Trump has done much to deepen his country's political divide, not least on issues relating to women's rights.

---

[61] Pressman and Chenowith, 500 marches (2017).

[62] Donald Trump address via video-link to the March for Life, 19 January 2018.

[63] Susan B Anthony (SBA) press release, 17 January 2018.

However, it may be possible to move beyond the antagonistic rhetoric and political manoeuvres to consider how his administration might bring some practical improvements to the lives of American women. Donald Trump is first and foremost a business man, and as president, it is evident that there are certain topics, including the economy and jobs, that are authentic priorities for him. In addition, the influence of the First Daughter is noteworthy. Ivanka Trump's parental leave plan, for all of its shortcomings, is nonetheless a potentially significant step forward on behalf of a Republican party that has chosen to ignore or rebuke previous efforts on this front. It is possible that the president may listen to the arguments for the economic benefits of women maintaining bodily autonomy and being supported in balancing the needs of their family planning and careers. There is every sign to date that he is increasingly leaning towards the supporters on his religious right, with whom the above message does not resonate. It is clearly politically expedient for him to talk the pro-life evangelical talk. However, there is potential for him to marry these messages to working American parents with a practical aspect, letting them know that if they are going to give birth to children that there will be a federal parental leave plan in place to support them. There is scope here for a strand of unity via a government policy that is genuinely pro-family, rather than simply pro-birth. The nation is divided, and a majority of women voted against Donald Trump in 2016. Many are concerned about what the remainder of his presidency may mean for the social landscape of their country. Additional appointments of conservative justices to the Supreme Court along with federal level judicial appointees may result in the tightening of women's rights, reproductive and otherwise. It is no small irony that the Trump victory has galvanised progressive women in a way that Hillary Clinton would have struggled to. At this time of national rancour, the president has the opportunity to display political skill by offering some meaningful initiatives that could transcend the partisan divide and benefit children, parents and the national economy.

REFERENCES

Baker, Greg. 'The Final Year.' HBO Documentary, 2018.
Trump, Donald. *The Art of the Deal.* New York: Ballantine, 1987.
Trump, Ivanka. *Women Who Work: Rewriting the Rules for Success.* Portfolio, 2017.

CHAPTER 9

Trumpism, Conservatism and Social Policy

Alex Waddan

Through the 2016 election campaign, there was a constant commentary that candidate Donald J. Trump was running as a populist, challenging the established norms of contemporary political behaviour. Often this challenge simply took the form of provocative performance as he belittled political opponents and media outlets in a manner designed to maximize controversy and therefore garner even more publicity. There was also a sense, however, that he was upsetting the ideological rules that arranged the partisan apple cart. While he doubled down on conventional Republican thought in some areas, such as increasing spending on the military, in others he appeared to rebuke Republican orthodoxy. These instances rarely stretched beyond rhetoric into carefully crafted statements of policy, but the cases where he did step away from prevailing conservative ideas did fit with the notion that he was advancing a populist agenda.

Perhaps the most explicit example of this was his attack on the merits of free trade, but there was also an underlying message that he was not a small government conservative in the mould of the Republican Party's leaders in Congress, particularly House Speaker Paul Ryan who

A. Waddan (✉)
University of Leicester, Leicester, UK
e-mail: Aw148@leicester.ac.uk

© The Author(s) 2019
M. Oliva and M. Shanahan (eds.), *The Trump Presidency*,
The Evolving American Presidency,
https://doi.org/10.1007/978-3-319-96325-9_9

was committed to reform of the major social programmes, including the highly popular programmes serving the country's seniors, Medicare and Social Security. Hence, candidate Trump appeared to be shifting away from the model of conservatism that had been at the core of Republican thinking since the Reagan era. This message was delivered most forcibly in the early stages of the campaign when Trump criticized his rivals for the Republican nomination who did support the party's long-term plans to reform the big entitlement programmes. Positioning himself in more traditionally Democrat territory, he declared that these programmes, the bulwark of the American welfare state, should not be downsized. On the other hand, Trump did not align with the Democrats on other fundamentals of social policy. Echoing Republican memes of the previous six years, he constantly attacked the Affordable Care Act (ACA), almost always derisively referred to as "Obamacare", whatever the evidence that this law benefitted many of those Americans that he claimed to want to help. Trump's preference, in a previous life, for government-run health care, as expressed to Larry King in 1999, had long gone: "If you can't take care of your sick in the country, forget it, it's all over. I mean, it's no good. So I'm very liberal when it comes to health care. I believe in universal health care. I believe in whatever it takes to make people well and better." (Politico Staff 2017)

Given these inconsistencies, the purpose of this chapter is to investigate how consistently and successfully Trump's candidacy transferred into his presidency. First, did he stick with his campaign goals of a "terrific" health care replacement for the ACA and persuade Speaker Ryan to keep his hands off Social Security and Medicare? Second, did his actions amount to an identifiable Trumpism in social policy? And, if so, to what extent did it diverge from, or converge with, the party of Reagan?

CONSERVATISM AND SOCIAL POLICY FROM REAGAN TO TRUMP

The significance of Trump's supposed populism, his capture of the Republican Party, and what this might mean for the development of social policy, is best understood in the context of the opposition to "big Government" that had become conservative orthodoxy since the 1980s. In a clear statement of intent, if not what always turned out to be practice, President Reagan's first inaugural address defined the mood of contemporary conservatism: "In this present crisis, government is not the solution to our problem; government is the problem". The new president went on to add, "We are a nation that has a government—not the other way around. … It is time to check and reverse the growth of government, which shows signs of having grown beyond the consent of the governed" (Reagan 1981).

President Reagan's success in implementing his preferred agenda, transforming the American political and policy landscape in the manner of a president of reconstruction (Skowronek 1993), remains contested even over 25 years after he left office. In an oft-cited interpretation of the 1980s, Paul Pierson (1994) makes a powerful case for emphasizing the durability of social policy programmes and the limits of a "Reagan revolution". Key figures involved in promoting the original project were divided as to their own success, with some disappointed (Stockman 1986), but others more willing to celebrate the changes that did take place (Anderson 1988). What is clear, however, is that the "age of Reagan" (Wilentz 2008), which continued long past his presidency, witnessed an emboldened conservative movement that promoted ideas associated with thinkers such as Milton Friedman (1962) and pushed Republicans to roll back the state in key areas of social policy, rather than seeking to win office and accommodate to a liberal consensus on the appropriate role of government in the manner of Presidents Eisenhower and Nixon. According to one conservative commentator, Henry Olson (2017), conservatives had in fact over interpreted Reagan and moved to a more anti-government position than he properly occupied, but even if this is an accurate portrayal of Reagan's personal beliefs, the Reagan legacy within conservative circles has been an emphasis on cutting taxes whenever possible and rolling back the major programmes of the American welfare state.

Ironically, perhaps the most significant example of the ideology of Reaganism bearing legislative fruit came when a Democrat occupied the White House. As a candidate in 1992, Governor William J. Clinton had tried to occupy a political space that simultaneously drew on areas of traditional Democratic strength, while also acknowledging the enduring importance of the Reagan legacy in both political and policy terms. This strategy secured a path to the White House, but in Skowronek's typology (1993), this cast Clinton as a pre-emptive president, benefitting from favourable weather at the time of the election but needing to navigate in what was still a hostile climate. One central feature of Clinton's efforts to establish a political identity that suited this environment was his campaign promise to "end welfare as we know it"; here, welfare referred specifically to the Aid to Families with Dependent Children (AFDC) programme, which paid cash benefits to very low-income households with children, most of whom were families led by single mothers.

As it was, Clinton's own legislative proposal, advanced in 1994, made minimal impact, but once Republicans captured Congress in the 1994 mid-term elections, the movement towards a path-breaking reform of the welfare system gathered real momentum. The final legislative path to reform was tortured and Clinton did twice veto bills that emerged from the Republican Congress, but in August 1996 Clinton finally signed the Personal Responsibility and Work Reconciliation Act (PRWORA) (see Weaver 2000, for a full account of the history of welfare reform efforts and the legislative process through 1995 and 1996). This reform, which imposed much tougher work requirements on welfare recipients and placed lifetime time limits on beneficiaries, was a triumph of conservative ideas (Béland and Waddan 2012) and belatedly reinforced Reagan's legacy (Davies 2003).

Yet, while rolling back welfare in the form of AFDC was a significant win for conservatives, the major pillars of the American welfare state, Social Security and Medicare remained firmly in place as President Obama left the White House. And, unlike AFDC, these two programmes were very popular and had proven resilient in the face of retrenchment efforts. Moreover, the Medicaid programme, sometimes referred to as "welfare medicine", had also not only survived through the Reagan and Bush presidencies, but it had been significantly expanded as part of the ACA, aka "Obamacare". Leading post-Reagan conservatives, however, lamented these developments and, at least in principle, wished to reform these programmes in ways that increased the level of individual choice.

Early in his presidency, Reagan himself had broached the idea of reducing Social Security benefits, even for some current recipients. This plan was justified on the basis that the programme was in financial distress. The economic downturn of the 1970s had undermined the sustainability of the so-called Trust Fund whereby the benefits paid out by the programme, which were indexed to increases in the cost of living, were funded by the payroll taxes collected from employees and employers. As inflation had hit hard in the middle and latter part of the decade, the overall volume of payments to Social Security beneficiaries had risen, but the revenues coming in to the Trust Fund did not keep pace. This was a real, rather than a politically constructed, problem, but there was little appetite for the Reagan administration's proposed method of stabilizing the programme. This distaste for cuts to benefits extended to congressional Republicans as well as Democrats (Derthick and Teles 2003: 184), forcing the administration to step away from its proposals and to establish the bipartisan National Commission on Social Security reform, better known as the Greenspan Commission with reference to its chair, Alan Greenspan, and charging that body to identify solutions. After complex negotiations, the Greenspan Commission's report provided the basis for the 1983 amendments to the Social Security Act (Berkowitz 2003). These changes did include some retrenchment of the programme by increasing the retirement age to 67 over time, but, critically, reinforced the underlying principles of the Social Security system by increasing the payroll tax rather than cutting benefits in order to provide increased fiscal stability.

This episode was particularly damaging to conservative visions of downsizing the US welfare state's largest programme, establishing Social Security's reputation as the "third rail" in American political life ("touch it and die"). According to Martha Derthick and Steven Teles (2003: 182), the administration's "Ill-conceived proposals … brought a savage Democratic counter-attack and made Republican politicians vulnerable on the issue for decades to come". As Andrea Campbell (2003) has persuasively argued, Social Security is an exemplar of a policy creating an activist community of supportive constituents, who are primed to mobilize if they feel that their benefits are threatened. In this context, the difference between the political fates of AFDC, which did not generate an equivalent body of support with the capacity for effective political organization, and Social Security, is very evident.

Despite this evidence, however, by the end of the Clinton presidency conservative voices were again making the case for Social Security reform, and this was a cause adopted by the Bush administration. The rationale for reform was once again that the Trust Fund was running into financial trouble, though that was a much longer-term prospect than had been the case in the early 1980s and was really an effort to construct a "need to reform" (Cox 2001), in order to justify an ideological project. In order to avoid a repeat of the 1980s, however, the Bush administration hoped that it would avoid a backlash from existing Social Security recipients by leaving the system in place for existing beneficiaries, while offering more choice for current workers planning their retirement options.

The Bush plan, delayed from his first term but announced as a priority after his re-election, was designed to alter both the fiscal and philosophical logics underpinning the programme's arrangements over the long term, while avoiding short-term pain. One primary reason for Social Security's popularity is that it is widely perceived to be an "earned entitlement", as people pay into the system while working and therefore earn the defined benefits they get later in life. In the language of social policy, this means that Social Security is a social insurance programme rather than a universal one (Béland and Waddan 2017), but in reality nearly all Americans do qualify for payments and the federal government is at the centre of the programme's organization as it collects and distributes the monies involved. At the heart of the Bush plan, however, was a proposal to give individuals the opportunity to "carve out" a proportion of their payroll tax contributions, allowing them to invest that money in an individual retirement account. Such a change would have constituted a partial privatization of the scheme and fundamentally undermined its inherent social solidarity.

President Bush had earlier explained his ambitions in his 2004 State of the Union address: "Younger workers should have the opportunity to build a nest egg by saving part of their Social Security taxes in a personal retirement account. We should make the Social Security system a source of ownership for the American people" (Bush 2004). This concept of "ownership" was central to conservative thinkers in the 2000s, as it promised an alternative, individualized, model, to that of state-provided benefits. Fred Barnes, a conservative advocate and champion of the Bush administration, even suggested that "the phrase *ownership society* could someday enter the lexicon of presidential trademarks" and stand alongside the New Deal and Great Society (Barnes 2006: 126). Less enthusiastically, E. J. Dionne (2006) summed up the "ownership society" as "a political project designed to increase Americans' reliance on private markets for their retirements … The idea was that broadening the 'investor class', a totemic phrase among tax-cutting conservatives, would change the economic basis of politics – and create more Republicans".

As it was, President Bush's decision to prioritize Social Security reform in 2005 marked the beginning of the end stage of his domestic presidency. Despite strong support from conservative groups and think tanks and a concerted effort by the White House to promote the plan, including a 60-day presidential tour, described by presidential scholar George Edwards as "perhaps the most extensive public relations campaign in the history of the presidency" (Edwards 2007: 284), congressional Republicans, just as they had in the 1980s, kept their legislative distance from their president. In fact, the more the administration publicized its plan, the more hostile public opinion became (Ross 2007: 423). Hence, even for those Republican members of Congress supportive of the principles behind a partial privatization of Social Security, the evidence was clear that the third rail was still electrified and still highly politically dangerous.

Overall, therefore, Republican efforts to smoothly navigate the distance between small government lip and existing government programme cup sometimes left much spilt on the floor. Nevertheless, it remained the case that if Republicans wanted to be regarded as serious minded conservatives, then they would still push a small government agenda calling for reform of entitlement programmes: and, through the Obama presidency, Paul Ryan from Wisconsin, first from his position as chair of the House Budget Committee and then as Speaker of the House, emerged as the leading intellectual and political figurehead promoting these ideas (Chait 2012). Mitt Romney chose Ryan as his running mate in 2012, and in his speech to the Republican national convention accepting the nomination as Vice Presidential candidate, Ryan (2012) spoke in the most Ayn Randian terms: "None of us have to settle for the best this administration offers – a dull, adventureless journey from one entitlement to the next, a government-planned life, a country where everything is free but us".

As Romney and Ryan slipped to defeat in 2012, it looked as if this meant that a further extension of government's role in socio-economic in the shape of the ACA would become firmly entrenched before the GOP was in an institutional position to repeal that law. As it was, however, just as they had been since the early 1990s, Republicans continued in their effective opposition to efforts by Democrats to reform the US health care system. Through 1993 and 1994, this opposition helped see off President Clinton's reform effort, and, even though they were unable to stop the passage of the ACA in 2010, the party maintained its opposition to the new law, with many Republicans at state level doing much to obstruct the implementation of key aspects of the law (Béland et al. 2016). In addition, the party continued to campaign against "Obamacare" in federal and state elections from the 2010 mid-terms onwards, with evidence that this was a particularly effective ploy in 2010, helping the party to sweeping gains in all levels of election (Saldin 2010).

Before moving on to look at the methods employed by Republicans to oppose the ACA, it is worth delving into the reasons for conservative angst about the prospects of Democrats successfully bringing about reform. Much, of course, lies with objections in principle to the idea of greater government intervention in and regulation of any area of socio-economic policy. In addition, a more basic political instinct was in play. Republicans feared that if Democrats were successful, then that would not only expand the tentacles of the welfare state but in doing so would expand the appeal of the Democratic Party. The implications of this potential double whammy were explicitly addressed in a memo sent around in December 1993 by the highly influential conservative commentator, Bill Kristol. Kristol, widely respected amongst Republican leaders for the "power of his ideas" (Johnson and Broder 1997: 233), was adamant that President Clinton's Health Security Act had to be beaten back by any means necessary. Kristol (1993, 2013) insisted that legislative negotiation was not an option and that Republicans should "adopt an aggressive and uncompromising counterstrategy designed to delegitimize the proposal and defeat its partisan purpose". Kristol's fear was that an expansion of the government's role in the American health care system could "revive the reputation of the party that spends and regulates, the Democrats, as the generous protector of middle-class interests".

A similar logic was again a feature of the Republican response to President Obama's reform effort in 2009. Steven Brill recounts events at a gathering of Republican luminaries on the night of Obama's inauguration. Gathered at the home of Republican pollster Frank Luntz, discussion turned to health care with agreement on the need to defeat any plan that would expand government-funded entitlements. According to Brill (2015: 93), Luntz explained how those present expected that some of the more moderate members of the congressional caucus might start to negotiate with the Democrats, but that these efforts would lead nowhere. The prevailing "sense was that we'd let them play along but then come up with the arguments and the polling that would get them to drop out". Furthermore, ideological discipline would be enforced by outside groups such as the Club for Growth, which had emerged as a major player in conservative circles during the Bush era, who were quite prepared to fund advertising campaigns against Republicans contemplating co-operating with Democrats (Hulse 2009).

Importantly, even after the passage of the ACA and the re-election of President Obama in 2012, opposition to its implementation remained vigorous, with all means of obstruction employed. This involved imme-diate legal challenges with half the states' attorney generals joining in suits filed against the law. Most state governments refused to co-operate in establishing state-level health insurance marketplaces, which placed the federal government under pressure to set up online systems that it initially could not cope with (Kliff 2013). Even more consequentially, after a Supreme Court decision in summer 2012 ruled that the ACA's intended means of expanding the Medicaid programme constituted fed-eral government over-reach (Waddan 2013), many states controlled by Republicans chose not to participate in the Medicaid expansion, which had been seen by the law's framers as a critical way of providing health insurance to people living below or close to the poverty line. Thus, at the start of 2018, there were 4 million people across 19 states that remained ineligible for Medicaid, but who would have qualified for the programme if the ACA had been implemented as it was intended to be by the Obama administration and congressional Democrats (Garfield and Damico 2017).

In addition to these actions, congressional Republicans repeatedly voted to "repeal" Obamacare during Obama's presidency. While much of this was more performance art than serious legislating, since any-thing that arrived on President Obama's desk would be vetoed (Harris 2016), it did send the message that the ACA was not settled law and that Republicans would still try to repeal it should they take all the levers of power again in Washington, DC.

CANDIDATE TRUMP AND THE 2016 CAMPAIGN

As commentators on American politics prepared their briefings on the upcoming Republican Party presidential primary battle in spring of 2015, there seemed little likelihood of much rhetorical dissent from the Ryanesque social policy agenda, whatever the problems in terms of how that might actually be implemented. Candidates were always more likely to display their fidelity to tax cuts and the mantra of repealing Obamacare more prominently than giving details of plans for entitle-ment reform, but the all round commitment to "small government" was an established part of conservative and Republican ideology. There was a reticence to go back to the Bush blueprint for Social Security reform from 2005, but if mostly dressed up as plans to save Social Security, vari-ous candidates expressed their support for either introducing an element of personal accounts into Social Security or pursuing other reforms that would undo the collectivist foundations of the programme.

Amongst those who were expected to be serious candidates for the nomination, Senator Ted Cruz of Texas announced one of the more aggressive reform plans for the Social Security programme, which included both benefit retrenchment and the introduction of a form of personal accounts: "for younger workers we should gradually raise the retirement age, we should have benefits grow more slowly, and we should allow them to keep a portion of their taxes in a personal account that they control, and can pass on to their kids" (Cruz 2015). Florida's Senator Marco Rubio talked of the need to save Social Security by increasing the retirement age, "reducing the growth of benefits for upper income seniors" and encouraging people to save in a wider portfolio of accounts (Rubio 2015). Former Florida Governor Jeb Bush shied away from following in his brother's footsteps on Social Security, but talked of raising the retirement age and talked, if somewhat imprecisely, about increasing the choice of plans available under Medicare (Killough 2015b). New Jersey's Governor, Chris Christie, staked out his ground as the person who would tell the hard truths about the need for entitlement reform, "I will not pander. I will not flip-flop. I am not afraid to tell you the truth as I see it, whether you like it or not", which included reducing or even eliminating Social Security benefits for wealthier Americans (Killough 2015a). Kentucky's Senator Rand Paul (2015) reflected that raising eligibility ages was "the only way you fix Medicare, the only way you fix Social Security". He also insisted, "You will also have to means-test the benefits". The surgeon Ben Carson spoke, if in rather vague terms, of giving people the chance to opt out of the Medicare programme, explaining that once people saw the details of his plan they would support his ideas: "When people are able to see how much more freedom they will have, and how much more flexibility they will have, and how much more choice they would have, I think it's going to be a no-brainer" (quoted in Cheney and Millman 2015).

These collections of sentiments did not exactly amount to a consensus on how to move forward with entitlement reform, but they generally paid homage in one way or another to the idea that even popular entitlement programmes needed reforming. Into this intellectual and ideological tangle stepped Donald Trump, in full populist mode, denouncing as nonsense plans to scale back the schemes benefitting American seniors. In fact, this was a stance that Trump had previously articulated. Speaking at the high profile annual Conservative Political Action Conference meeting in 2013, shortly after the 2012 defeat of Mitt Romney with Paul Ryan on the ticket, he had told his audience, "As Republicans, if you think you are going to change very substantially for the worse Medicare, Medicaid and Social Security in any substantial way, and at the same time you think you are going to win elections, it just really is not going to happen", adding that amongst those opposed to any such reform efforts were many Tea Party supporters (McLaughlin 2013).

Interestingly, the political scientists Theda Skocpol and Vanessa Williamson backed up Trump's contention that opposition to entitlement reform went beyond Democrats and liberals. In their examination of the Tea Party, Skocpol and Williamson (2012: 60–64) found that many of those who identified themselves with the Tea Party saw Social Security and Medicare as earned benefits, which beneficiaries were properly entitled to receive, and which they did not want changing. Furthermore, this attitude was not based on liberal stereotypes of Tea Partiers as people ignorant about the government's role in these social programmes. Skocpol and Williamson found that their respondents were largely aware that leaving Social Security and Medicare in their existing form ran counter to conservative orthodoxy about the merits of programme privatization. Hence, Trump's strategy in the primary of emphasizing that he differed from the Republican conventional wisdom with regard to entitlement programmes was not misplaced: And he clearly stated that he was not going to threaten these popular pillars of the American welfare state. As early as May 2015, he tweeted, "I was the first & only potential GOP candidate to state there will be no cuts to Social Security, Medicare & Medicaid" (Trump 2015). When a poll in October 2015 showed Trump trailing Ben Carson, Trump promptly attacked Carson's ideas for Medicare reform: "You know, Ben wants to knock out Medicare, I heard that over the weekend … I think abolishing Medicare, I don't think you're going to get away with that one" (Gass 2015).

On the other hand, while Trump ploughed his own furrow on the established entitlement programmes, he was very much in tune with Republican, and Tea Party, attacks on Obamacare. In July 2015, he blasted the programme, declaring, "It's gotta go… Repeal and replace with something terrific" (Ferris 2015). Towards the end of the general election campaign, at a campaign rally in Florida, he promised that reform would be quickly done:

Together we're going to deliver real change that once again puts Americans first. That begins with immediately repealing and replacing the disaster known as Obamacare. My first day in office, I'm going to ask Congress to put a bill on my desk getting rid of this disastrous law and replacing it with reforms that expand choice, freedom, affordability. You're going to have such great health care, at a tiny fraction of the cost—and it's going to be so easy. (Fox News 2016)

Overall, therefore, the Trump campaign sent a series of mixed messages on social policy. Like all Republicans over the previous six years, he campaigned hard against Obamacare, but, particularly during the primaries, he had been keen to distinguish himself from other Republicans with regard to Social Security and Medicare, as he promised that he would not look to bring change to those programmes. As he took office in January 2017, it was the first of those promises that quickly came into focus as a Republican President, with Republican majorities in both House and Senate, was expected to do what the party's leaders had been promising since the spring of 2010.

PRESIDENT TRUMP, CONGRESS AND HEALTH CARE

The effort through the spring and summer of 2017 to actually "repeal and replace" Obamacare reinforced how much easier it is to oppose, than constructively to propose, change in complex areas of public policy. In addition, as congressional Republicans struggled to find a formula to replace, rather than simply repeal, the 2010 health care law, President Trump's detachment from the details of policy and general disinterest in what that replacement might actually look like became increasingly evident. When pressed during the campaign for more details on what his "terrific" plan might be, he vaguely answered, "If somebody has no money and they're lying in the middle of the street and they're dying, I'm going to take care of that person". In case anyone mistook the meaning of that answer he added, "That doesn't mean single payer" (Richardson 2016).

In office, his language was barely more precise. At the end of February 2017, in a meeting with the chief executives of leading insurance companies the president told them once again how bad Obamacare was: "Obamacare has been a disaster and is only getting worse". He then promised that he would soon reveal a "fantastic plan", which "will be a great plan for the patients, for the people, and hopefully for the companies …It's going to be a very competitive plan", which would help reduce health care costs (Luhby 2017). Bizarrely, however, this came at the almost the exact time that he told a meeting of the country's governors, "We have come up with a solution that's really, really I think very good", infamously going on to say of the health care system, "Now, I have to tell you, it's an unbelievably complex subject … Nobody knew health care could be so complicated" (Liptak 2017). While this last remark was presumably a throwaway line rather than a considered one, it is suggestive of someone who had not closely followed the tortured, over a year long, process that led to Obamacare in the first place.

Nevertheless, the intensity of Republican opposition to Obamacare since 2010 seemed to indicate that the law had little shelf life to come once the GOP controlled the White House and Congress. House Speaker Paul Ryan had explicitly predicted as much in January 2016 when President Obama had been forced to use his veto to preserve the law after Congress had used the reconciliation process to repeal the ACA. Hence, although the ACA did survive, Ryan was able to reflect: "We have now shown that there is a clear path to repealing Obamacare without 60 votes in the Senate… So, next year, if we're sending this bill to a Republican president, it will get signed into law. Obamacare will be gone" (Harris 2016). And, fifteen months later, if unconvincingly, Ryan did manage to corral his caucus into action. In early spring of 2017, the original moves in the House to enact a repeal and replace measure were withdrawn due to unanimous opposition from Democrats and a combination of complaints from moderate Republicans and their conservative counterparts in the House Freedom Caucus. Eventually, however, enough concessions were made to the latter group to move the American Health Care Act (AHCA) through the House. There was little love for the AHCA, but the bill was welcomed by conservatives as a staging post, and as something that could be significantly refined after Senate passed its version of a bill, leaving a Conference Committee with the task of coming to a satisfactory settlement. The President was so enamoured of this development that he organized a Rose Garden ceremony of the sort normally reserved for when a final bill has been passed (O'Keefe et al. 2017).

Yet, notwithstanding this excitement, there was not a further Rose Garden moment to celebrate actual Obamacare repeal in 2017.

The Senate failed to match the House's action, despite multiple itera-
tions of reform bills and even after employing the reconciliation process, which meant that only 50 votes were needed since Vice President
Mike Pence would be able to cast a decisive vote. The GOP did only
have a slender 52-48 majority in Senate, and since there was little effort
to reach across the aisle to win over any moderate Democrats, the task
was to find a compromise that would keep those members together,
which was always likely to be problematic. The difficulty for the Senate
Majority Leader, Mitch McConnell from Kentucky, who had developed
a reputation as a formidable tactician, willing to push the boundaries
of accepted congressional practise (Weissmann 2017), was to maintain
harmony between the more hard line conservative and moderate wings
of the party. The latter was a much-diminished grouping from decades
gone by, but with the chamber's vote counting maths so tight the legislative process depended on virtual GOP unanimity, thus empowering the
handful of moderate voices left in the caucus.

An underlying problem for Republicans was that the Congressional
Budget Office (CBO) repeatedly estimated that the plans under consideration would end up leaving over 20 million more Americans uninsured (Kaplan and Pear 2017). In this context, the issue was how to
construct a replacement bill that would not have such potentially damaging impact, which satisfied conservative principles: And here, the problem was exacerbated by the reality that Obamacare was itself based on
a pre-existing conservative framework (Quadagno 2014), which had
been developed in the early 1990s at the conservative think tank, the
Heritage Foundation, as an alternative to President Clinton's then plan.
The ACA was certainly not a replica of that plan, but key parts of the
ACA borrowed from ideas about how to extend insurance while limiting
the extent of direct government encroachment into the health insurance
market.

Through the Obama presidency, however, Republicans had vigorously
denounced Obamacare as a government takeover, regardless of the manner in which the ACA did try to use market mechanisms as well as government spending to reduce uninsurance. Hence, at least to some extent,
Republican efforts to devise replacement, as well as repeal, plans were
stymied by their own rhetoric attacking ideas previously seen as passing
a conservative smell test. Adding to this problem, Republicans needed
to find ways of preserving the very popular aspects of the ACA and this
proved more problematic than might have been expected because of the

interlocking nature of the ACA; for example, it would have been politically highly risky to repeal the bar on insurers discriminating against individuals with pre-existing conditions, yet keeping this part of the ACA in place meant that they would also have to find ways of helping insurers cover the costs of patients who were very likely to be loss bearing.

The first major push by the Republican leadership to devise a package that achieved all these objectives was known as the Better Care Reconciliation Act (BCRA), but this in fact managed to antagonize both conservatives, such as Senator Mike Lee from Utah, as well as the moderates, notably Senators Susan Collins from Maine and Lisa Murkowski of Alaska, and fell some way short of passage, going down 57 votes to 43. One feature of the BCRA effort was the manner in which the normal Senate legislative procedure, which would involve lengthy committee hearings with the possibility of multiple amendments, was effectively short-circuited. This by passing of so-called regular order was also used for subsequent efforts and itself became a point of contention. Indeed, it helped defeat the bill known as "skinny repeal", which turned out to be the closest vote in Senate. This bill, which simply repealed some of the mandates in the ACA and in fact left much of the law intact, was designed to allow Republicans to move on to a Conference Committee where they would try again to put together a package. This effort was knocked back by 51 votes to 49, with much publicity centred on Senator John McCain's dramatic, middle of the night vote against that doomed the bill (Pear et al. 2017). McCain did not give a particularly clear explanation of his motives, but his vote seemed to hinge on the matter of process and the neglect of "regular order". The focus on McCain, if understandable given that he had recently been diagnosed with a likely fatal cancer, somewhat ignored the fact that Collins and Murkowski also voted against the bill, once again proving to be the resilient opponents of their party's efforts to leave potentially many millions of Americans again struggling to afford adequate health insurance (McCarthy 2017).

One of the ironies of the efforts to repeal the ACA through 2017 was that it seemed to make the existing law more popular. From the passage of the law through to the end of the Obama presidency the ACA was underwater in terms of its popularity. As Obama prepared to leave office in December 2017, the Kaiser health tracking poll found unfavourable opinion of the ACA outrunning favourable opinion by 46% to 43%, which was consistent with its findings from May 2010, and indeed a more positive result for the law that at some of the peaks of its unpopularity; for example, from late 2013, as the insurance exchanges had a particularly shaky roll out, the poll found the ACA was often 10 points underwater. Yet, from early 2017 the ACA found itself in positive territory, with net favourable ratings peaking over the summer of 2017 as Senate discussions about repeal gathered publicity (Kaiser Family Foundation 2018).

It is important to understand, however, that the increased popularity of the ACA and failure to pass legislation in Congress repealing the law did not mark the end of the matter. The ACA is a complex arrangement and requires active government effort, rather than mere quiescence, to make it work effectively. For example, a key means by which the ACA extended insurance to low income, but not poor, households was through the so-called individual insurance marketplaces, whereby people could choose an insurance plan and receive a federal government subsidy, with the amount depending on their income, to help pay for the package they preferred. In the early years, the federal government spent generously on advertisements and outreach navigators to increase awareness of this scheme and help people complete the registration process. In summer of 2017, however, the Trump administration announced massive cuts to the advertising budget and significant reductions in funding for the navigator projects (Seervai 2017).

More directly undermining the ACA, the Tax Cut and Jobs Act (TCJA), passed in December 2017, effectively brought an end to the controversial "individual mandate", through which the ACA had ruled that people who could afford to buy insurance must do so or face a fine. This had always been the least popular part of the ACA, but by incentivizing healthy people to buy insurance the mandate helped offset costs for insurers who were now being forced to insure unhealthy individuals. Hence, the TCJA by revising the penalty to "zero" threatened the stability of insurance markets in the long term (Pear 2017). In addition, in autumn 2017 the administration declared that it would no longer continue to pay so-called cost sharing reduction (CSR) payments. CSR payments were made to insurers who participated on the individual marketplace. The nature of these plans meant that they would often include potentially significant out of pocket expenses for consumers. In order that these expenses did not deter some of those households with incomes below 250% of the federal poverty line from using their insurance, the ACA required insurers to cover some of these costs. The CSR payments were made to insurers to help reimburse them for this (Scott 2017).

The insurers were still in fact required to cover the out-of-pocket expenses, so bringing concerns that ending CSR payments would force insurers to raise premiums for other households to cover any losses.

When announcing that the government would cease CSR payments, President Trump ridiculed the payments as a "bail out" for insurance companies, but this suggested a misunderstanding of the purpose of the payments and the interlocking design of the ACA (Mangan 2017). This failure to grasp the importance of detail and comprehend how the ACA worked was seen again in his claim that repealing the individual mandate was tantamount to repealing the whole law. After the passage of the TCJA, he made the following comments to reporters:

> The individual mandate is being repealed .... that means Obamacare is repealed. Because they get their money from the individual mandate... So in this bill... we have essentially repealed Obamacare and will come up with something that will be much better, whether it's block grants or whether it's taking what we have and doing something terrific. (quoted in Wolf 2017)

It is certainly true that the individual mandate was an attempt to share risk within the American health insurance system and so effectively repealing the penalty for people, betting on their good health, who chose to forgo insurance might destabilize insurance markets, especially in the individual marketplace, but that, in itself, did not constitute Obamacare repeal. Moreover, in the months after the passage of the TCJA, there was little sign of the administration developing a coherent reform plan of its own to deal with the ongoing problems of many millions, unwillingly, being without insurance and a series of arrangements placing a huge strain on the budgets of American families, businesses and government.

TRUMPISM: BEYOND HEALTH CARE

The effort to pass a straightforward repeal of Obamacare was thwarted despite the fact the President Trump, Speaker Ryan and Majority Leader McConnell were all on the same page in their desire to achieve that goal. In this context, action on entitlement reform, where Trump had diverged so publicly from the congressional leadership, would seem unlikely. Ryan did, however, have a powerful potential ally in his cause in Mick Mulvaney, an ideologically conservative congressman from South Carolina, who had developed a reputation as a fierce deficit hawk, keen to cut entitlement programmes, and who was Trump's pick to be Director of the Office of Management and Budget (OMB). The Senate hearings to discuss Mulvaney's nomination were marked by Republican Senators, such as Tennessee's Bob Corker, urging Mulvaney to stick to his principles and to tell the new president that some of the things that he had said on the campaign trail about Social Security and Medicare were "Totally unrealistic" (quoted in Berman 2017).

As it was, the first year of the Trump administration did not see any effort at reducing or privatizing benefits for seniors, but in autumn 2017 Politico ran a report on how Mulvaney was at least still trying to push the president to alter his position. Furthermore, sourcing the story to Mulvaney himself, the report explained how earlier in the year the OMB director had proposed Social Security and Medicare reforms to the president only to be rebuffed by Trump, "No! I told people we wouldn't do that" (Grunwald 2017). Next, Mulvaney offered "disability insurance", which he described as "welfare", and the President agreed that this could be cut. Yet, the programme Mulvaney was referring to was in fact part of the broader Old Age Social security and Disability Insurance (OASDI) programme. Hence, it was not "welfare" in the same way as AFDC was described as welfare. The cuts, amounting to $70 billion over ten years, were then included in the Trump administration's budget proposal. Those cuts did not get enacted into law, but the story is another testament to Trump's inattention to detail. It also shows that Trump's desire to protect social programmes did not extend beyond the popular ones. This was also reflected in a proposal floated by the administration to reform the Supplemental Nutrition Assistance Programme (SNAP), by replacing the benefit payments with food parcels (Kirby 2018), and by plans to allow states to use waivers to introduce work requirements for the Medicaid programme.

CONCLUSION

A year into the Trump administration, the social policy record was difficult to easily summarize in either substantive or ideological terms. Despite the failure of the repeal and replace effort, the importance of the social policy changes that did take place in 2017 should not be underestimated. The salami slicing tactics with regard to the implementation of the ACA leave the stability of insurance markets in question, and the future of Medicaid looked uncertain. In fact, Trump's attitude towards the Medicaid programme offers a useful indicator of the confusion surrounding policy development. During the campaign, Medicaid would intermittently appear in Trump's speeches alongside Social Security and Medicare as a protected species, yet the Trump administration has consistently run with conservative voices in treating Medicaid as a welfare programme, which can be subject to cuts and tougher eligibility requirements. This suggests that Trump is happy to accommodate the small government party of Reagan when it seems to carry a lesser political risk and resonates with the party's base support. On the other hand, if Paul Ryan is seen as the modern manifestation of Reagan style conservatism, much remains to be done. In April 2018, Speaker Ryan announced that he would not be seeking re-election in the November 2018 mid-term elections. At the time he said that much of his agenda had been accomplished, yet the reality was that his ambitious plans for major entitlement reform of Social Security and Medicare remained a distant prospect.

REFERENCES

Anderson, Martin. *Revolution*. New York: Harcourt Brace, 1988.

Barnes, Fred. *Rebel in Chief: Inside the Bold and Controversial Presidency of George W. Bush*. New York: Crown Forum, 2006.

Béland, Daniel, and Alex Waddan. *The Politics of Policy Change: Welfare, Medicare and Social Security Reform in the United States*. Washington, DC: Georgetown University Press, 2012.

Béland, Daniel and Alex Waddan. "Why are there no universal social programs in the United States." *World Affairs Journal*, 180 (1) (2017): 64–92.

Béland, Daniel, Philip Rocco, and Alex Waddan. *Obamacare Wars: Federalism, State Politics, and the Affordable Care Act*. Lawrence: University Press of Kansas, 2016.

Berman, Russell. "Will Trump Cut Medicare and Social Security?" *The Atlantic*, 24 January 2017. https://www.theatlantic.com/politics/archive/2017/01/will-trump-cut-medicare-and-social-security/514298/.

Campbell, Andrea Louise. *How Policies Make Citizens: Senior Political Activism and the Welfrare State*. Princeton, NJ: Princeton University Press, 2003.

Chait, Jonathan. "The Legendary Paul Ryan." *New York*, 29 April 2012. http://nymag.com/news/features/paul-ryan-2012-5/.

Cheney, Kyle, and Jason Millman. "Dr. Ben Carson's Prescription: Abolish Medicare." *Politico*, 22 October 2015. https://www.politico.com/story/2015/10/ben-carson-medicare-medicaid-215055.

Cox, Robert. "The Social Construction of an Imperative." *World Politics*, 53 (2001): 463–98.

Cruz, Ted. http://www.ontheissues.org/2015_FoxBiz_GOP.htm. *Fox Business/ Wall Street Journal Two-Tier 2015 GOP Primary Debate*, 2015.

Davies, Gareth. "The Welfare State." In W. Elliot Brownlee and Hugh Davis Graham, eds., *The Reagan Presidency: Pragmatic Conservatism and Its Legacies*, 209–32. Lawrence, KS: University Press of Kansas, 2003.

Derthick, Martha, and Steven Teles. "Riding the Third Rail: Social Security Reform." In W. E. Brownlee and H. Davis Graham, eds., *The Reagan Presidency: Pragmatic Conservatism and Its Legacies*, 182–208. Lawrence, KS: University Press of Kansas, 2003.

Dionne, E. J. "Rove's New Mission: Survival." *Washington Post*, 21 April 2006: A23.

Ferris, Sarah. "Trump: I'll Replace Obamacare with Something Terrific." *The Hill*, 2015. http://thehill.com/policy/healthcare/249697-trump-replace-obamacare-with-something-terrific.

Fox News. "How the ObamaCare Lie Is an Opportunity for Trump; Trump Family Talks Importance of Millennial Vote." *Transcript of the 'Hannity Show'*, 25 October 2016. http://www.foxnews.com/transcript/2016/10/25/how-obamacare-lie-is-opportunity-for-trump-trump-family-talks-importance.html.

Friedman, Milton. *Capitalism and Freedom*. Chicago: University of Chicago Press, 1962.

Garfield, Rachel, and Anthony Damico. *The Coverage Gap: Uninsured Poor Adults in States that Do Not Expand Medicaid*, 2017. https://www.kff.org/uninsured/issue-brief/the-coverage-gap-uninsured-poor-adults-in-states-that-do-not-expand-medicaid/.

Gass, Nick. "Trump Attacks Carson: Ben Wants to Knock Out Medicare." *Politico*, 27 October 2015. https://www.politico.com/story/2015/10/donald-trump-criticize-ben-carson-medicare-medicaid-215181.

Grunwald, Michael. "Mick the Knife." *Politico Magazine*, September/October, 2017. https://www.politico.com/magazine/story/2017/09/01/mick-mulvaney-omb-trump-budget-profile-feature-215546.

Harris, Gardiner. "Obama Vetoes Bill to Repeal Health Law and End Planned Parenthood Funding." *New York Times*, 8 January 2016. https://www.nytimes.com/2016/01/09/us/politics/obama-vetoes-bill-to-repeal-health-law-and-end-planned-parenthood-funding.html.

Hulse, Carl. "Conservative Group Takes Aim at Gang-of-Six Republicans." *New York Times*, 20 August 2009. https://prescriptions.blogs.nytimes.com/2009/08/20/conservative-group-targets-gang-of-6-republicans/.

Johnson, Haynes, and David Broder. *The System: The American Way of Politics at the Breaking Point*. Boston: Little, Brown and Company, 1997.

Kaiser Family Foundation. *Kaiser Health Tracking Poll: The Public's Views on the ACA*, 2018. https://www.kff.org/interactive/kaiser-health-tracking-poll-the-publics-views-on-the-aca/#?response=Favorable--Unfavorable&a-Range=all.

Kaplan, Thomas, and Robert Pear. "Senate Health Bill in Peril as C.B.O. Predicts 22 Million More Uninsured." *New York Times*, 26 June 2017. https://www.nytimes.com/2017/06/26/us/politics/senate-health-care-bill-republican.html?mcubz=3.

Killough, Ashley. "In New Hampshire, Chris Christie Spells Out Entitlement Reform Plan." *CNN Politics*, 15 April 2015a. https://edition.cnn.com/2015/04/14/politics/chris-christie-new-hampshire-2016-elections/.

Killough, Ashley. "Jeb Bush Rolls Out Proposals for Social Security, Medicare." *CNN Politics*, 27 October 2015b. https://edition.cnn.com/2015/10/27/politics/jeb-bush-entitlement-plan-social-security-medicare/index.html.

Kirby, Jen. "Trump Wants to Replace Food Stamps with Food Boxes, for Some Reason." *Vox.com*, 13 February 2018. https://www.vox.com/2018/2/13/17004636/snap-trump-budget-food-stamps-food-boxes.

Kliff, Sarah. "Inside the Obamacare War Room, HealthCare.gov's Launch Was Chaos." *Washington Post*, 6 November 2013. https://www.washingtonpost.com/news/wonk/wp/2013/11/06/inside-the-obamacare-war-room-healthcare-govs-launch-was-chaos/?noredirect=on&utm_term=.129f48762552.

Kristol, William. *Memorandum to Republican Leaders*, 2 December 1993. Reprinted https://www.scribd.com/document/12926608/William-Kristol-s-1993-Memo-Defeating-President-Clinton-s-Health-Care-Proposal.

Liptak, Kevin. "Trump: Nobody Knew Health Care Could Be so Complicated." *CNN Politics*, 28 February 2017. https://edition.cnn.com/2017/02/27/politics/trump-health-care-complicated/index.html.

Luhby, Tami. "Trump Promises Health Insurance Ceos Will Like His 'Fantastic Plan' for Obamacare." *CNN Money*, 27 February 2017. http://money.cnn.com/2017/02/26/news/economy/health-insurers-trump-obamacare/index.html.

Mangan, Dan. "Trump Is Wrong—The Government Wasn't Giving Obamacare Insurers a 'Bailout'." *CNBC*, 18 October 2017. https://www.cnbc.com/2017/10/18/trump-is-wrong-obamacare-insurers-werent-getting-a-bailout.html.

McCarthy, Tom. "Susan Collins and Lisa Murkowski: The GOP Senate Duo Keeping Trump in Check." *The Guardian*, 27 July 2017. https://www.theguardian.com/us-news/2017/jul/27/susan-collins-lisa-murkowski-senate-republicans-healthcare.

McLaughlin, Seth. "CPAC 2013: Donald Trump: Immigration Reform Is a 'Suicide Mission' for GOP." *The Washington Times*, 15 March 2013. https://www.washingtontimes.com/news/2013/mar/15/cpac-2013-donald-trump-immigration-reform-suicide-/.

O'Keefe, Ed, Paige Winfield Cunningham, and Amy Goldstein. "House Republicans Claim a Major Victory with Passage of Health-Care Overhaul." The *Washington Post*, 4 May 2017. https://www.washingtonpost.com/powerpost/republicans-plan-health-care-vote-on-Thursday-capping-weeks-of-fits-and-starts/2017/05/03/e7dd7c28–306d-11e7-9dec-764dc781686f_story.html?noredirect=on&utm_term=.eb9ab17c421b.

Olsen, Henry. *The Working Class Republican: Ronald Reagan and the Return of Blue-Collar Conservatism*. New York: Harper Collins, 2017.

Pear, Robert. "Without the Insurance Mandate, Health Care's Future May Be in Doubt." *New York Times*, 18 December 2017. https://www.nytimes.com/2017/12/18/us/politics/tax-cut-obamacare-individual-mandate-repeal.html.

Pear, Robert, Thomas Kaplan, and Emily Cochrane. "Health Care Debate: Obamacare Repeal Fails as McCain Casts Decisive No Vote." *New York Times*, 27 July 2017. https://www.nytimes.com/2017/07/27/us/politics/senate-health-care-vote.html.

Pierson, Paul. *Dismantling the Welfare State? Reagan, Thatcher, and the Politics of Retrenchment*. New York: Cambridge University Press, 1994.

Politico Staff. "18 Confusing Things Donald Trump Has Said About Health Care." *Politico*, 20 July 2017. https://www.politico.com/magazine/story/2017/07/20/18-confusing-contradictory-and-just-plain-kooky-things-donald-trump-has-said-about-health-care-215402.

Quadagno, J. "Right-Wing Conspiracy? Socialist Plot? The Origins of the Patient Protection and Affordable Care Act." *Journal of Health Politics, Policy and Law*, 39 (1) (2014): 35–56.

Reagan, Ronald. "Inaugural Address." Online by Gerhard Peters and John T. Woolley. *The American Presidency Project*, 20 January 1981. http://www.presidency.ucsb.edu/ws/?pid=43130.

Richardson, Bradford. "Trump Promises to 'Work Something Out' on Health Care." *The Hill*, 31 January 2016. http://thehill.com/blogs/ballot-box/presidential-races/267673-trump-promises-to-work-something-out-on-healthcare.

Rubio, Marco. "Saving Social Security in the 21st Century." *National Review*, 15 August 2015. https://www.nationalreview.com/2015/08/saving-social-security-21st-century-marco-rubio/.

Ryan, Paul. "Transcript: Rep Paul Ryan's Convention Speech." *NPR*, 29 August 2012. https://www.npr.org/2012/08/29/160282031/transcript-rep-paul-ryans-convention-speech.

Saldin, R. "Healthcare Reform: A Prescription for the 2010 Republican Landslide?" *The Forum*, 8 (4) (2010).

Scott, Dylan. "Trump Is Readying His Nuclear Option on Obamacare." *Vox*, 31 July 2017. https://www.vox.com/policy-and-politics/2017/4/20/15306068/ trump-obamacare-hostage-threat-cost-sharing-explained.

Scott, Dylan. "Read: Paul Ryan's Announcement That He Will Retire from the House." *Vox*, 11 April 2018. https://www.vox.com/policy-and-politics/2018/4/11/17224976/paul-ryan-retiring-statement.

Seervai, Shannor. "Cuts to the ACA's Outreach Budget Will Make It Harder for People to Enroll." *The Commonwealth Fund*, 11 October 2017. http://www.commonwealthfund.org/publications/features/2017/slashing-aca-funding.

Skocpol, Theda, and Vanessa Williamson. *The Tea Party and the Re-making of Republican Conservatism*. Oxford: Oxford University Press, 2012.

Stockman, David. *The Triumph of Politics: The Crisis in American Government and How It Affects the World*. London: Coronet Books, 1986.

Waddan, Alex. "Health Care Reform After the Supreme Court: Even More Known Unknowns." *Journal of Health, Economics, Policy and Law*, 8 (1): 139–43.

Weaver, R. Kent. *Ending Welfare as We Know It*. Washington, DC: Brookings Institution Press, 2000.

Weissmann, Jordan. "Mitch McConnell, Master Tactician: The Majority Leader Shreds Senate Norms and Gets His Way." *Pittsburgh Post-Gazette*, 22 June 2017. http://www.post-gazette.com/opinion/Op-Ed/2017/06/22/Mitch-McConnell-master-tactician/stories/201706220042.

Wilentz, Sean. *The Age of Reagan: A History, 1974–2008*. New York: Harper Collins, 2008.

Wolf, Byron. "Donald Trump Thinks He Just Quietly Repealed Obamacare." *CNN*, 21 December 2017. https://edition.cnn.com/2017/12/20/politics/donald-trump-thinks-he-tricked-everyone-into-repealing-obamacare/index.html.

PART III

Winning Away

CHAPTER 10

"Stability Not Chaos"? Donald Trump and the World—An Early Assessment

Maria Ryan

When the businessman Donald J. Trump campaigned for the Presidency of the USA, he presented himself as a radical and disruptive outsider in almost every respect. Trump's popularity with his core Republican base was premised on his willingness to speak frankly about what he, and they, saw as the corruption of Washington by vested interests—pledging to "drain the swamp" of lobbyists—and the influence of a cosmopolitan liberal elite that was responsible for the displacement of American workers and the rise of a "politically correct" multiculturalism that supposedly displaced and devalued white Americans and privileged non-whites and other minorities.[1] Trump's pledge to "Make America Great Again" also appeared to entail a rejection of what he called "the false

[1] On the economic, cultural and political reasons for Trump's victory see Davis, 'Election 2016'; Wypijewski, 'Politics of Insecurity'; Riley, 'American Brumaire?'; Zevin, 'De Te Fabula Narratur,' and Anderson, 'Passing the Baton' all contained in the special edition of *New Left Review* (January/February 2017).

M. Ryan (✉)
University of Nottingham, Nottingham, UK
e-mail: Maria.ryan@nottingham.ac.uk

M. Oliva and M. Shanahan (eds.), *The Trump Presidency*,
The Evolving American Presidency,
https://doi.org/10.1007/978-3-319-96325-9_10

song of globalism": the elite bipartisan consensus on US global leadership that had dragged the country into its longest running war to date in Afghanistan and a second quagmire in Iraq.[2] While these conflicts drained blood and treasure "everyday," Americans struggled in an austere economy with wage stagnation and a rising cost of living.[3] Trump promised national renewal—ostensibly nation-building at home and an end to what he referred to in his inauguration speech as "this American carnage."[4] He was sceptical of international commitments "that tie us up and bring America down." Against the prevailing globalism of the established order, Trump claimed that it was "The nation-state [that] remains the true foundation of happiness and harmony."[5] As such, Trump declared, "I'm not isolationist but I am America first."[6]

The use of the phrase "America first," which was closely associated with pre-World War Two isolationism in the USA (and even tinged with anti-Semitism), ostensibly signalled a sharp departure from the existing norms of US foreign policy.[7] Trump's nationalist rhetoric suggested to many that, as President, he would drastically re-orient the country's economic and political priorities. A rupture in the Western world order was widely expected.[8] For many, Trump's first year did indeed entail a substantive shift in US policy.[9] For others, Trump's nationalism seemed to signal "an abrupt turning inward, entailing a narrower definition of the national

---

[2] Hattem, 'Trump Warns Against "False Song" of globalism.'

[3] Shambaugh and Nunn, 'Why Wages Aren't Growing in America' and Stokes, 'Trump, American Hegemony, and the Future…'.

[4] Trump, Inaugural Address. Dueck asserts that nation-building at home was at the core of the "Obama Doctrine." See his *Obama Doctrine*.

[5] Hattem, 'Trump Warns Against "False Song" of Globalism.'

[6] Trump, Transcript: 'Donald Trump Expounds on His Foreign Policy Views,' henceforth Trump *NYT* interview.

[7] Calamur, 'A Short History of America First,' Doenecke, ed., *In Danger Undaunted*.

[8] See, for example, Ikenberry, 'The Plot Against American Foreign Policy'; Quinn, 'With Trump in Charge, the World Will Change'; Keylor, 'The Future of the Atlantic Alliance Under President Trump'; Anon., 'Donald Trump and the New World Order.'

[9] Barry Posen claims Trump has 'Ushered in an Entirely New U.S. Grand Strategy: Illiberal Hegemony.' See 'The Rise of Illiberal Hegemony.' According to Adam S. Posen, Trump "challenges almost all the fundamental aspects of the United States' global role and the values the country has professed for the last 70 years." See "The Post-American World Economy." See also Margon, 'Giving Up the High Ground: America's Retreat on Human Rights.'

interest."[10] Within three months of his inauguration, however, Trump had begun to revert, on issue after issue, to policies much closer to the recent historical norm, that is to the pursuit of global primacy within an economic and political order conducive to the interests of the West.[11] This chapter will argue that despite Trump's nationalistic *rhetoric* and his unprecedented tendency towards impetuous showmanship, which would at times prove destabilising, in substantial policy terms the Trump administration largely defaulted to existing—and usually long-standing—US policy on an array of issues in its first year. I argue here that the seeds of this lie not in "luck" or in a realisation that governing was more difficult than campaigning (although it's certainly possible that Trump thought this).[12] The roots of his conventional foreign policy lie in Trump's own foreign policy preferences, as expressed in his Presidential campaign, though often obscured by his nationalist rhetoric. While Trump the candidate could not necessarily speak in coherent or very knowledgeable terms about grand strategy, the policies he did espouse did not eschew US global leadership and did not offer a radical or serious alternative to the established norms of US foreign policy in the post-Cold War world. Moreover, several of his key cabinet appointees were conventional conservatives when it came to foreign policy, and they reinforced Trump's own tendency towards more conventional foreign policy options. This meant that on almost every international issue it dealt with in the first year of office, the new administration reverted on a case-by-case basis to policy more in line with the Obama and Bush years. The net result of this was an approach that was not necessarily identical to his predecessors, but did nevertheless lead to the de facto continuation of the existing global order. Whether this will last for the duration of Trump's tenure—however long that may be—is an open question. The biggest threat to Trump's objectives is the President himself, whose course personal style and tendency towards knee-jerk and impetuous reactions may undermine the global leadership he claims to aspire to.

[10] Haslam, 'The Significance of the Trump Presidency.'

[11] Eliot Cohen makes this point but claims that Trump's "Version of the Republican Normal" was down to "good fortune, not restraint, and the resistance of subordinates rather than the boss' growth." See his "Trump's Lucky Year." On the history of the Western liberal order and its beneficiaries, see Stokes and Raphael, *Global Energy Security and American Hegemony*, Bacevich, *American Empire*; Ikenberry, *Liberal Leviathan*.

[12] On "luck" see Cohen, 'Trump's Lucky Year.' On being President, Trump admitted after 100 days in office that 'I Thought It Would Be Easier.' See Adler, Mason and Holland, 'Exclusive: Trump Says He Thought Being President...'.

THE ELITE CONSENSUS AND THE TRUMP CAMPAIGN

Since the end of the Cold War, an elite consensus on the fundamental objectives of US foreign policy has proved remarkably durable.[13] While Republicans and Democrats have often differed on the methods that should be utilised to achieve US goals, more often than not they agreed on the basic objectives of global strategy. Since the end of the Cold War, both Republicans and Democrats have been committed to the preservation of the USA's position as the world's sole superpower.[14] Even with the rise of other "great" powers—like China, India and Russia—the USA's determination to extend its hegemony for as long as possible led both parties in Washington to endorse the maintenance of a worldwide military establishment comprised of more than 700 bases in over 70 countries and military interventions in every region of the world.[15] US military power ultimately undergirds an "open" economic system that relies on freedom of the seas, political stability (though not necessarily democracy) and the unimpeded transfer of goods and capital around the world.[16] In doing this, Washington has shaped and guaranteed an economic order from which it and its allies derive disproportionate benefits.

Trump's nationalistic rhetoric during the 2016 Presidential campaign ostensibly suggested a radically different course of action. Over the course of two interviews with the *New York Times* devoted exclusively to foreign policy in March 2016, Trump first eschewed the "isolationist" label in favour of an "America first" approach. Although as a candidate he did not rule out foreign interventionism per se—notoriously pledging to "bomb the shit out of [ISIS] ... and take the oil"—Trump had come to the conclusion that "We should never have been in Iraq."[17] He wanted to re-negotiate the terms of America's engagement

---

[13] On elites and on the historical parameters of US policy, see Parmar, *Foundations of the American Century*, Abelson, *A Capitol Idea*; Kuklick, *Blind Oracles*; Ikenberry et al., *Crisis of American Foreign Policy*; Bacevich, ed., *Short American Century*.

[14] See Bacevich, 'Ending Endless War.' See also Brands, *Making the Unipolar Moment*, pp. 336–62 and Kagan, *Paradise and Power*.

[15] Vine, *Base Nation*; Salazor Torreon, '"Instances of Use of United States" Armed Forces Abroad.'

[16] See Stokes and Sam Raphael, *Global Energy Security and American Hegemony*; Agnew *Hegemony*.

[17] Trump, Remarks on ISIS. *Politico* Staff, Full Transcript.

with the world. The two core elements of US foreign policy that Trump disputed concerned alliances and free trade. Security alliances had traditionally been viewed as a way of anchoring other states into the American-led order, but Trump focused on the cost to the USA of maintaining an expansive overseas military presence capable of defending US allies. Under a Trump administration, he claimed, countries that had historically relied on an American security guarantee—such as South Korea, Japan and members of the North Atlantic Treaty Organization (NATO)—would have to contribute more financially to the cost of their own defence. He told the *New York Times* "we're not being reimbursed for the kind of tremendous service that we're performing by protecting various countries."[18] Trump derided NATO—America's foremost and oldest security alliance—as "obsolete": "When NATO was formed many decades ago we were a different country. There was a different threat." The demise of the Soviet Union brought the continued existence of the anti-communist alliance into question.[19]

Trump also disputed elements of the neoliberal trading regime the USA had been instrumental in extending. The North American Free Trade Agreement (NAFTA) , in effect since 1994, and the Trans-Pacific Partnership (TPP), which the Obama administration had spent six years negotiating, were bad for America, sending "our jobs, our wealth and our factories... overseas."[20] "This wave of globalization has wiped out totally, totally, our middle class" he claimed.[21] Trump was not wrong to point out that neoliberal globalisation had caused the rise of widespread economic precariousness and inequality in the West, and the outsourcing of blue-collar industrial jobs to Asia, leading to the deindustrialisation of parts of the USA (the so-called rust belt). Globalisation had been promoted by US elites because, as Hal Brands remarks, it had been "rejuvenating for American power"—but it was also "excruciating for many Americans."[22] When Trump won the Presidency, his victories in the previously Democratic "Mid West" states of Iowa, Wisconsin, Michigan,

[18] Trump *NYT* interview.

[19] Ibid.

[20] Gillespie, 'Trump Hammers America's "Worst Trade Deal"'; Woolf, McCurry, Haas, 'Trump to Withdraw from Trans-Pacific Partnership,' Trump, Speech on Trade.

[21] Trump, Speech on Trade.

[22] Brands, *Making the Unipolar Moment*, p. 346. See also Spence, 'Globalization and Unemployment.'

Ohio and Pennsylvania indicated the salience of economic insecurity to his appeal in the rust belt, where the Electoral College votes turned the national election decisively in his favour.[23] In the context of a bipartisan embrace of neoliberalism since the 1980s—NAFTA was signed by a Republican President and passed through Congress under a Democratic President—Trump's repeated questioning of the free-trade agenda resonated profoundly with Americans who had suffered decades of wage stagnation, disappearing jobs and growing inequality.

A Revisionist Interpretation of Trump's Campaign

On the basis of his comments about US allies, NAFTA and the TPP, the incipient Trump approach to the world was labelled "isolationist" (or "neo-isolationist"), "transactional" and "protectionist"—all of which were viewed as serious challenges to the existing order.[24] Yet the perception that Trump the candidate offered a substantive departure (as opposed to a stylistic one) from existing US foreign policy was inaccurate. To be sure, Trump could be inconsistent and appeared completely unembarrassed about contradicting himself (and remains so as President).[25] He could not speak coherently about grand strategy. Nevertheless, Trump the candidate did possess a recognisable and distinct global outlook. He was an internationalist, who believed that US interests were global in scope and that protecting them required the projection of US power, but also a realist: he firmly rejected what he saw as the nation-building and democracy promotion of the Bush and Obama administrations.

Trump's positions on alliances and global trade were critical to the perception that he rejected a business-as-usual foreign policy. Yet a detailed examination of his statements demonstrates that he did not reject the *concept* of alliances or the *principle* of free trade. With regard to alliances, what Trump claimed he wanted was for these to be fully reciprocal. US allies, he claimed, "look at the United States as weak and

---

[23] Brownstein, 'How the Rustbelt Pave Trump's Road to Victory.'

[24] Krauthammer, 'Trump's Foreign Policy Revolution'; Keylor, 'The Future of the Atlantic Alliance'; Hadar, 'The Limits of Trump's Transactional Foreign Policy'; Graceffo, 'Trump's New Protectionism.'

[25] *Washington Post*, Trump Fact Checker.

forgiving and feel no obligation to honor their agreements with us."[26] Of the US–Japanese alliance, he said: "If we are attacked, they don't have to do anything. If they're attacked, we have to go out with full force... That's a pretty one-sided agreement."[27] His objection to NATO was not because he favoured isolationism or rejected the principle of multilateralism, but on the basis that the alliance was designed during the Cold War to fight the Soviet Union, that it was allegedly not doing enough to fight terrorism, and because "the United States bears far too much of the cost." Trump argued that the principal threat facing the West had changed. Apparently unaware of NATO's role in Afghanistan and its members' contributions to the campaign against ISIS, Trump claimed that the Organization "has to be changed to include terror." He subsequently even suggested establishing "a new institution" to fight terrorism but one that "would be more fairly based... from an economic standpoint."[28] In fact, Trump claimed, "We should work together with any nation in the region that is threatened by the rise of radical Islam. *But this has to be a two-way street*" (my italics).[29] In other words, Trump accepted the principle of collective international action but was concerned with burden-sharing. This complaint from American leaders with regard to the NATO alliance was not uncommon or unprecedented.[30] In 2006, NATO members agreed that each state should aim to spend 2% of GDP on national defence, but by 2016 only five countries, including the USA, were actually doing so.[31] In April 2016, President Obama spoke

[26] Trump, 'Foreign Policy Speech,' 27 April 2016, https://www.nytimes.com/2016/04/28/us/politics/transcript-trump-foreign-policy.html?_r=1 (30 November 2017).

[27] Trump *NYT* interview.

[28] Trump *NYT* interview. Obama noted in 2016 that all 28 Nato member states were contributing to the campaign against ISIS. See Remarks by President Obama in Address to the People of Europe, Hannover, Germany, 25 April 2016, https://obamawhitehouse.archives.gov/the-press-office/2016/04/25/remarks-president-obama-address-people-europe (28 November 2017).

[29] My emphasis. Trump, speech April 2016.

[30] As Keylor comments, Presidents Eisenhower and Kennedy also complained about the European allies' preference for butter over guns at the expense of the American taxpayer. See 'The Future of the Atlantic Alliance.' More broadly, Joyce P. Kaufman notes that there have always been transatlantic disputes in Nato. See 'The U.S. perspective on Nato Under Trump.'

[31] Appathurai, Press Remarks. Page, 'Defence Expenditure: Nato 2% Target.'

in Hannover, Germany, and chided NATO members for "complacency" about their own defence and not "contributing [their] full share—2% of GDP—towards our common security."[32] Trump's delivery of this message was less diplomatic than Obama's, but on the substance of the message there was bipartisan agreement.

Trump was also asked in his long *New York Times* interview whether he would be willing to withdraw US forces from Japan and South Korea "if they don't increase their contribution significantly" to the cost of the US military presence there. "Yes, I would" said Trump, but "*I would not do so happily*, but I would be willing to do it. *Not happily*" (my italics). This suggested that Trump's preference was to remain in Asia but with a greater financial contribution from its allies. When asked whether he would object to Japan and South Korea developing nuclear weapons to counter the North Korean threat, Trump suggested that if this occurred it would reflect poorly on the USA as an ally:

> ...if the United States keeps on... its current path of weakness, they're going to want to have [nuclear weapons] anyway... because I don't think they feel very secure in what's going on with our country... You know, if you look at how we backed our... allies – it hasn't exactly been strong. When you look at various places throughout the world, it hasn't been very strong. And I just don't think we're viewed the same way that we were 20 or 25 years ago, or 30 years ago.[33]

In a campaign speech in September 2016, he claimed he would "be uncompromising in the defence of the United States and our friends and allies."[34] Under Obama, he claimed, "our friends are beginning to think they can't depend on us.... To our friends and allies, I say America is going to be strong again."[35] This suggested that Trump believed that the USA had global interests and that the credibility of American power was determined by the support it gave to its allies worldwide—a long-standing premise of US internationalism.

---

[32] Obama, Address to the People of Europe.
[33] Trump *NYT* interview.
[34] Trump, Address to American Legion Convention.
[35] Trump speech April 2016.

Often Trump seemed less inclined to sanction major military interventions, especially the use of ground troops. He told the *New York Times* "we cannot be the policeman of the world." Yet here too his position was far from radical. Trump pledged to continue fighting ISIS in Iraq and Syria, but would avoid seeking to topple the Assad regime because ISIS was the greater problem.[36] This was essentially the same as the Obama administration's position: avoid dragging the USA into a costly ground war against ISIS, conduct drone strikes against alleged extremists and attempt to arm the anti-ISIS opposition but not with weapons that would constitute a threat to the regime.[37] Trump was reluctant to outline the precise circumstances under which he would deploy US troops abroad arguing "You cannot just say that we have a blanket standard all over the world because each instance is totally different." In other words, foreign interventionism was not off the table but just depended on the circumstances—hardly an unconventional position. Similarly, Trump refused to rule out using force in the South China Sea in order to maintain a sense of strategic ambiguity over US intentions—the long-standing US policy towards China's maritime claims.[38] In fact, Trump even claimed he would not rule out humanitarian intervention. When asked whether he was in favour, he replied "Yes, I would be... depending on where and who and what. And, you know, again generally speaking – I'd have to see the country; I'd have to see what's going on in the region and you just cannot have a blanket [standard]."[39]

However, the most salient characteristic of Trump's international outlook was his rejection of nation-building. He expressed admiration for the realist internationalism of President George H. W. Bush and his handling of the Persian Gulf War in 1991: "he did the right thing. He went in, he knocked the hell out of Iraq and then he let it go, O.K.? He didn't

---

[36] Trump told the *NYT*: I'm not saying Assad is a good man, "cause he's not, but our far greater problem is not Assad, it's ISIS...." For similar comments, see Trump speech April 2016 and Trump, President-Elect Rally in Cincinnati.

[37] Blanchard and Belasco, *Train and Equip Program for Syria*, p. 10. Allinson argues that withholding MANPADS was a sign that the US did not want to topple Assad lest it end up dragged into another ground war in the Middle East. See his "Disaster Islamism" pp. 132–33.

[38] Trump *NYT* interview and Bernkopf Tucker, 'Strategic Ambiguity Or Strategic Clarity?'

[39] Trump *NYT* interview.

go in... He didn't get into the quicksand and I mean, history will show that he was right."[40] In Cincinnati in September 2016, Trump claimed: "We are going to end the era of nation-building, and create a new foreign policy – joined by our partners in the Middle East – that is focused on destroying ISIS and Radical Islamic Terrorism." This approach, not isolationism, was "the cause of Americanism."[41] In a post-election victory rally, again in Cincinnati, he was even more explicit: the Trump administration would "stop looking to topple regimes and overthrow governments... Our goal is stability not chaos, because we want to rebuild our country."[42] The Bush and Obama years had "made the Middle East more unstable and chaotic than ever before." "It all began" he claimed, "with a dangerous idea that we could make western democracies out of countries that had no experience or interest in becoming a western democracy." This had created "confusion and disarray, a mess" and so "We're getting out of the nation-building business and instead focusing on creating stability in the world." In other words, the goal to which the US global presence was directed would change under Trump, but foreign policy would remain global. An "America first" foreign policy did not mean a rejection of global activism where the objective was the protection of US interests, but it did mean a rejection of regime change and nation-building.

Trump's most ostensibly radical commitment was to economic protectionism. This was not a wholesale rejection of neoliberal trade in all circumstances, but he pledged to impose import tariffs on goods from Mexico (35%) and China (45%) unless China revalued its currency and Mexico re-negotiated the NAFTA on terms more favourable to the USA.[43] How this protectionism would work in practice—in other words, how Trump would avoid spiralling into trade wars—and how he could marry his protectionism with some form of international cooperation with regard to security affairs was never explained. Trump's anti-NAFTA rhetoric, which converged easily and conveniently with his anti-Clinton hyperbole (on account of her long-standing support for free-trade agreements and her husband's stewarding of NAFTA through Congress), was a

---

[40] Ibid.

[41] Speech: Trump Addresses American Legion Convention.

[42] Trump, 'President-Elect Rally in Cincinnati.'

[43] Haberman, 'Donald Trump Says He Favours Big Tariffs on Chinese Exports' and Lawder and Rampton, 'Trump's Tariff Plan Could Boomerang, Spark Trade Wars.'

prominent feature of Trump's campaign. His proposed alternative received relatively little attention during the campaign because Trump spent most of his time criticising existing free-trade agreements rather than discussing what might actually replace them. Again, however, his proposed alternative was not a major departure from the *status quo*. "I'm a big believer in free trade. I like free trade," Trump told a campaign rally in Iowa.[44]

However, instead of multilateral free-trade agreements like NAFTA and the TPP, Trump favoured *bilateral* free-trade agreements on the grounds that multilateral accords—especially large ones like the TPP—required more compromises and were difficult to disengage from, whereas agreements with only one other party required fewer compromises were easier to leave and were therefore "fair" to the USA.[45] In his inimitable style, Trump explained that the rejection of the TPP paved the way for

> one-on-one trade deals that protect and defend the American worker... but they'll be one-on-one. They won't be a whole big mash pot....And if that particular country doesn't treat us fairly we send them a 30-day termination... And then they'll come and say 'please don't do that' and we'll negotiate a better deal during that 30 day period. The other way [multilateral] you can't get out of it. It's like quicksand.[46]

Negotiating new unique free-trade agreements with all eleven TTP participants (never mind re-negotiating them within 30 days if necessary) was an ambitious goal that would likely take many years—if other countries would agree to it. Nevertheless, this was not a rejection of free trade itself but of the current form of trade liberalisation. As so often in the campaign, Trump's nationalist language obscured a policy position that was far from radical.

Summarising his world view, Trump claimed "We're going to be friendly with everybody, but we're not going to be taken advantage of by anybody. We won't be isolationists – I don't want to go there because I don't believe in that. I think we'll be very worldview [*sic.*], but we're not going to be ripped off anymore." Trump's nascent global outlook was therefore characterised by three interlocking premises: a belief that

[44] Anon., 'Trump Has Attacked China This Week...'.

[45] Reuters Staff, 'Trump Calls for Trade Deals with Individual Countries' and Trump, 'Speech on Trade.'

[46] Anon., 'Trump: 30-Day Termination of "Unfair" Trade Deals.'

the USA had a set of interests that were global in scope; a realist's rejection of nation-building; and an insistence that the USA was consistently being "ripped off" by others, politically, militarily and economically—in other words, he claimed, US global commitments needed to be met with greater reciprocity by its allies.

Although this approach did not depart significantly from the established parameters of post-1989 US foreign policy, there was, nevertheless, a great deal of unease and even alarm in the Republican establishment about Trump's nomination as candidate for President. Much, though not all, of this stemmed from Trump's personal conduct and his temperament as opposed to policy specifics. Two days before the 2016 Presidential election, *The Atlantic Monthly* compiled a list of 85 prominent Republicans who declared they would not vote for Trump. Many cited his personal conduct, such as his "demeaning comments about women and his boasts about sexual assaults" (John McCain) and his "constant stream of cruel comments and his inability to admit error or apologize" (Susan Collins).[47] The most withering criticism came from a group of fifty former Republican national security officials. In a public letter released in August 2016, the group claimed that Trump "lacks the character, values, and experience to be President." "He continues to display an alarming ignorance of basic facts of contemporary international politics." Lambasting his temperament and personal conduct, the officials stated that Trump

> is unable or unwilling to separate truth from falsehood. He does not encourage conflicting views. He lacks self-control and acts impetuously. He cannot tolerate personal criticism. He has alarmed our closest allies with his erratic behavior. All of these are dangerous qualities in an individual who aspires to be President and Commander-in-Chief, with command of the U.S. nuclear arsenal.[48]

Trump's personal conduct and his temperament were, undoubtedly, deeply concerning and deserving of all the opprobrium they received. It seems likely, however, that Trump's erratic and undiplomatic behaviour combined with his heightened nationalist rhetoric distracted from and obscured what was, in many ways, a relatively conventional foreign policy

[47] Graham, 'Which Republicans Oppose Donald Trump?'
[48] Ayer et al., 'Letter from G.O.P. National Security Figures Opposing Donald Trump.'

agenda. That is not to say that there were no differences between Trump and Obama or Trump and Bush or, indeed, either of the Clintons, but these differences did not amount to a radical rejection of the existing bipartisan consensus in US foreign policy. As Inderjeet Parmar has argued, the Republican establishment's dismay with Trump was likely based less on his policies and more on the belief that his "brutal rhetorical style undermines the international credibility of U.S. power [and] brings it into disrepute."[49] Trump's unique selling point constituted little more than a set of grievances based on the notion that America "has been disrespected, mocked, and ripped off for many many years"—but these grievances were not translated into a strategy that repudiated the established international system.[50]

THE FIRST YEAR

Personnel Matters

By the time the novice President was inaugurated, he had appointed advisors and cabinet members that fell roughly into two groups: the equally inexperienced but highly influential close personal advisors, and the more seasoned cabinet appointees, who generally had somewhat less access to Trump but often brought government or military service to bear. The political novices included "first daughter", Ivanka Trump, appointed as special assistant to the President; her husband and Trump confidante, Jared Kushner, also a senior advisor to the President; and Steve Bannon, a former film producer and head of the ultra-conservative website Breitbart News, appointed as Trump's chief strategist.[51] Less close to the President but equally devoid of government experience was Rex Tillerson, the former CEO of Exxon Mobil, appointed as Secretary of State. These advisors' complete lack of government experience compounded Trump's own ignorance and led to chronic disorganisation in the administration's first year in office. By mid-April, there were still 108 unfilled policymaking positions at the State Department.[52]

---

[49] Parmar, 'By Refusing to Recertify Nuclear Deal...'.

[50] Trump *NYT* interview.

[51] Beavers, 'Ivanka Trump Will Have an Official White House Position'; Anon., 'Steve Bannon: Who Was Trump's Key Advisor?'

[52] Schoen, 'Help Wanted.'

By November, 60% of the Department's top-ranked diplomats ('career ambassadors') had left, 42% of the second highest rank ('career ministers') were gone, and applications to work at the Department had dropped by half—the combined result of a hiring freeze, a colossal decline in staff morale and the shuttering of whole departments by Tillerson.[53] By February 2018, there were still 227 policymaking positions across the administration (out of a total of 636) with no nominee, while a further 144 were still awaiting confirmation by the Senate (with just 236 confirmed).[54]

The second group of more experienced appointees included Trump's first National Security Advisor, Michael Flynn—the man who tweeted that fear of Islam was "RATIONAL"—who lasted less than a month after it became clear that he had lied about his ties to Russia. Flynn was replaced by the highly respected and much more conventional H. R. McMaster, a career army officer with a reputation for speaking truth (or, at least, his mind) to power.[55] With General James Mattis serving at the Department of Defense, Trump's two most important foreign policy appointees were men with military backgrounds and conventional conservative views about the US role in the world.[56] Neither offered Trump any radical foreign policy options during the first year, and at times both acted as a restraining influence on him. Both spoke openly in favour of remaining a party to the international Comprehensive Joint Plan of Action on the Iranian nuclear programme.[57] When North Korea tested a nuclear weapon apparently capable of reaching the continental USA, Trump responded that if Pyongyang launched such a weapon, "they will be met with fire and fury like the world has never seen."[58]

---

[53] Beauchamp, 'New Data Shows How the Trump Administration Is Destroying the State Department.' Trump's first budget also recommended slashing the State Department's budget by a third. See Thrush and Davenport, 'Donald Trump Budget Slashes Funds.'

[54] *Washington Post*/Partnership for Public Service, 'Tracking How Many Positions Trump Has Filled So Far.'

[55] Gibbons-Neff, 'Fear of Muslims is Rational'; Borger, 'Trump Security Adviser Flynn Resigns'; Browne, 'Who Is H.R. McMaster.'

[56] Filkins, 'Warrior in Washington.'

[57] Gibbons-Neff and Sanger, 'Mattis Contradicts Trump on Iran Deal Ahead of Crucial Deadline'; Eli Watkins, 'Tillerson: US Trying to Stay in Iran Deal,' *CNN*, 16 October 2017, http://edition.cnn.com/2017/10/15/politics/rex-tillerson-iran-nuclear-agreement-cnntv/index.html, 4 February 17.

[58] Borger and McCurry, 'Donald Trump Vows to Answer North Korea...'.

However, Tillerson reassured Americans that they could "sleep well at night" and that the President was "just reaffirming that the United States has the capability to fully defend itself from any attack." Mattis, while noting that Pyongyang "would lose any arms race or conflict it initiates," also affirmed that "our State Department is making every effort to resolve this global threat through diplomatic means."[59] Finally, Steve Bannon, the White House Chief Strategist, was demoted from his brief stint on the National Security Council (NSC), leaving McMaster in full control of the NSC.[60] This further diminished the likelihood of Trump receiving any radical policy suggestions when it came to foreign affairs.

The combination of inexperienced personal advisors, more seasoned cabinet members with conventional conservative views and a relatively conventional pre-existing foreign policy agenda as laid out in the Presidential campaign meant that Trump's first year in office was more moderate—at least when it came to foreign policy—than his nationalist rhetoric suggested it might be.

Policy Matters

Examples of Trump's reversion to existing US policy were visible at an early stage in his tenure. In his State of the Union address in February, Trump firmly rejected isolationism and again endorsed a version of realist internationalism, calling for "stability, not war and conflict" and "American leadership based on vital security interests that we share with our allies all across the globe."[61] Trump called again for NATO partners to "meet their financial obligations" agreed in 2006, but also expressed "stron[g] support [for] NATO, an alliance forged through the bonds of two world wars... and a Cold War, and defeated communism."[62] On a trip to Europe in July, he explicitly endorsed NATO's collective defence guarantee.[63] After meeting the organisation's Secretary General, Jens

---

[59] Reuters Staff, 'Factbox: Key Trump Administration Figures Shaping the North Korea Debate'; Mattis, 'Statement by Secretary of Defense.'

[60] Costa and Phillip, 'Steve Bannon Removed from National Security Council.'

[61] Trump, Joint Address to Congress.

[62] Ibid.

[63] Herb, 'What Is Article 5?'

Stoltenberg, Trump reversed his criticism of NATO, telling reporters that it "is not obsolete" and that he and Stoltenberg had had a "productive discussion about what more NATO can do in the fight against terrorism." He also acknowledged that he had made his original comments about the alliance "not knowing much about NATO" but "now I know a lot about [it]."[64] That same month Trump gave official US approval for Montenegro's accession to the alliance.[65]

Trump also committed in explicit terms to the defence of Japan when Prime Minister Shinzo Abe visited the White House shortly after the inauguration. While Trump politely called for "*both* Japan and the United States to continue to invest very heavily in the alliance to build up our... defensive capabilities" (my italics) he also stated that "The US-Japan alliance is the cornerstone of peace and stability in the Pacific region," that Washington was "committed to being an active and fully engaged partner" that would work towards an "even closer" relationship, and that the US security commitment to Japan extended to "all areas under its administrative control"—meaning it encompassed the disputed islands in the East China Sea known in Japan as the Senkaku Islands (and in China as the Diaoyu Islands).[66] When North Korea tested a ballistic missile in March, Trump pledged Washington's "ironclad commitment to stand with Japan and South Korea in the face of the serious threat posed by North Korea."[67] Secretary of Defense, Mattis, had reaffirmed the US commitment to Seoul on his trip there in February, while Vice President, Mike Pence, visiting South Korea in April, reiterated the "unbreakable bond" between the two countries and affirmed "We are with you 100%."[68]

After threatening to label China a currency manipulator during the Presidential campaign, Trump also appeared to question the long-standing "One China" policy (i.e. US non-recognition of the Taiwanese government) by taking an unprecedented congratulatory phone call from the President of Taiwan after the US election. However, in a telephone call with Chinese President, Xi Jinping, three weeks after his inauguration,

---

[64] Bertrand, "Trump: I Said Nato Was Obsolete 'Not Knowing Much About Nato'"

[65] Mitchell, 'Trump Approves Montenegro's Nato Membership.'

[66] See video clip and report in Hirschfeld and Baker, 'In Welcoming Shinzo Abe...'.

[67] Office of the Press Secretary, 'Readout of the President's Calls.'

[68] Gordon and Sang-Hun, 'Jim Mattis Seeks to Sooth Tensions'; Anon., 'Pence to South Korea.'

Trump endorsed the "One China" policy.[69] He also backtracked on a pledge to label Beijing a currency manipulator, now arguing that it was not possible to condemn the Chinese in an economic sense and also ask for their help with North Korea. ("It doesn't work that way.")[70] Despite his criticisms of China for its trade deficit with the USA during the campaign—when he called the deficit "one of the greatest thefts in the history of the world"—when Trump visited China in November 2017, he claimed that it was his predecessors in the USA who were to blame for "allowing this out-of-control trade deficit" to grow and that "I don't blame China. After all, who can blame a country for being able to take advantage of another country to the benefit of its citizens?"[71]

Despite his rejection of multilateral free-trade agreements, Trump called for bilateral agreements with Britain and Japan. Rather than abandoning NAFTA, Trump attempted to negotiate a more favourable version of the free-trade agreement.[72] Excluding Mexico and Canada, the USA had 18 other bilateral free-trade deals also in place and there were no signs in Trump's first year that the President sought to re-negotiate any of them.[73] The US remained a leading member of the World Trade Organization, which exists to promote freer trade. It was even reported in April that Trump was considering the resumption of talks on the Transatlantic Trade and Investment Partnership (TTIP) with the EU after German Chancellor Merkel made it clear that members of the EU do not sign bilateral trade deals with other countries.[74] Commerce Secretary, Wilbur Ross, commented that "the EU is one of our largest trading partners, and any negotiations legally must be conducted at the EU level and not with individual nations... Thus, it makes sense to continue TTIP negotiations and to work towards a solution that increases overall trade while reducing our trade deficit."[75]

[69] Landler and Forsythe, 'Trump Tells Xi Jinping U.S. Will Honour One China Policy.'

[70] Associated Press, Transcript of Interview with Trump.

[71] Stracqualursi, '10 Times Trump Attacked China.'

[72] Office of the United States Trade Representative, *Summary of Objectives.*

[73] Rayner, 'Donald Trump Vows to Sign "Very Big, Very Powerful" Trade Deal with UK'; Anon., 'Trump to Seek Bilateral Trade Deal With Japan...' Office of the United States Trade Representative, Free Trade Agreements.

[74] *Financial Times*, 'US Reopens Door to Reviving EU Trade Talks'; *The Times*, 'Trump Puts EU Ahead of Britain in Trade Queue.'

[75] LaRocco, 'Wilbur Ross Says He's "Open to Resuming" talks.'

Other aspects of Trump's foreign and security policies also appeared to be arcing back towards established conventions. In early February, his United Nations ambassador, Nikki Hayley, condemned Russia's activities in the Crimea, and the Obama-era sanctions against Moscow remained in place.[76] In response to Russia's interference in the 2016 US Presidential election, Congress passed a further round of sanctions against Moscow, which were denounced by the Russians as "a full scale trade war."[77] The serious and substantial allegations about the Trump campaign's collusion with Moscow during and after the Presidential election campaign made it impossible for Trump to "reset" the relationship with Russia as Obama had attempted in 2009, and as Trump himself had suggested during the campaign.

Instead, Russia, alongside China, was framed as a new great power adversary. The National Defense Strategy, released at the end of Trump's first year, painted a stark picture of a hostile world in which "inter-state strategic competition, not terrorism, is now the primary concern in US national security." The resurgence of "long-term strategic competition" by "revisionist powers"—namely China and Russia—had created "global disorder" and "a security environment more complex and volatile than any we have experienced in recent memory." In this environment, the USA would seek to "remain the preeminent military power in the world, ensure the balances of power remain in our favour, and advance an international order that is most conducive to our security and prosperity."[78] This meant a revival of US global leadership. According to the National Security Strategy: "the whole world is lifted by America's renewal and the re-emergence of American leadership" because "when America does not lead, malign actors will fill the void." The formal enunciations of US purpose under Trump thus re-framed engagement with the world through a realist lens that focused on nation states and vital interests and precluded the destabilisation associated with regime change and nation-building: "We are realistic and understand that the American way of life cannot be imposed upon others" the NSS stated.[79]

[76] Gaouette and Roth, 'UN Ambassador Hayley Hits Russia Hard on Ukraine.'

[77] Rampton and Zengerle, 'Trump Signs Russia Sanctions Bill…'.

[78] Department of Defense, Summary of the 2018 National Defense Strategy of the United States of America: 1, 2, 4.

[79] National Security Strategy of the United States of America: foreword II, 3, 4.

The renewed focus on long-term interstate competition did not mean that the administration wound down its fight against ISIS. Defeating the group remained a priority. During the campaign, Trump had claimed repeatedly that he had a secret plan to defeat ISIS that he could not reveal because "I don't want the enemy to know what I'm doing."[80] No such plan emerged in Trump's first year, which was characterised instead by a great deal of continuity with Obama's approach. The campaign of targeted assassination, via drones, continued and in some cases intensified. As well as conducting ongoing combat operations from the air in Iraq, Syria and Afghanistan, additional areas of Somalia and Yemen were declared "areas of active hostilities"—a practice inherited from the Obama administration, meaning that war zone targeting rules applied for 180 days thus giving commanders greater freedom to carry out offensive strikes.[81] In Yemen, there was a dramatic increase in the number of drone strikes: in eight years, the Obama administration conducted 162 bombings there; in just one year, the Trump administration conducted 126.[82] Extending Obama's designation of Libya as a fourth combat zone, the administration killed around 17 alleged ISIS militants in Libya in September.[83] Mattis' and Tillerson's staunch public defence of the September 2001 Congressional Authorization for the Use of Force, which came into effect seven days after 9/11, indicated the administration's determination to continue relying on Bush- and Obama-era justifications of the "war on terror" as global in scope and targeting any group that might now be linked to al-Qaeda, including groups that did not exist when the Authorization was passed.[84]

[80] Tan, 'A Timeline of Trump's Clearly Made-Up 'Secret Plan' to Fight ISIS.'

[81] Department of Defense, Operation Inherent Resolve. Bureau of Investigative Journalism, Strikes in Afghanistan. Savage and Schmitt, 'Trump Eases Combat Rules in Somalia'; Savage and Schmitt, 'Trump Administration Said to Be Working...'; Savage and Schmitt, 'Trump Poised to Drop Some Limits...'.

[82] Bureau of Investigative Journalism, Strikes in Yemen, January 2009–January 2017, and Strikes in Yemen, January 2017–Now. Zenko, 'The (Not So) Peaceful Transition of Power.'

[83] Schmitt, '17 ISIS Fighters Reported Killed.'

[84] Public Law 107–40. Senate Foreign Relations Committee, 'The Authorizations for the Use of Military Force.'

Conclusion

At a purely rhetorical level, Trump remained a hyper-nationalist in his first year, but the rhetorical nationalism that appeals so much to his base obscured an internationalist foreign policy, consistent with the basic world view he expressed during the Presidential campaign, that amounted to a realist vision of American global hegemony, characterised by a focus on material interests, a rejection of nation-building and an insistence that political, economic and military alliances be fully recipro-cal. "Stability not chaos" was always Trump's global objective.

For any other President, this might be an eminently achievable goal given the relative strength of the USA in the global order—and, indeed, at the end of his first year, Trump had not done irreparable damage to the US position. Yet the President's careless and impulsive style is a constant threat to his professed goal of US leadership. The main threat to "stability" may well come from Trump himself. His reckless tweeting in response to North Korea's missile tests could easily be misinterpreted by the paranoid regime in Pyongyang.[85] His recognition of Jerusalem as the capital of Israel—a goal espoused by other Presidents but never actually enacted—seems likely to make a peace agreement that is acceptable to the Palestinians hard to achieve.[86] Trump's personal conduct at both home and abroad undermines America's soft power appeal. In June 2017, a Pew survey across thirty-seven countries found that a median of just 22% had confidence in Trump to "do the right thing when it comes to international affairs" (compared to 64% for Obama in the final year of his Presidency).[87] Occasionally, even close allies were forced to openly condemn Trump's Twitter commentary, as did British Prime Minister, Theresa May, when the President retweeted anti-Muslim videos by the far-right xenophobic fringe group, Britain First in November 2017.[88] If Trump continues in this vein—and there is no reason why he should not give the force of his personality—it may well start to undermine the stability and leadership he claims to seek.

[85] Ryan, 'Message Confusion.'

[86] Public Law 104–45. Bump, 'In 1995, Congress Reached a Compromise...'; Khalidi, 'Trump's Error on Jerusalem Is a Disaster...'.

[87] Wike, Stokes, Poushter, and Fetterolf, 'U.S. Image Suffers.' See also Dupuy, 'Donald Trump a Loser...'.

[88] Weaver, Booth, and Jacobs, 'Theresa May Condemns Trump's Retweets.'

REFERENCES

Abelson, Donald E. *A Capitol Idea: Think Tanks & US Foreign Policy.* Montreal: McGill-Queen's University Press, 2006.

Agnew, John. *Hegemony: The New Shape of Global Power.* Philadelphia: Temple University Press, 2005.

Anderson, Perry. "Passing the Baton." *New Left Review,* 103 (January/February 2017): 41–64.

Bacevich, Andrew J. *American Empire: The Realities and Consequences of U.S. Diplomacy.* Cambridge, MA: Harvard University Press, 2002.

Bacevich, Andrew J., ed. *The Short American Century: A Postmortem.* Cambridge, MA: Harvard University Press, 2012.

Bacevich, Andrew J. "Ending Endless War: A Pragmatic Military Strategy." *Foreign Affairs,* 95, No. 5 (September/October 2016): 36–44.

Bernkopf Tucker, Nancy, ed. *Dangerous Strait: The U.S.-Taiwan-China Crisis.* New York: Columbia University Press, 2005.

Blanchard, Christopher M., and Amy Belasco. "Train and Equip Program for Syria: Authorities, Funding, and Issues for Congress." Congressional Research Service, 9 June 2015. https://fas.org/sgp/crs/natsec/R43727.pdf.

Brands, Hal. *Making the Unipolar Moment: U.S Foreign Policy and the Rise of the Post-Cold War Order.* Ithaca and London: Cornell University Press, 2016.

Doenecke, Justus D., ed. *In Danger Undaunted: The Anti-interventionist Movement of 1940–41 as Revealed in the Papers of the America First Committee.* Stanford, CA: Hoover Institution Press, 1990.

Dueck, Colin. *The Obama Doctrine: American Grand Strategy Today.* Oxford and New York: Oxford University Press, 2015.

Ikenberry, G. John. *Liberal Leviathan: The Origins, Crisis, and Transformation of the American World Order.* Princeton: Princeton University Press, 2011.

Ikenberry, G. John. "The Plot Against American Foreign Policy: Can the Liberal Order Survive?" *Foreign Affairs,* 96, No. 3 (May/June 2017): 2–9.

Ikenberry, G. John, et. al. *The Crisis of American Foreign Policy: Wilsonianism in the Twenty-First Century.* Princeton: Princeton University Press, 2009.

Kagan, Robert. *Paradise and Power: America and Europe in the New World Order.* London: Atlantic Books, 2004.

Kaufman, Joyce P. "The U.S. Perspective on Nato Under Trump: Lessons of the Past and Prospects for the Future." *International Affairs,* 93, No. 2 (2017): 251–66.

Kuklick, Bruce. *Blind Oracles: Intellectuals and War from Kennan to Kissinger.* Princeton: Princeton University Press, 2007.

Parmar, Inderjeet. *Foundations of the American Century: The Ford, Carnegie, and Rockefeller Foundations in the Rose of American Power.* New York: Columbia University Press, 2012.

Riley, Dylan. "American Brumaire?" *New Left Review*, 103 (January/February 2017): 21–32.

Ryan, Maria. "Message Confusion and Risk of Accidental War in North Korea." *The Globe Post*, 11 August 2017. http://www.theglobepost.com/2017/08/11/accidental-war-north-koreaa/, 7 December 2017.

Salazor Torreon, Barbara. "'Instances of Use of United States' Armed Forces Abroad, 1798–2016." Congressional Research Service, 7 October 2016. https://fas.org/sgp/crs/natsec/R42738.pdf, 12 May 2017.

Savage, Charlie, and Eric Schmitt. "Trump Administration Said to Be Workingto Loosen Counterterrorism Rules." *New York Times*, 12 March 2017.

Savage, Charlie, and Eric Schmitt. "Trump Eases Combat Rules in Somalia Intended to Protect Civilians." *New York Times*, 30 March 2017.

Stokes, Doug. "Trump, American Hegemony, and the Future of the Liberal International Order." *International Affairs*, 94, No. 1 (January 2018): 133–50.

Stokes, Doug, and Sam Raphael. *Global Energy Security and American Hegemony*. Baltimore: Johns Hopkins University Press, 2010.

Zevin, Alexander. "De Te Fabula Narratur." *New Left Review*, 103 (January/February 2017): 35–39.

CHAPTER 11

Trump and China:
Much Ado About Nothing

Mara Oliva

"Our President has allowed China to continue its economic assault on American jobs and wealth, refusing to enforce trade rules – or applying the leverage on China necessary to rein in North Korea."[1]

Candidates do not win elections by endorsing their predecessor's policies or their opponents' agendas, but Donald J. Trump's attacks on the Obama administration and Democratic nominee, Hillary R. Clinton, have ensured that the 2016 presidential election campaign will be remembered as one of the harshest in US history. By exploiting fear, anger and hatred, his inflammatory rhetoric often made bold but unrealistic promises of a new dawn for the country where American interests will come first. Accuracy of facts was often ignored.

---

[1] Remarks on Foreign Policy at the National Press Club in Washington, DC, 27 April 2016, http://www.presidency.ucsb.edu/index.php [accessed 1 May 2018].

M. Oliva (✉)
Department of History, University of Reading,
Reading, Berkshire, UK
e-mail: m.oliva@reading.ac.uk

© The Author(s) 2019
M. Oliva and M. Shanahan (eds.), *The Trump Presidency*,
The Evolving American Presidency,
https://doi.org/10.1007/978-3-319-96325-9_11

In the case of Sino-American relations, his message focused on Beijing's lack of respect for the USA because of President Obama's weakness and Secretary of State Clinton's incompetence. Accusing China of being a currency manipulator, a theft of intellectual property and a cyber-terrorist, he also showed a certain level of admiration for the Communist giant for being able to get away with hundreds of billions of dollars in trade deficit every year; "if they can get away with that, then hat's off to them," he declared during a press conference.[2] This trade disaster would only get worse, if the USA decided to go ahead with the Trans-Pacific Partnership (TPP), a twelve nations trade deal created by the USA to contain China's economic rise. According to Trump, the Obama administration's cornerstone of its pivot to Asia strategy would ship millions of American jobs abroad and surrender Congressional power to an international foreign commission.[3] The extreme rhetoric extended to climate and environmental issues too. After tweeting his belief that "the concept of global warming was created by and for the Chinese in order to make US manufacturing non-competitive," he repeatedly blasted Obama for wasting over $70 billion dollars on climate change activities and not prioritising the war on terror.[4]

A Trump presidency, however, would fix all these problems by keeping America out of the TPP, instructing the US Trade Representative to bring trade cases against China, withdrawing from the Paris agreement and finally, by abolishing the Environmental Protection Agency (EPA). Once in the White House, these bold statements did not survive the inevitable reality check.[5] True, during the transition period, Trump took a phone call from Taiwan president, Tsai Ing-wen, to congratulate him on his victory. But that was a "diplomatic gaffe" rather than a revolutionary move to break off with the 1972 Shanghai Communiqué' issued during Richard M. Nixon's historic visit to China.[6] On his third day in office,

---

[2] New Conference, Florida, 27 July 2016, http://www.presidency.ucsb.edu/index.php [accessed 1 May 2018].

[3] Remarks at Trump Soho in NYC, 22 June 2016, http://www.presidency.ucsb.edu/index.php [accessed 1 May 2018].

[4] Trump's tweets on 6 November 2012; 14 October 2014; and 17 November 2014.

[5] Remarks at the Economic Club of NY at Waldorf Astoria, 5 September 2016, http://www.presidency.ucsb.edu/index.php [accessed 1 May 2018].

[6] The communiqué was issued during President Richard M. Nixon's historic visit to China and effectively established a "One China" policy whereby the USA did not formally recognise the Taiwanese government; Mark Landler and Jane Perlez, 'Trump's Call with Taiwan: A Diplomatic Gaffe or a New Start?' *The New York Times*, 5 December 2016.

Trump withdrew from the TPP, only to signal fifteen months later that he might be interested in rejoining the trade partnership soon. In June 2017, then, in a speech in the White House Rose Garden, he announced the USA would withdraw from the Paris Climate Accord too. Despite these headline-grabbing declarations, in practice, Sino-American relations have more or less conformed to pattern throughout Trump's first year.[7]

After a brief discussion of the evolution of US-Chinese ties, this chapter will argue that Trump's China policy lacks a clear strategy. This uncertainty about the US role in the Pacific and its intention towards the Communist giant has not only led to a failure to implement campaign promises and thus continuity of previous administrations' policies; it has also often led to US abdication of power in the region, leaving a vacuum that Beijing has been quick to fill and leaving US long-term allies confused.

HISTORICAL CONTEXT

America's fascination with the myth of the emerging China market dates back to the nineteenth century, when traders and Christian missionaries crossed the Pacific ocean hoping to spread the American way of life to the Asian continent and, at the same time, contain the world's most populous nation by integrating it into the liberal capitalist system. The duality of this strategy often led to strained relations between Washington and Beijing, which culminated in a total breakdown in 1949, when the Chinese people favoured the Communist regime of Mao Zedong to the Nationalist government, and US ally, of Generalissimo Jiang Jieshi.[8]

Throughout the 1950s and 1960s, at the height of the Red Scare, US-China policy was caught in the Cold War game and Senator Joseph McCarthy's (R-WI) crazy anti-communist witch-hunt. Fearing the Senator might end their careers, State Department Far Eastern desk officials either left their posts or advocated support for a policy of "containment by isolation" of the newly established People's Republic of China (PRC). The lack of expertise and debate around the China question froze Sino-American relations for over twenty years. Washington refused to establish diplomatic relations with Beijing, implemented a total trade

---

[7] Michael Shear, 'Trump Will Withdraw US from Paris Climate Agreement,' *The New York Times*, 1 June 2017.

[8] Mara Oliva, *Eisenhower and American Public Opinion on China* (New York: Palgrave, 2018), pp. 15–16.

embargo following the outbreak of the Korean War in 1950 and recognised Jiang Jieshi's regime on the island of Taiwan as the only representative of the Chinese people. Only Richard M. Nixon, with his staunch anti-communist reputation, could break the "bamboo curtain" when he travelled to China in 1972. In what turned out to be the most strategic shift of the Cold War era, Washington and Beijing acknowledged that they could benefit both from a relaxation of tension and a "tacit alliance" in fighting a common enemy: the Soviet Union. Since then, all US administrations from Nixon via Clinton and Bush to Obama have followed a policy of "containment by integration" towards China. The main challenge of this approach has been to devise a strategy that would allow the USA to regain access to the China market, while at the same time preventing a rise of China that would jeopardise US hegemony in the Asian Pacific.[9]

For George W. H. Bush, the priority was to stabilise US-China relations without antagonising what the administration considered to be the other major power in Asia: Japan. Despite a few troublesome issues, such as: China's human rights record and Beijing's sale of Silkworm missiles to Iran, overall diplomatic, military and economic ties improved between 1989 and 1992. The president was especially keen on avoiding a trade war with China, which could damage US prestige and economic interests in the Pacific. Indeed, the administration set the foundations to eventually let Beijing enter the General Agreement on Tariffs and Trade (GATT).[10]

When Clinton took office in 1993, he fundamentally continued Bush's strategy, but focused predominantly on bolstering America's economic revitalisation. His national security strategy of engagement and enlargement clearly stated that it was in US interests to "further integrate China into a market-based world economy system," even if that meant sacrificing human rights issues. Indeed, while initially the administration made the renewal of the Most Favoured Nation (MFN) status dependent on China improving its human rights record, by 1994, the two were delinked and the MSF status renewed.[11]

[9] Ibid.; Evelyn Goh, *Constructing the US Rapprochement with China, 1961–1974* (Cambridge: Cambridge University Press, 2009).

[10] Michael Green, *By More Than Providence: Grand Strategy and American Power in the Asia Pacific Since 1783* (New York: Columbia University Press, 2017), p. 439.

[11] Nana de Graaff and Bastiaan van Apeldoorn, 'US-China and the Liberal World Order: Contending Elites, Colliding Visions?' *International Affairs*, 92 (2018), 113–31.

For the George W. Bush administration, the China market represented more of "serious long term challenge" rather than an opportunity for the expansion of US capital. Still, the president concurred that isolating Beijing would not be beneficial for the USA. Instead, making it part of the US-led liberal order through increased trade relations would allow Washington to keep it in check. During this time, Washington initiated more free-trade agreements in Asia than any previous administrations. It also approved China's entry into the World Trade Organisation (WTO), a process started during the Clinton years, and laid the groundwork for the TPP.[12]

Obama took the concept of engagement to the next level. Partly because of the need to shift the focus from the US disastrous involvement in the Middle East, and partly because of recognition of the rising strategic and economic importance of Asia, the administration announced a "pivot" to Asia, later renamed "rebalance." Supported by US public opinion, Obama became the first president to implement an Asia-first policy. This meant engaging unconditionally with authoritarian regimes, such as Cuba, Syria, Iran and North Korea, develop multilateralism and emphasise transnational challenges such as climate change. As his predecessor, Obama saw China both as a challenge and as an opportunity. Thus, his Asia-first policy aimed at managing this ambivalent relationship with "every element of American power." On the one hand, he tried to prevent the rise of a Sino-centric economic area by championing the TPP. He also tried to reassure other Asian countries, especially Japan, of American continuous support for stability in the area. Indeed, Secretary of State, Hillary Clinton's first trip abroad was to Asia with a first stop in Japan. He also reinforced US presence in the Pacific to deter China from its ambitious territorial plans in the South China Sea. But on the other hand, he engaged on great diplomacy on climate change.[13]

[12] Green, *By More Than Providence: Grand Strategy and American Power in the Asia Pacific Since 1783*, p. 483.

[13] Green, *By More Than Providence: Grand Strategy and American Power in the Asia Pacific Since 1783*, pp. 518–40; Campbell Kurt, *The Pivot, the Future of American Statecraft in Asia* (New York: Twelve, 2016); Badger Jeffrey, *Obama and China's Rise* (Washington: Brookings Institution Press, 2012).

Retreat and Chaos

Trump's inauguration on 20 January 2017 seemed to promise a complete rejection of all the previous administrations' efforts to facilitate US engagement in the Asia-Pacific, especially Obama's "pivot" or "rebalancing" strategy. However, besides withdrawing from the TPP on the third day in office and expressing doubts about US alliances with Japan, South Korea and Australia, the president and his team are still to formulate a coherent and clear strategy for the US role in the Pacific and their plans vis-à-vis China.

Trump rejects the US-led global liberal order on the basis that globalisation has done more harm than good to US economy. For the president, trade is both the source of all problems and source of all solutions for "American survival." He does not seem to be persuaded by the argument that trade is only one aspect of a more multifaceted foreign policy tradition that is at the core of US national security. Export of American values and democracy and anything that could be classified as "soft power" are often too costly and risky for Trump. Instead, focusing on "America first" means withdrawing US leadership, severing all expensive commitments abroad, renegotiating trade agreements and turning to protectionism to kick-start the regeneration of US manufacturing industry.

His attempts at banning immigrants from several Muslim-majority countries were followed by disengagement from UN talks on migration and a reduction of US contribution to the UN by 40%. He has withdrawn financial support for many of the World Bank-sponsored development projects. In March 2017, as his first step to disengage the USA from climate change leadership, he issued executive order 13783.[14] This fundamentally instructed EPA director, Scott Pruitt, to dismantle Obama's Clean Power Plan, which Trump had repeatedly called "stupid" and "job killing." The order was followed a few months later by the announcement to withdraw from the Paris Climate Accord. And finally, at his first UN speech in September speech in 2017, he firmly stated: "As president of the United States, I will put America first."[15]

---

[14] Executive Order 13783, 28 March 2017, http://www.presidency.ucsb.edu [accessed 3 May 2018].

[15] Evan Osnos, 'Making China Great Again,' *The New Yorker*, 8 January 2018, pp. 36–45.

Withdrawing from international affairs has been made easier by the State Department's lack of foreign policy direction. Following his campaign promises to "drain the swamp" and cut the budget, Trump appointed chairman of Exxon Mobil, Rex Tillerson as Secretary State. A successful oil executive, Tillerson was tasked with a complete reorganisation of the State Department to reduce costs and simplify bureaucracy. With the help of business consulting firms Insigniam and Deloitte, his plan focused on micromanaging small areas of the department while missing out on the bigger picture of diplomacy. While a few high-level diplomats have been fired, many more have offered their resignations and dozen of key positions remain unfulfilled, including a permanent undersecretary for arms control and international security affairs, as well as a permanent assistant secretary for East Asian and Pacific Affairs. These vacancies have put a strain on relationships with key allies and have created a "paralysis that has left the department crippled" and confined to a secondary role.[16] The vacuum was quickly filled by the White House and in particular, the National Security Council, and by the Defence Department. Tillerson became more and more isolated, until eventually he was fired in March 2018 and replaced by former CIA director Mike Pompeo.

For Asia policy, the situation is further complicated by the lack of senior appointments with proven Asian expertise and institutional memory. At the time of this manuscript completion, the administration is still to appoint an Ambassador to South Korea. Victor Cha, a former official in the George W. Bush administration and a distinguished expert on North Korea, was dropped in January 2018 because of his public disagreement with the president's views on Pyongyang.[17] For his presidential bid, Trump had appointed Peter Navarro, professor of economics and public policy at the University of California, Irvine, as part of his economic team. Having firmly established his credentials as an anti-China hardliner by publishing three books denouncing Beijing's trade crimes and militaristic ambitions, he gave credence to Trump's campaign

---

[16]'Is Rex Tillerson Destroying the State Department in Order to Save It?' *Vanity Fair*, August 2017, https://www.vanityfair.com/news/2017/08/rex-tillerson-state-department-reorganization.

[17] *The Hill*, 30 January 2018—*The Washington Post*, 30 January 2018.

rhetoric by arguing that China and "its bad practices are the world's central problem."[18] His radical views were endorsed by another anti-China hawk, Trump's campaign manager, Steve Bannon. But while threats of a trade war made great campaign speeches and slogans, once in the White House, Navarro's influence on the administration faded quite quickly. He was appointed head of the newly created National Trade Council, but the management of Sino-American relations was assigned to the president's thirty-seven years old son-in-law, Jared Kushner.[19]

Kushner epitomises the administration's approach to diplomacy. While less aggressive than his father-in-law, like Trump, he believes in the "art of the deal" and confidential relationships rather than the traditional Washington's diplomatic game. He joined the new administration during the transition period. By his own admission, his experience in diplomacy was very limited. But through his position as a CEO of his family real-estate empire, he had established firm links with China.

Concerned about the campaign rhetoric and especially by Steve Bannon's potential role in the new White House, the Chinese contacted former Secretary of State Henry Kissinger to enquire about a less hostile representative of the Trump team. Kissinger recommended Kushner. As Michael Pillsbury, a former Pentagon aide on Trump's transition team, reported, pretty quickly Kushner became "Mr China."[20] Indeed, Kushner met at least three times with Cui Tiankai, the Chinese Ambassador to the USA, during the transition period. Once in the White House then, the two met on a fairly regular basis to discuss the future of US-Chinese relations and arrange a meeting between the new president and Chinese Prime Minister Xi Jinping as soon as possible. Kushner often received the Chinese Ambassador without Washington's top China experts or senior officials. To the dismay of Foggy Bottom and the intelligence community, they also met at least on one occasion alone.

[18] Davidson Adam, 'Trump's Muse on US Trade with China,' *The New Yorker*, 12 October 2016, https://www.newyorker.com/business/currency/trumps-muse-on-u-s-trade-with-china [accessed 25 April 2018].

[19] 'One China, Once Again: Donald Trump Grants China's Fervent Wish,' *The Economist*, 15 February 2017, https://www.economist.com/china/2017/02/13/donald-trump-grants-chinas-fervent-wish.

[20] Quoted in Adam Entous and Evan Osnos, 'Soft Target,' *The New Yorker*, 29 January 2018, pp. 20–24.

While these meetings were taking place, the administration was seeking security clearance for Kushner, his wife Ivanka Trump and Donald Trump Jr and Eric Trump who had become part of the new White House too. The process revealed, among other critical issues, some of Kushner's and Ivanka's business deals with China. As reported by *The New Yorker*, in early 2017, after Trump took office, Ivanka's fashion company was given the green light to sell bags, jewellery and spa-services in China and a number of trademark applications by the Trump Organisation received approval by Beijing regulators. By March 2017, the FBI was warning Kushner about the danger of foreign influence operations. Although US intelligence was unable to find any conclusive evidence of Chinese attempts at exploiting Kushner's position in the White House through business ties, permanent security clearance was eventually denied.[21]

Besides the US intelligence community's concerns over China's undue influence on policy-making via Kushner's business interests, his appointment as the president's special advisor and confidant has had further serious repercussions on US foreign policy in general, and in the Pacific in particular. Like with other members of Trump's family, his position fuels rumours of nepotism and incompetence within the upper levels of the White House and makes the executive's relationship with other departments more difficult. An article by *The Wall Street Journal* reported that Trump and his team had assumed the West wing had a permanent staff, which they would inherit once he entered office. In the absence of this presumed group of experts, he filled the vacant positions with members of his family. Though successful at their business activities, none of them has any government experience. Very much like the president, their approach to governing is more similar to running a business than running a country. They favour short-term transactions rather than long-term grand strategies. Inevitably, family members also receive preferential treatment over staff. Indeed, appointees favoured by Kushner and Ivanka seemed to be "on the rise." And despite the constant carousel of departures and firings, Trump is not going to lay off his daughter or son-in-law. The best example being Bannon's departure following his "civil war" with Kushner.[22]

[21] Ibid.

[22] Sarah Ellison, 'The Inside Civil War Between Kushner and Bannon,' *Vanity Fair*, April 2017, https://www.vanityfair.com/news/2017/04/jared-kushner-steve-bannon-white-house-civil-war [accessed 3 February 2018].

Appointing inexperienced family members, shifting foreign policy-making into the White House and the chaos generated by the business-like restructuring of the State Department have created confusion and uncertainty among allies. The rejection of expert advice might give the impression to voters that the administration is keeping its campaign promise to "drain the swamp" but in reality, it undermines its ability to think strategically about the US role in the world and its long-term goals in specific regions. So far Trump has failed to fully transition from businessman to commander-in-chief. His first fifteen months in the White House have shown how unprepared he was for the job. He has often relied on short-term solutions and quick fixes. His private character and operating style, for example, the reckless use of twitter, have left allies and enemies puzzled, to say the least, about the president's knowledge and understanding of his role. The US president is by far the important actor influencing views of the US abroad. These perceptions have significant implications for how the USA is treated and other countries engage with it.

China has welcomed America's retreat from international affairs. In a speech to Communist party officials in January 2018, Major General Jin Yinan, a strategist at China's National Defense University, happily remarked to his audience: "As the US retreats globally, China shows up." Beijing has worked hard in the last few decades on an ambitious plan to replace the "American Dream" with the "Chinese Dream." In May 2013, PRC President Xi Jinping, called upon young Chinese "to dare to dream, work assiduously to fulfil the dreams and contribute to the revitalization of the nation."[23] According to Robert Lawrence Khun, an investment banker and long-term adviser to China's leaders and the Chinese government, this dream needs to focus on developing four key aspects to be fulfilled. In *The New York Times*, he wrote:

> The Chinese Dream has four parts: Strong China (economically, politically, diplomatically, scientifically, militarily); Civilized China (equity and fairness, rich culture, high morals); Harmonious China (amity among social classes); Beautiful China (healthy environment, low pollution).[24]

[23]'Xi Jingping and the Chinese Dream,' *The Economist*, 4 May 2013, https://www.economist.com/leaders/2013/05/04/xi-jinping-and-the-chinese-dream [accessed 16 January 2018].

[24]Robert Lawrence Khun, 'Xi Jinping's Chinese Dream,' *The New York Times*, 4 June 2013, https://www.nytimes.com/2013/06/05/opinion/global/xi-jinpings-chinese-dream.html [accessed 5 April 2018].

To achieve this, China needs to regain its position as leading power in the sciences, technology and business. It also needs to "export" Chinese civilisation and culture and finally, it must engage actively in global issues. To this end, it has already become one of the key financial contributors to the UN and its peacekeeping corps and has shown initiative and leadership on terrorism, nuclear proliferation and climate change issues. Its Belt and Road Initiative, seven times more expensive that the Marshall plan of 1947, is building infrastructure and trade links across Asia and Africa.[25]

While initially impressed by Trump's victory, and somehow respectful of what he had achieved, Beijing quickly learnt that the new president presented an invaluable opportunity for China's rise. Yan Xuetong, dean of Tsinghua University's Institute of Modern International relations, told Evan Osnos of *The New Yorker*, that the Chinese leadership thinks "Trump is the America's Gorbachev," as in the man responsible for the collapse of the Soviet Union. They have been very good at reading the US president and seeing him exactly for what he is: a deal-maker, keen on bargaining and short-term transactions, but unable to see the bigger picture of diplomacy.

Trump has given China the perfect opening to speed up its plan of breaking the Western domination of international institutions and markets. Withdrawing from the TPP allowed Beijing to reopen negotiations with sixteen countries in the Asia Pacific to form the Regional Comprehensive Economic Partnership, which China had launched back in 2012 to counterweight the TPP. If successful, this would exclude the USA from the world's largest trade bloc (by population). The withdrawal has also damaged US credibility among the allies. The Prime Minister of Singapore, Lee Hsien Loong, also interviewed by Evan Osnos, stated that Trump's decision will have significant impact in the long term. In the short term, in the absence of US leadership, Asian countries are already looking at China for guidance. It is, perhaps, no surprise that in January 2018, in a *CNBC* interview, Trump declared he might be open to reconsider the partnership.[26]

---

[25] Evan Osnos, 'Making China Great Again,' *The New Yorker*, 8 January 2018, pp. 36–45.

[26] 'Trump: I Would Reconsider a Massive Pacific Trade Deal If It Were Substantially Better,' https://www.cnbc.com/2018/01/25/trump-says-he-would-reconsider-trans-pacific-partnership-trade-deal.html [accessed 1 May 2018].

The TPP is not the only casualty in what the media have called a "trade war." The Chinese have been studying Trump's rhetoric carefully and have understood that he uses it as a weapon for bargaining. Many of his campaign and twitter threats have actually not been followed through once he took office. So when Trump decided to place tariffs on imports of Chinese steel and aluminium in early 2018, Beijing called his bluff and retaliated by imposing duties on about $3 billion in US exports. Trump's impulsive response placing further 25% tariffs on some $50 billion in Chinese imports to hit China's industrial base and expose alleged tech theft, not only forced Beijing to raise the stakes by imposing new tariffs on US products, including soyabeans, but it has also shown how unpredictable the American president can be.

China is indeed a thief of tech and intellectual property and is damaging US economy. There is no doubt about it. But imposing tariffs will not solve this problem. On the contrary, it has given Beijing a great opportunity to drive a wedge between the USA and its closest partners by casting US policy as unilateralist because of the consequences these tariffs will have on global trade. Its firm response has also further consolidated Chinese strength in international affairs and is deterring other countries from following US lead. Washington might not be in a trade war with China, as Trump tweeted in April 2018, but it is locked down in an almost impossible situation. It cannot back down, otherwise US credibility and prestige will suffer. But if tariffs are imposed the American economy will definitely be hit hard.

Some have suggested that in launching this attack on China, the president was trying to appease his disappointed political base. But even if this were true, this shows the president has not fully transitioned from the campaign trail to commander-in-chief. More importantly, it confirms the perception that he is unable to think strategically and broadly, but he approaches each issue as an individual business transaction without considering repercussions in other areas.

On 1 June 2017 in the White House Rose Garden, Trump announced that the USA would withdraw from the Paris Climate Accord and end its financial contribution to the Green Climate Fund because these would greatly damage US industry and would diminish US economic production. Singling out China and India as the only two countries, which would actually benefit from the Accord, he declared his aim was to renegotiate an "entirely new transaction on terms that are fair to the United States, its business, its workers, its people, its taxpayers."[27] The intention of "renegotiating" the Accord left the international community baffled because the original negotiations had entirely been driven by the USA and the final agreement very much favoured accommodating US requests on the right to set its own targets and impose the same obligations on developing countries.[28]

The speech also cherry-picked one particular set of data according to which compliance with the commitments would cost the US economy $3 trillion in lost GDP and 6.5 million in industrial jobs. This scenario seems highly unrealistic. At the moment, the US clean technology industry employs more than 3 million people whereas the coal industry only employs a couple of hundred thousand. The clean technology sector is growing twelve times faster than any other sectors, so it is in the interests of the US economy for Washington to retain its leading position on climate change. But misuse of data and information to confuse the public on the impact of climate change is not something new for the president. His tweets often blur the theory behind climate change and weather. Either he is unaware of the difference between the two or he is deliberately creating confusion to appeal to his electoral supporters.

The decision has harmed America's soft power, prestige and global leadership. The USA is now the only country in the world, together with Syria and Nicaragua, not in the agreement. Syria is going through a horrific civil and Nicaragua had not signed the Accord in the first place because it thought it was too weak. It is unlike that other countries will follow the US lead and join a minority group. Plans to reduce emissions in the USA will continue anyway at state level, but Trump has created a leadership vacuum that China has been quick to fill. Immediately after the November 2016 election, Beijing signalled the world that it was ready to take the lead. At the COP22 in Marrakesh, the Chinese vice-foreign minister Liu Zhenmin rebuked Trump's campaign attacks by reminding him that climate change was not a Chinese hoax. It was actually President Ronald Reagan who had put it on the international agenda back in the 1980s.

---

[27] Statement by President Trump on Paris Accord, 1 June 2017, https://www.whitehouse.gov/briefings-statements/statement-president-trump-paris-climate-accord/ [accessed 13 May 2018].

[28] Ibid.

He also declared "any change in US policy won't affect China's commitment to support climate negotiations and also the implementation of the Paris Agreement."[29]

China's climate policy has come a long way and it has become a priority for the next phase of its growth, prosperity and fulfilment of the Chinese Dream. Chinese leaders have acknowledged the detrimental impact of their reliance on high-carbon growth on the economy, the environment and society. Xi Jinping's government has embraced an "ecological civilisation" vision that aims at reversing these effects. Key to this is investment in new clean technologies that would also establish China as a primary innovator in the field. China already possesses the world's biggest installed capacity of wind and solar power, which is now sharing with the developing world.[30]

The difference between the two approaches: Trump's denial that climate change even exists and China's investment in new technologies would not only create more economic opportunities for the Communist country, but it will also allow Beijing to claim the moral high ground on an issue that affects the entire planet, thus strengthening Chinese soft power and influence in the world.[31]

PERSONAL DIPLOMACY

Trump and Xi's "friendship" has been the subject of much news reporting, especially since their first meeting in April 2017. Both men have embraced the art of personal diplomacy. Since Xi came to power in 2012, he has been very open to using more informal style to nurture friendships with foreign leaders. Trump has often stated that he considers himself and his style the best assets in any transaction, whether business or diplomatic.

---

[29] 'China Emerges as Global Climate Leader in Wake of Trump's Triumph,' *The Guardian*, 22 November 2016, https://www.theguardian.com/environment/2016/nov/22/donald-trump-success-helps-china-emerge-as-global-climate-leader.

[30] Rob Bailey, 'What Trump's Withdrawal from Paris Means for Global Climate Action,' Chatham House Report, 2 June 2017, https://www.chathamhouse.org/expert/comment/what-trump-s-withdrawal-paris-means-global-climate-action [accessed 7 May 2018].

[31] Ibid.

On Jared Kushner's suggestion, he invited Xi to his golf course resort Mar-a-Lago, or as he calls it: the Winter White House, in Florida. The idea was praised by many experts as a smart one. In both American and Chinese culture to welcome someone in your home as a guest is a sign of great respect. But it has also raised some ethical questions, especially because the meeting took place at a time when several members of the Trump family were being scrutinised over business ties with China. Trump is no longer president of the club; he gave up that position before inauguration. His son Donald Trump Jr. now holds the title. Still, as Kathleen Clark, a government ethics specialist, pointed out in an interview on *CBS* news, a foreign leader's visit attracts lot of domestic and international attention, if the meeting takes place at one of Trump's branded properties, "he is actually using government office for private gain."[32]

Xi and his wife, Peng Liyuan, a Chinese contemporary folk singer and performing artist, spent just over 24 hours in Florida. They were greeted by Secretary of State, Rex Tillerson, at the airport and then escorted to a candlelit private dining room at the president's private residence where they dined on pan-seared Dover sole and New York strip stake with Trump, first lady Malania, the president's daughter Ivanka and her husband Jared Kushner. Arabella and Joseph Kushner, Ivanka's children, then entertained the guests after dinner reciting poetry and signing a classic Chinese ballad "Jasmine Flower."[33] Beyond the lavish hospitality and symbolism, were they actually able to establish a working relationship?

Whether the president was successful in impressing Xi with his personal style diplomacy and wealth is not known. Xi is a man of great self-control and confidence and seldom reveals his personal feelings. The two have also had very different upbringings. Xi grew up in poverty in the countryside of Shaanxi, after his father was persecuted during the Mao Zedong era. Trump grew up in real-estate paradise and celebrates wealth. He could certainly not charm him with a round of golf. Xi is an

---

[32] 'Trump's Mar-a-Lago Meeting with China's Xi Jinping Raises Ethics Concerns,' *CBS News*, 6 April 2017, https://www.cbsnews.com/news/president-trump-china-xi-jinping-mar-a-lago-meeting-ethics-expert/ [accessed 7 May 2017].

[33] 'Trump Hails "Tremendous" Progress in Talks with China's Xi,' *BBC News*, 7 April 2017, http://www.bbc.co.uk/news/world-us-canada-39517569 [accessed 7 May 2017].

avid fan of swimming and soccer and as many of the Communist party leaders, he considers golf a game for rich people. Indeed, in an attempt to crack down corruption, he shut down plenty of golf courses in China and has forbidden party officials to play.

For sure, Trump was very impressed by Xi. The president has often expressed admiration for leaders with strong personalities. From Turkey to the Philippines, via Moscow, he has professed admiration for state officials who do not often value the law or democratic principles. "We had a great chemistry, I think. I mean, at least I had great chemistry – maybe he did not like me," he said to *Fox Business Network* after Xi's visit. He also thought that "tremendous progress" had been made. Exactly what kind of "progress" is not clear, but overall, the visit was quite cordial. Trump's rhetoric certainly did not mirror his campaign threats. Xi avoided commenting on the US air strike on air bases in Syria, which had taken place the night before his arrival, he urged cooperation on trade and invited his host to China.[34]

In private, however, Chinese officials agreed that Trump is a "paper tiger." The president's interview with the *Wall Street Journal* where he declared how little he understood of China's relationship with Korea did not go unnoticed in Beijing. This coupled with Trump's failure to actually deliver on many campaign promises, such as: the wall in Mexico and repeal of Obamacare and the fact that he is under investigation boosted Chinese confidence. In Mar-O-Lago, Xi also learnt that flattery goes a long way with Trump. When his turn came to host the US president, he arranged for a "state-visit plus."[35]

When Trump landed in Beijing in November 2017, his political leverage was certainly not the same as during the previous US-China meeting. His approval rating was 37%, lowest than any of his predecessors at that point in their tenure. The Republicans had lost the governors' elections in Virginia and New Jersey. And three of his former aides had been charged in the investigation into Moscow's role in the 2016 presidential campaign. Xi pulled out all the stops to impress Trump and maximise the propaganda opportunity at home. After a sunset tour of the Forbidden

[34]Brian Klass, *The Despot's Apprentice, Donald Trump's Attack on Democracy* (London: Hurst & Company, 2017), p. 17.

[35]Evan Osnos, 'Making China Great Again,' *The New Yorker*, 8 January 2018, pp. 36–45.

City, he invited the president and first lady Melania to a special opera performance at the Pavillion of Pleasant Sounds. The following day, the Chinese military bands and firing cannons welcomed Trump to the Great Hall of the People while school children yelled "Uncle Trump." Government censors helped control social media messages that might be critical of Trump. A video of the president's granddaughter, Arabella Kushner, singing a 1953 Chinese song went viral on the Internet and the Chinese celebrated it as a sign that Chinese culture had made it to the international stage.[36]

For his part, Trump never missed a chance to praise Xi publicly. At one point he declared: "You are really a special man." He took repeatedly to twitter to thank the Chinese leader for his hospitality. "Looking forward to a full day of meetings with President Xi and our delegations tomorrow. Thank you for the beautiful welcome China! @flotus Melania and I will never forget it!" he tweeted on November 8. The following day, he added: "President Xi thank you for such an incredible welcome ceremony. It was a truly and memorable display."[37]

In a complete reversal to his campaign threats and first 100 days rhetoric, he upheld the One China policy and blamed previous American presidents for the massive trade deficit between the USA and China. "I don't blame China - after all, who can blame a country for taking advantage of another country for the benefit of its citizens... I give China great credit," said Trump during one of his meetings with business leaders. Trump tried to put North Korea on top of the visit agenda. Xi diplomatically declared that China would "continue to work towards" fully implementing UN sanctions and "enduring peace" on the peninsula but he did not make any further commitments.[38]

THE REST OF ASIA

Xi's reticence in making significant commitments towards reining in North Korea sums up China's strategy in the Pacific. Like Washington, Beijing is in favour of a denuclearisation of the Korean peninsula but at the same time, it wants to prevent turning Pyongyang into an enemy or

[36] Ibid.

[37] President Trump's twitter account.

[38] Evan Osnos, 'Making China Great Again,' *The New Yorker*, 8 January 2018, pp. 36–45.

pushing it and the USA close. Trump's approach to North Korea has been, to say the least, as erratic as Kim's approach to international relations. From declaring it a state sponsor of terrorism, increasing economic sanctions against it, to threatening it with nuclear bombing to unexpectedly accepting an innovation to meet the North Korean leader, the US president has injected much uncertainty in the Pacific area.

Despite his campaign promises, in the first fifteen months of his administration, he has continued previous presidents' efforts to improve relations with other countries. Indeed, not wanting to alienate US long-term allies, immediately after Xi's visit in April 2017, Trump called Japan and South Korea and reassured both countries of US commitment to their defence. Very much like during the Obama years, the administration's first official visits were in Asian countries. In February 2017, Secretary of Defence, Jim Mattis, travelled to Japan and South Korea and proposed the deployment of THHAD missiles to South Korea in order to defend the area from possible North Korean attacks. A month after, Secretary of State Tillerson visited Japan, South Korea and China. And in April, Vice-President Mike Pence made a similar tour extending it to Indonesia and Australia.

US-Japanese relations have improved in the last years and despite Trump's protestations that if Japan and South Korea did not pay their fair share, he was willing to withdraw US forces, things are not set to change in the foreseeable future. Following US new strategic defence commitments in 2015, Japan is now home to more US military personnel than any other foreign countries. In 2016, acknowledging the improvement of US-Japanese relations, President Obama was the first sitting president to visit Hiroshima. This was followed a few months after by Prime Minister Abe visit to Pearl Harbour.

The Trump administration's trips to Asia carried the same objective to reassure and cultivate US-Japanese relations. The administration shares Japan's concern that a rising China might pose a threat to the balance of power in Asia, especially if it joins forces with North Korea, and oust both Japan and the USA from the area. This common interest in containing China has made Trump's approach to Japan much softer and friendly than his campaign rhetoric proclaimed and led to a few actions to show unity against China. First of all, Trump met Abe before meeting Xi. Secondly, the USA showed much support for Japan in the perennial dispute between Japan and China in the East China Sea. Both Beijing and Tokyo claim the Senkaku/Diaoyu islands. Military tensions have risen accordingly. The situation is quite difficult in the South China Sea too.

A US-Japanese joint operation in May 2017 set China on alert. At the same time, Tokyo, very much like Trump, blames China for failing to exercise enough influence to rein in North Korea.

The same concern is shared by South Korea. As North Korea has increased its nuclear development programme and Beijing has failed to rein in, Washington-Seoul relations have improved and become tighter. In March 2016, the USA and South Korea initiated discussion on deploying THAAD anti-missile system in Korea for defence purposes. Trump supports the plan and despite Beijing's protestations in March 2017, initial elements of THAAD system were being deployed in South Korea.

Trump's decision to accept, via twitter and without consulting his advisors, Kim's invitation has certainly damaged the strengthening of this alliance and has given China an opportunity to drive a wedge between the USA and Japan and South Korea. As Michael Green, a former Asia advisor to President George W. Bush, stated: "the abrupt decision on steel tariffs (which included Japan and South Korea) and now the summit with Kim will inevitably raise questions in Tokyo and other allied capitals about how decisions are made by this administration that affect their interests."[39] A meeting between Trump and Kim means de-escalating tensions and abandon the bellicose rhetoric, thus removing the necessity of having to cooperate with other Asian countries to contain North Korea.

Although relations between Beijing and Pyongyang have not always been easy, the two still share the strategic objective of breaking the US-South Korean alliance and remove US presence in the southern part of the peninsula. Indeed, on 26 March 2018, Kim travelled to Beijing to get China's support before meeting South Korean President Moon and then Trump.

The Trump administration has not surprisingly been busy in claiming the credit for this breakthrough. Accordingly, it was Trump's pressure on implementing extensive economic sanctions through the UN that brought Kim to the table. But in truth, much of the credit should go to South Korean leader Moon Jae-in who faced with an unpredictable ally, the USA, and a nuclear North Korea, staked his political career on engaging the North at the Winter Olympics. Kim accepted because his bargaining position has greatly improved in the last year. As he declared on 1 January 2018: "North Korea has at last come to possess a powerful and reliable war deterrent, which no force and nothing can reverse."

---

[39] Motoko Rich, 'Trump's Unpredictability on Trade and North Korea Opens a Door for China,' *The New York Times*, 10 March 2018, https://www.nytimes.com/2018/03/10/world/asia/china-north-korea-trump-tariffs.html.

A meeting with Trump would only help to consolidate his legitimacy. Indeed, he had invited previous US presidents too, but they all refused on the basis that North Korea's concept of "denuclearisation" differs from the American definition. In this sense, Trump made a great concession.

CONCLUSION

In its first fifteen months in office, the Trump administration has failed to implement a cohesive and effective China policy. While on the one hand, the president has continued his predecessors' pursuit of improved relations with long-term allies, such as Japan and South Korea; on the other, he has often acted impulsively and unpredictably towards the key Asian player: Beijing. Previous administrations recognised the importance of engaging with China as a way to preserve access to its market but most of all, to maintain US hegemony in that area. They have also avoided trade wars because they would clearly damage US economy and prestige. This unclear vision for the US role in the Pacific is partly due to the fact that the administration officials, including the president, lack the expertise and experience necessary to formulate adequate foreign policy and a tendency to address diplomatic issues as business transactions. But history has shown that this can have serious long-term consequences in international affairs. Indeed, Trump's State Department Far Eastern desk is a frightening reminder of the McCarthy era.

The administration's priority has been to maintain support form its isolationist electoral base. In this sense, Trump has never really left the campaign trail and he has easily sacrificed strategic interests in Asia to appease those who voted for him because of his promises to put "America first" and "drain the swamp." But withdrawing US leadership from the international liberal order, refusing to engage with global issues and starting a trade war with China are not the solution to "make America great again," quite the contrary, they seem to be the quickest way to make China great again. Trump's bold statements have certainly symbolic value that can have, and have had, a significant influence on domestic politics. But rolling back Obama's "disastrous" foreign policy needs to be supported by an actual plan. This is something the administration has failed to do. In the meantime, Beijing has been very skilful in presenting itself as the best option to lead a new Asian century.

Finally, with the spotlight being constantly on Trump's erratic moves and provocative tweets, in the last fifteen months, Beijing has been able to get away with many actions that in other circumstances would have been condemned by the international community, such as: build up on the islands in the South China Sea and Xi's lifetime appointment to power.

References

Badger, Jeffrey. *Obama and China's Rise.* Washington: Brookings Institution Press, 2012.

Campbell, Kurt. *The Pivot, the Future of American Statecraft in Asia.* New York: Twelve, 2016.

De Graaff, Nana, and Bastiaan van Apeldoorn. "US-China and the Liberal World Order: Contending Elites, Colliding Visions?" *International Affairs,* 92 (2018): 113–31.

Goh, Evelyn. *Constructing the US Rapprochement with China, 1961–1974.* Cambridge: Cambridge University Press, 2009.

Green, Michael. *By More Than Providence; Grand Strategy and American Power in the Asia Pacific Since 1783.* New York: Columbia University Press, 2017.

Klass, Brian. *The Despot's Apprentice, Donald Trump's Attack on Democracy.* London: Hurst & Company, 2017.

Oliva, Mara. *Eisenhower and American Public Opinion on China.* New York: Palgrave, 2018.

CHAPTER 12

Conclusion

Mark Shanahan and Mara Oliva

Writing in the middle of May 2018, the memory of Donald Trump's first year in the White House is already receding fast. The struggles to establish an Executive team to pass any useful legislation and to heal the divides that blighted the USA through the 2016 campaign already seem of another age as the Trump bandwagon rolls on, its strategy simple and its impact, at home and abroad, ever-more divisive. What has emerged is an 'honest Presidency': focused solely on delivering campaign promises and rolling back all and any Obama-era strategies.

The Trump model is billed as, and built around, America First. But it's not an America for all. Rolling back regulation and cutting corporate taxes delivers a disproportionate benefit to the wealthiest individuals and most powerful corporations in the nation. The hawkish hike in military spending is lining the coffers of the defence sector and its stockholders while the MAGA rhetoric emboldens the narrow tract from white conservatives

M. Shanahan (✉)
Department of Politics and International Relations,
University of Reading, Reading, Berkshire, UK
e-mail: m.j.shanahan@reading.ac.uk

M. Oliva
Department of History, University of Reading,
Reading, Berkshire, UK
e-mail: m.oliva@reading.ac.uk

© The Author(s) 2019   249
M. Oliva and M. Shanahan (eds.), *The Trump Presidency*,
The Evolving American Presidency,
https://doi.org/10.1007/978-3-319-96325-9_12

to white supremacists, while widening the gulf with liberals at home. But the rifts in American society are far less binary than a simple liberal-conservative axis. Women, the LGBT+ community, immigrants, African Americans, poor non-white Americans, Muslims, experts, academics, the media and more or less any citizens outside the 1% or the Trump base have found themselves dismissed, denuded or displaced by Trumpism. What is emerging in the Trump USA is divides as deep as the worst days in the 1960s and early 1970s when civil rights and Vietnam delivered the fracture lines in American society.

But the Trump presidency, 16 months in, has the potential to be far more destructive than even the dying days of Nixon's imperial presidency. This is the ratings presidency, where, reinforced by his experience of a year in the White House, Trump has concluded that his greatest impact remains in the headlines he garners in the news cycle that deliver the short-term 'winning' moments seemingly beloved of those who voted him into office in the first place. It is a strategy unchanged from the campaign trail—owning the news agenda through the early-morning tweets that often herald another presidency-as-reality—TV moment as Trump strides to the microphone again to deliver soundbite policy. In recent weeks, we have seen the dangerously short-sighted step of withdrawing from the Iran nuclear deal; the heralding of a June summit with 'Little rocket man' Kim Jong Un of North Korea; the imposition of tariffs on imports of goods and materials from solar panels to steel; and the opening of the US Embassy in Jerusalem. All played extremely well with those minded to vote for Trump at home and appeared key steps both in delivering on his campaign promises and in establishing his credentials as a strong leader.

But what has been the effect of this wave of action from Year-2 Trump? Over 60 Palestinians were killed by Israeli troops in the 48 hours after the Embassy opened. Meanwhile Trump's plan for peace in Israel is nowhere to be seen. American business is rounding on Trump because he has failed to note that tariffs are not a one-way street, and for every job in the steel industry he is saving at home, he is potentially losing several more elsewhere across US industry as exporters are finding it more expensive to get their goods into overseas markets. Kim Jong Un appears less than reconciled to an America First strategy for the Korean Peninsula which would, in a Libya-like plan, see North Korea give up its nuclear and ballistic capabilities, while Japan and South Korea would sit serenely under the US nuclear umbrella. And as for Iran? The other five international signatories to the JCPOA remain committed to an agreement designed as a first step in a long-term strategy to reintegrate Iran into the norms and legalities of the community of nations. But Trump's actions immediately saw the Tehran regime revert to rocket attacks on Israel, and there is a palpable fear that the already fever-pitch tensions in the region could explode into a full-scale regional war. With offensive realists such as National Security Advisor John Bolton now having the President's ear, the prospects of the USA being embroiled in another conflict it can't win, despite Trump's natural isolationism, must be increasing.

Of course, one continues to wonder if Trump is playing the long game at 1600 Pennsylvania Avenue at all. Having appeared bored and deflated by the travails of actually having to do the job of president, he seems to have found a second wind. But how long will that last? Again, the analogy of the TV presidency comes forth. The salacious soap opera of Stormy Daniels and why the president first paid an actress who makes pornographic films $130,000 following a sexual encounter he asserts never happened plays to the base instincts of gossip-hungry Americans. If the money trail leads to illegal campaign financing, it could bring him down. So too could the links to Russian influence on the 2016 Presidential Election being pursued by the Mueller Inquiry. By spring 2018, this appeared to be circling ever-closer and Trump's ever-more shrill denials, such as: "It's a witch hunt, that's all it is. There was no collusion with Russia, you can believe this one"[1] were wearing paper-thin. Whatever happens, the outcome of the Mueller investigation will define Trump's presidency—will he simply be the disruptor who changed the way we thought about presidential politics, or the head of a kleptocracy fuelled by instincts to ignore the rules and shape executive office to his personal benefit?

Following his dismissal as Secretary of State, Rex Tillerson warned of a 'growing crisis of ethics and integrity' that threatened democracy.[2] While not mentioning Trump, his target was clear. What distinguishes the Trump presidency most from his predecessors so far is the president's

---

[1] From News conference following meeting with German Chancellor Angela Merkel, 27 April 2018, sourced from CNN footage, https://edition.cnn.com/2018/04/27/politics/collusion-donald-trump-answer/index.html [last accessed 17 May 2018].

[2] Rex Tillerson, Commencement Speech to Virginia Military Institute Graduating Class, 16 May 2018.

propensity to lie whenever it suits him, and for too many Americans to normalise those lies. Far from 'draining the swamp', the Trump presidency so far has been built on a crony-Camelot where the structures of his mid-ranking New York development business have been replicated in the Executive. Power is not administered through expertise, but by having the ear of the president, an ear that is attuned to flattery and offended by anything other than his version of the truth. We now look to property rental heir Jared Kushner to bring peace to the Middle East, while a slew of Fox News pundits have been appointed to key roles across Government with the headliner being John Bolton as National Security Adviser.

Where might this disruptive presidency turn next? Perhaps we should revisit our contributors and consider the character of the president in the context of some of his most illustrious predecessors and then project forward on his ability to be 'winning' at home and abroad. As Mark Shanahan stated, if Trump is ever to emerge as a statesman rather than a presidential accident, he will have to demonstrate his ability to wage peace. Intemperate in his own character, and surrounded by hawkish throwbacks to a Cold War era, the chances of a major breakthrough in the Middle East, on the Korean Peninsula or even in the global economic environment, seem slim. Clearly, he covets a Nobel Peace Prize. For now, it remains a distant prospect. There again, in 2015, a Trump presidency was equally laughable.

What made the president was the media, and as Mark White notes, it may yet bring him down. Unlike the days of Camelot, press deference has disappeared. What Trump describes as 'fake news' is so often simply reporting that does not fit his gilded narrative. Today, his every move is analysed endlessly; his road to the White House, seemingly playing fast and loose with rules, regulations and propriety, is picked over on a daily basis, and inquiries into his personal, professional and political life have become a soap opera staple. As with any soap opera, there is a point where the ratings turn south and the networks pull the plug. We are not there yet, but prospects for future seasons of the Trump story are a little less rosy. It may be, as Iwan Morgan discusses, because what America fears most is a hit in the wallet. Trump's much-vaunted tax reforms appear to be ushering in a new era of Reaganomics where Wall Street Republicans are rejoicing, but Main Street's Joe and Jessica GOP continue to struggle. The Reagan era did much to denude the American Middle Class. The danger for Trump is that his appeasing the rich will lock away the American Dream for too many for ever.

As Lee Marsden showed, at home, Trump has kept on winning through rhetoric aimed straightforwardly at religious Americans and the Alt-right—and the strong crossover between evangelicals and more politically fundamentalist conservatives. For someone whose own character is far removed from the 'Strict Father Mentality' he espouses, it will be a constant challenge for a highly swampish House of Trump Cards to inspire the Heartland to raise a barn again. So far, the rhetorical connection has been one of the president's greatest achievements. Does it truly have legs, or will it be revealed as snake oil from the Reality TV huckster? For the moment, those white Americans, bypassed by globalisation and out of love with the state, are foursquare behind Trump. They may yet prove to be his last bastion.

Certainly, as articulated by Richard Johnson, Trumpism has applied a choke-hold to expanding the franchise to the other America—those separated from the base by colour, creed or residency status. The effect appears to be another loosening of the bricks in the wall of American democracy. In further politicising the franchise, Trump's zero-sum mentality further emboldens the white right and stokes the fires of resentment from Black Lives Matter to the Mexican border. Of course, it is on this border where Trump's vision of a big beautiful wall is the most concrete example of his philosophy of demonising the 'other'—the existential threat he uses to stoke a climate of fear among those most likely to vote for him. Kevern Verney's distillation of his antagonism towards Mexican immigrants offers little hope for the healing of America's divides.

But could his Achilles' Heel prove not to be an existential threat but a grouping much closer to home. As Clodah Harrington told us, Trump's actions so far in leaning towards social conservatives have already had the effect of galvanising more women to protest, to oppose and even to run for political office. Hillary Clinton proved to be far too divisive to even unite women to vote for her in 2016. But could the personal strength of feeling against Trump the man, supported by a growing recognition of the impact of his policies and appointments on womens' rights turn women who voted for him into opponents should he stand in 2020?

Perhaps, as Alex Waddan highlighted, his salami slicing of social policy may even raise the spectre of large numbers in his base also abandoning him, seeing as it seems that by not-very-well-hidden stealth, Trump's embrace of a small-state Reagan type government carries the threat of rapidly dismantling the US' social support structure. No amount of barn raising in Kansas can replace the losses of health and welfare care so many Trump supporters rely on.

Thus, the picture at home remains one of ifs and buts. Appeasing the base may actually reduce support from the wider Trump-voting group. As his majority in key states was so thin, the risk of losing the 2020 election may actually prompt a decision not to run. Trump likes winning, not losing.

Can he keep on winning overseas? The risk with foreign policy is not that different from what he faces at home. Maria Ryan compares his hypernationalist rhetoric with an ongoing internationalist need. At present, decisions on Iran, Jerusalem and global trade deal all point to the business dealmaker, comfortable with bilateral arrangements, but only on his terms. America First is beginning to bite in the international community, and Trumpism may be remembered for its diminution of the power of America projected globally. And who will be the winner? If Trump's strategy for America in the world remains so fractured and flawed, the rising power will most probably be China, as calculated by Mara Oliva. Impulsiveness and unpredictability do not play well in the global order, and rhetoric intended for the anti-globalist masses at home could, and probably will, be construed quite differently from Paris, to Berlin to Seoul, Tehran, Pyongyang and Beijing. Who knew that the inadvertent effect of the Trump Presidency would be to Make China Great Again?

The Trump presidency may yet not turn out to be greatly different from those before it, but Trump is a very different president. He is changing the way Americans normalise unacceptable behaviour. Future writers will be able to reflect on whether this was a short-lived blip, or the tipping point taking the USA into a new, darker and more dangerous age. The only certainty is that Trump's time in the White House will remain the age of unpredictability.

INDEX

Printed by Printforce, the Netherlands